ONE NATION INDIVISIBLE

One Nation Indivisible

THE UNION IN AMERICAN THOUGHT

1776-1861

Paul C. Nagel

NEW YORK   OXFORD UNIVERSITY PRESS
1964

for Joan

Copyright © 1964 by Oxford University Press, Inc.

Library of Congress Catalogue Card Number: 64-11235

Printed in the United States of America

Preface

Although scholars busily have been reconstructing ideas important in American history, no one has done more than acknowledge the dynamic character of Unionism.[1] Long ago, in saying that our Constitutional story "is in no small degree taken up with tracing opinion and assertion as to the actual character of Union," Andrew McLaughlin could better have argued that no idea said more to Americans or they to it, than did the guises of Union between 1776 and 1861.[2] The reasons for examining this meaning seem so many as to justify surprise at the tardiness of anyone to undertake the task. The pages following attempt to portray the complex of beliefs which made up Union's ideology.

An analysis of this sentiment must first recognize that the setting is an era wherein the political activist, that day's entertainer, shaped public attitudes. But while politicians generally dominate this book, many other voices are heard. The notes at the volume's close should reflect my sampling of public and private expression as found in the records of Congressional debates, in newspapers and periodicals, in essays and orations, and in diaries and correspondence. From the sentiments found in these can be delineated Union's representational qualities. It is these forms into which people generally put their thoughts about Union which tell us as much about the time as would speculation about the sincerity of an oration or the motive behind an editorial. For now the

v

study of history seems to have bridged the artificial dichotomy between words and reality.

My methods have been unabashedly impressionistic, since the amount of material inviting attention would endure as long as patience or a lifetime might tolerate. However, the major sources have shown me the pattern of a persisting Union cult. They reveal how America, uneasy in the midst of political and technological change, struggled to remain agreed on the tactics and goals of man in political society. The Union became a supreme ideal and image, as it increasingly answered this desire to elude personal and national peril. It proved a reassuring symbol of the American dream in the nation's first age of insecurity.[3] In a succeeding study, I intend to explore the broader dimensions of American nationalism in the nineteenth century, concentrating on this subsoil of terror.

This book's completion met the sequence of barriers peculiar to the academy. That these difficulties were finally eluded is due to many persons scattered across America. Naming them all would seem to boast. Yet some debts I must gladly acknowledge. Especially am I grateful for unending help and patience from my wife; for encouragement from Thomas D. Clark, my department chairman; and for superb guidance from Sheldon Meyer, editor for the Oxford University Press. Many librarians brought me cheer as well as sources, especially in the University of Kentucky, Amherst College, Vanderbilt University, and the Library of Congress. For these, I express thanks, as I do for the diverse and subtle aid over several years from my colleagues, Clement Eaton and Enno E. Kraehe, from the late George M. Stephenson, and from my friends, Daniel J. Boorstin and John William Ward. Finally, I salute the energy and devotion of my typists, Miss Dorothy Leathers and Mrs. Neva Armstrong.

Lexington, Kentucky   P. C. N.
May 1963

Contents

vii

ONE NATION INDIVISIBLE

Prologue

In 1851, the citizens of Capon Springs provided Virginia hospitality for Secretary of State Daniel Webster. In return, Webster lavished his unrivaled oratory upon a topic central to the nation's thought. Saluting "THE UNION OF THE STATES!" Webster posed a favorite question: "What mind can comprehend the consequences of that Union, past, present, and to come?" His Virginia audience, remembering the recent 1850 compromise, agreed when he asserted, "The Union of these States is the all-absorbing topic of the day; on it all men write, speak, think, and dilate, from the rising of the sun to the going down thereof." [1] Nevertheless, many would quarrel with Webster's—or their neighbor's—notion of Union's quality and purpose.

The Union meant many things to many Americans from 1776 to 1861. Yet, despite Webster's accuracy in calling Union "the all-absorbing topic of the day," scholars have studied this ideology largely as federalist theory instead of recognizing the Union's semblances as a treasure-trove of the values and images by which Americans sought to comprehend their nature and destiny. One commentator lamented the failure of historians to become "familiar with the shifting responses, both intellectual and emotional, which at various times in our history have been evoked by terms like 'Federal Union.' " [2] It is this storehouse of ideas about Union which these pages will investigate.

The idea of Union had an extraordinary career in the brief interlude between the selection in 1776 of the motto, "*E Pluribus Unum*," and the Capon Springs occasion honoring Webster. Because it originated when localism prevailed, the change in Unionist ideology offers a significant measure of the increasing impact of technology on America. By giving Union the commanding physical presence which the Websterians desired for it in mood or spirit, this technological revolution drained Union's vital urgency as an idea. When the Civil War confirmed Union in fact, it made obsolete for two generations any serious thought about the unity of Americans. While this study stops with the year of Lincoln's inauguration, it begins in 1776. Before that, thoughts about unity had centered upon binding Great Britain and America in spite of the Atlantic. Already there has been much written about these ideas.[3]

A revolution in communication arrived too late for America and England to escape imperial disunion. Centralism, meaning absolute Union of one kind or another, was thus impossible in 1776 and 1787. This was no longer true in 1861. By then, centralism had a dramatic effect on Union's ideology.

An 1815 lecture, "The Permanency of the American Union," can stand as a microcosm of Union sentiment. The address was presented in Charleston, South Carolina, a community where the Union wavered constantly in its myriad roles. It appeared when a Union Absolute was becoming credible. The message, which remains anonymous, is emblematic of the supra-individual, near totalistic character of Union sentiment before 1861. Most important, it foreshadowed responses that Union would evoke from the American mind during the next half-century.

The oration was published in 1817 by Hezekiah Niles, possibly the most important journalist of the day and a militant nationalist. Niles merely noted that it had been submitted by the author after delivery before the Literary and Philosophical Society in Charleston.[4] Stressing the Union's immortality, the essay ascribed to it indeterminateness in time and space. It was an early declaration that history, inexorable progress, the popular will, and the coming of human interdependence through technological achievement might be seen in Union, presenting it as an awesome vehicle for American values.

First, the essayist dismissed the notion of temporary Union, or, "that as we increase in number we shall diminish in harmony—that the remaining days of our national love are but few." Despite numerous defenders, this idea in several forms became heresy, and finally, treason. Predictions of fratricidal conflict, common when New England fretted under Republican policy, were also rebuked. Surely liberty would not have given birth to an independent Union, only then to be "parent of our wretchedness." The author insisted that Union's immortality could be demonstrated in several ways, but especially by the manner in which heterogeneous groups had once converged to form units in Europe. These became great nations, despite beginning with less congenial elements than America's Union contained. Furthermore, in America "the real germ of union never was sown until 1765," and not until " '76" did the parts become "resolved to expire or to flourish together." After 1789, said Niles' contributor, this determination to be one people was confirmed by "wealth and happiness, the fruit of Union." This brought the orator to the explication of Union's character, to show what would prove to be for decades the idea's appealing qualities.

Affirming Union's uniqueness, the writer said that, while history showed unity was possible, its circumstances moved beyond history. Union resulted from "reason, sympathy, and general interest," whereas unity in the Old World had emerged out of "compulsion." Here the address reached what became a vital part of the ideology, the contention that Union was itself Spirit. In 1815, the circumstances of distance and diversity suggested that brotherly affinity was the real Union. The author announced that all things worked "to revive and animate affection," and nothing existed which "can irritate or provoke the anger of *any one* of its members." When the background of Europe's experience was combined with the fact that Americans "have known each other only as brothers," the author's conclusion was inevitable: "our union is not to dissolve, but to augment in vigor, and bear new blessings and new glories."

Having captured both past and spirit, the Charleston analyst enlisted another talent for Union. This was progress, embodied in Union because it was natural that great communities discover within themselves sources of continuity and growth. There followed an enumeration of these innate capacities, especially a predicted early technological triumph, which meant a more ready exchange of production. Here, dimly perceived, was an asset of Union which would cause the paths of men like Calhoun, Clay, John Quincy Adams, and Niles himself to converge as they pursued its implications. The essayist said, "Our wants make us mutually dependent, and by mutually supplying them, habits of amity and of intercourse are created." Consequently, what he simply called "commerce" had a "cementing quality." Its benefits inhered to Union, for the essayist invoked another powerful ally, a natural or divine decree. No other nation, said he, possessed sections "which seem to have been so *planned* for each other." As a result of this mutuality which communication now fostered, a "powerful band of union therefore exists, and is daily strengthening and enlarging."

Technology made for other happy prospects. Since Spirit and mutuality seemed the Union itself, a "uniformity of opinion and conduct" would obviously develop. For this, insisted the essayist, America had "a miraculous engine," the press, through which men shared ideas over vast physical distance. Also, the press meant the coalescence of centuries of genius, so that knowledge itself was employed to liberalize, soften, and refine the soul. Such, for instance, was the stability derived from distributing treatises on Union, like the *Federalist*. Niles' essayist observed that "we can never know how such works will impart stability . . . by giving new ideas to the rising generation, and by secretly dissolving the hopes of profligate ambition."

While admitting that greed would keep a few citizens out of step with the Union, the essayist predicted that a national consensus built upon equalitarianism would be yet another guarantor of Union. Among enlightened Americans, "social interests are understood," and "general affection" now prevailed, assuring Union in "our nobler days, when toleration was merged in an equal, indefeasible right of conscience and freedom." Each man accepted "his country as his impartially tender parent." This intuitive Union out of equalitarianism, with America's system of representation, allowed the "general interest" to triumph. Union was therefore described as being determined not to allow minorities to secure, "through plausible and deceptive measures," their own advantage "and not the general benefit."

Thus, a combination of technological growth with representative majoritarianism supplied Union's strength. "We are becoming as uniform in national feeling as we are in freedom and blessedness." The essay then returned to those who foresaw Union's decline. With science advancing on the physical front, why should it "retrocede in politics only?" The evidence to the contrary was overwhelming, so the author exulted confidently, "the amelioration of man is the design of Providence," and the Union's place in this had "been too much favored to dread unkindness hereafter."

Having ranged widely in demonstrating why history, science, and Providence all taught the triumph of Union, the writer could more confidently renew an earlier theme. First, the principle: "Another luminous truth which declares the perpetuity of our union is, that in all countries certain opinions become a national feeling and sentiment, and are consecrated by the devotion of the people." In the United States "the unspeakable importance of the Union . . . has become a national sentiment." From this it followed that only fools or traitors might dissent from Union, an argument destined for prominence in the 1850's. "An American would as soon reason with an atheist as with the idiot who could not see, or with the traitor who pretended he did not see its [Union's] vital importance." The writer pictured Union as sentiment which could "melt all hearts into one." He announced: "Next to the frown of Deity the loss of union would be our most awful visitation"; "the American will forgive any enemy, but that enemy who would assail the union of the states."

The ultimate "unextinguishable cause," proving that Americans "will never allow the sentiment of Union to be cold," was the widely affirmed faith in its inevitable "future grandeur." The essayist observed, "Whilst what has already been accomplished elevates every citizen, yet what will be performed inspires him with enthusiasm." The father now could portray for his son "the vision" of Union's role as wonder and example of mankind. Through a growing, free population, amidst advancing science and the arts, Union would fulfill its mission of guiding a darkened world to light.

Mission, Destiny, Providence, Nature, Spirit, Immortality—all would be themes prominent during Union's mastery over American thought; and each was identified. The essay concluded by again scolding doubters of Union's permanence. How could ambitious demagogues or immense physical possession prove dangerous when American opinion now accepted Union's vital qualities? The answer was a last reiteration of Union's uniqueness. Denouncing the argument that Union was impossible as "an old colonial prejudice inculcated by our foreign tyrant to render us more dependent," the writer presented an Emersonian plea. Just as America had dropped the old world's political shackles, let her "no longer be oppressed" with Europe's "senseless doctrines." Instead, guided by "our own judgment," let Union find, "imbibe, and diffuse those opinions which suit a great, free, and wise nation."

On this confident note, the Charleston Unionist closed his case. One other feature of this essay remains noteworthy. Rarely has scholarship considered Union sentiment anything more than a squabble over federal-state relationships, producing an appearance only of polity. The long essay reprinted by Niles barely mentions this aspect. Such disregard for Union's federal design was similarly manifested throughout the course of Unionist expression. Instead, Union was given roles such as a providential Agent, the legacy of inspired Founders, and the embodiment of a mystical popular Spirit. Not only did these motifs have broader appeal, they were much less technical and controvertible than a Union seen as a division of power. Abundant attention was showered upon the latter, of course; but the following pages will show that Union had even more significant roles in American thought, becoming a prime embodiment of America's major beliefs.

Although this sentiment was to lose its captivating quality when Union itself, through technology's aid, became manageable, for two generations Union was a verbal icon, merging both past and future with the present. It represented for that time a confused and apprehensive America's answer to the questions of order and security, purpose and achievement, glory and honor. There was nothing extraordinary in Webster's observation during the centennial of Washington's birth, that such as the Union "has happened once in human affairs, and but once." A miracle was involved, for Union "stands out as a prominent exception to all ordinary history," and Webster added, "unless we suppose ourselves running into an age of miracles, we may not expect its repetition." [5]

Union's many-sided ideology historically divides in three careers; these dominate this book. Initially, there are matters of form and function. From a sense of Experiment, the Union's role as a Polity and as a Spirit developed. These led to the supreme motif of an Absolute or an Ultimate. Second, there are the ways in which Union served as ideal and image, which included Mission, Legend, and Symbol. Third, there are the incessant misgivings about Union; the evils of remaining with it, or, conversely, the disasters of dismemberment.

A look at Union in its various roles should help make the reader of today sympathetic to the remarkable statement made in 1861, that the Union was "a holy instrument around which all American hearts cluster and to which they cling with the tenacity of a semi-religious attachment." The speaker, Illinois' radical Congressman Owen Lovejoy, asserted that, just as every nation had "some nucleas thought, some central idea, which they enshrine," so Americans embraced Union "with a spirit of superstitious idolatry." [6] Surely a century has been long enough to wait before reconstructing both the idea and the idolatry.

Of Form and Function

In the uncertain years after 1776, Union was generally accepted as a hopeful experiment, as a means of attaining security. Great changes in the nineteenth century, however, profoundly affected America's mingling of Union as Polity and as Spirit. Consequently, unity was enshrined as an Absolute barely a generation after its experimental quality had begun receding for most beholders. The evolution in the ideology of form and function discloses Unionism's triumph as well as its tragedy.

1: Experiment

For the men of '76, the Union's design was obscure, its intent uncertain. A succeeding age would proffer Union as an Absolute design. What Americans of the late eighteenth century considered to be simply one means for confronting common problems gradually became itself an end, an ultimate, an embodiment of society. To follow Union's transformation as sentiment, the qualities of its formulation as Experiment first must be reconstructed. They involve principally two ideas.

Uncertainty in the early national period encouraged a casual attitude toward Union. It was difficult to foresee what independence and national integrity would entail in organization. In these circumstances, Union seemed more like a means, like something tentative. Such a quality of Experiment especially pleased men who, while acknowledging that security and order required some sort of unity, could also see that such organization might destroy its own purpose.

When Union was considered a means, it was seen to be plastic or perhaps even expendable. For those who accepted this concept, Henry Clay's later insistence that man was nothing compared to Union would have been heretical or incomprehensible. Nevertheless, barely fifty years stood between moments when Union's experimental design prevailed and when an absolute image was invoked by the Clays and the Lincolns.

I

Historians once contended that Union was early and unreservedly embraced. It was asserted that by 1776 the idea of Union had become "the demand of the hour, to promote social, political, and national well-being, the path of duty and honor; the way pointed out by Providence to successfully resist aggression, and to obtain a redress of grievances." Delight in Union thus became "conviction, and this ripened into faith in its practicality. It was the religion of politics. Union became a fact, and had the moral force of unwritten law." [1]

Today we realize that the sense of Union before 1783 sprang essentially from emergency. Having proved itself in war, Union was somewhat coolly carried over into peace as an expedient response to a crisis of the moment, and "not as the natural outcome of a long historical development." [2] Certainly a sense of Union was part of the Revolutionary age when independence and national integrity were beclouded. However, after the Federal Constitution reiterated Union's presence, the ensuing political struggles found Union still tentative. Few men in Jefferson's day felt wholly confident about the cost and form of security. For most, Union was an Experiment.

Such uncertainty dominated the second Continental Congress' portrayal of Union during 1777. In asking state approval for the Articles of Confederation, Congress despaired of ever getting units so different "in habits, produce, commerce, and internal policy" to accept Union. Consequently, creating Union was "a work which nothing but time and reflection, conspiring with a disposition to conciliate, could mature and accomplish." When Congress begged the states to recognize "the absolute necessity of uniting," it also emphasized that Union was essentially an attitude. It depended upon the age's lodestone: men must be persuaded into congenial dispositions toward a social compact. Hopefully, such acceptance was more than merely revulsion from disastrous anarchy. In conceding Union as "essential to our very existence as a free people," the Revolutionary leaders preferred to stress the significance of attitude: "a liberality becoming brethren." Thus might comrades in danger wisely seek "ties the most intimate and indissoluble." [3]

This wistful note displayed America's awareness of its unprecedented career. The Union was no more sure than the tactics the United States used to defend itself. Union was, in fact, a stratagem for the occasion, as suggested in George Washington's oft-expressed warning that America might yet become foolish in Europe's eye and "the Sport of European policy." Prudence meant an "inviolable efficacious Union." But what a successful Union would be like, Washington did not know. He could only implore that Heaven might give the "wisdom to adopt the Measures" which would produce Union.[4] A few months later, Jefferson wrote that only in strengthening the deliberative process, itself "the band of Union," could the actual Union be preserved.[5]

Washington and Jefferson here expose the dominant feature of early Union sentiment—an awareness that Union, though necessary and useful, continued to be elusive in its form and function. Union represented an attitude. It brought Washington to observe: "If we are afraid to trust one another under qualified powers there is an end of the Union." If there was mutual sentiment, then let an effective mechanism be designed. If not, said Washington, then America must stop pretending at unity. Washington insisted, "We are either a United people or we are not." [6] Similarly distressed with the public's disregard of "everything that concerns the Union," Rufus King thought of discarding the experiment. He proposed that wise men "withdraw in season to effect if possible some sort of personal security." [7]

Men like Washington accepted Union as simply one means by which experiments in the New World might escape failure and ridicule. When it seemed there would be no unity, Washington planned to avoid the Philadelphia Convention, whose futility would only increase Europe's contempt. Yet the experimental mood helped persuade him to reconsider and attend, in spite of the uncertainty of achieving unity. While awareness of the need for Union prevailed in Philadelphia, many delegates feared their neighbors did not appreciate sufficiently the importance of collaboration. They also sensed the difficulty of conveying its utility, wondering if the public would learn the price of union only through sorrow. As Thomas Higginson put it early in the conclave: "Sad experience alone will fully satisfy the body of this people that the Sovereignty of the Several States must in a degree be transferred to the Union." [8]

Fear of the penalty of localism or anarchy tempted some men to recommend swift consolidation as the path into an uneasy future. Urging action other than the Constitution's adoption, Virginia's Governor Edmund Randolph asserted: "Our very quiet depends upon the duration of the Union." Without real Union uninhibited quarreling among the states would produce a "deep and deadly" hatred.[9] James Wilson, who was more optimistic about the experiment's outcome, said that ratification would "make us a nation, and put it in the power of the Union to act as such." As a result, "We shall regain the confidence of our citizens, and command the respect of others." [10] A similar urgency impressed James McHenry. He informed the Maryland House of Delegates that the country's affairs "were on the brink of ruin and desolation." Once the tie of Union was slipped, there would be bloodshed among domestic interests. Opportunity to preserve the tie was vanishing.[11]

Other men were suspicious of associating Union with an ordered and respectable future. A leading cautioner, Richard Henry Lee, conceded that "our greater strength, safety, and happiness depends on our union." Yet foreseeing that this dependence could transform Union beyond a means into a devastating ultimate, Lee hastily added: "I am as clear that this Union had infinitely better be on principles that give security to the just rights and liberties of mankind, than on such principles as permit rulers to destroy them." [12] The need was to balance Union as the hope of security against Union as the enemy of freedom. With liberty and security as the object of unity, Union seemed a means rather than an end. It was the object of such means which the era of Washington and Jefferson debated.

This quest for security and liberty relegated Union to the role of a common sense method, rather than an end in itself. Early in the Philadelphia Convention, a resolution was first worded to say that "The Articles of Confederation ought to be so corrected and enlarged as to accomplish the objects proposed by their institution, namely, common defense, security of liberty, and general welfare." Ultimately an altered resolution carefully left the purposes of Union unchanged, but emphasized that "a Union of the States merely federal will not accomplish the objects proposed by the articles of condeferation [sic]." [13] John Jay told John Adams that any feeble Union would be short-lived; its successor would require strength "as may be compatible with liberty . . . to give us national security and respectability." [14]

Through the pages of the *Federalist,* Hamilton and Jay praised Union as an interesting effort. Hamilton's tone was representative when he pleaded in the eighth number that the threat of disunion be avoided. Unsuccessful union would mean that "our liberties would be a prey to the means of defending ourselves against the ambition and jealousy of each other." A few issues later, he reiterated "the importance of the Union to your political safety and happiness," and projected it as a "sacred knot." [15]

It was James Madison who suddenly glimpsed danger in confining Union to a casual role. He urged his colleagues in the Virginia ratification debate "not to mistake the end for the means. The end is union." Simply agreeing to the Constitution and Union would not be enough. While Madison avoided designating Union as sheer sentiment, Sam Adams was less cautious during the Massachusetts debate when he argued: "It is of the greatest importance that *America* should still be united in sentiment." For the people "such a union" was essential "to preserve their valuable rights and liberties." [16] At the time, however, this Spirit version was rarely seen. More representative was Hamilton's expression in the New York convention: "I am persuaded that a firm union is as necessary to perpetuate our liberties as it is to make us respectable." [17]

While equating security with liberty was fashionable, such a view barely hid the inherent paradox. Georgia's William Jackson conceded that sinews of iron were needed for Union to avert dismemberment and not "bid adieu to all the blessings we have purchased," even though he feared that a demanding Union government might mean that "civil wars break out." To which dilemma Samuel Livermore of New Hampshire replied with what eventually was the bitter answer to Union's ambiguity. He insisted the majority would have to use force if necessary to compel obedience from a minority, for successful opposition from the latter "must destroy the Union." [18]

Inevitably, this antagonism between means and end grew. Authoritative voices sought to soften it. In a long essay of 1792, Madison continued his flirtation with Union's role as an Ultimate. Demanding to know who were the real friends of Union, he said they were hardly those "who would force on the people the melancholy duty of choosing between the loss of the Union, and the loss of what the Union was meant to secure." Bemoaning such a contrived distinction, Madison suggested that "in a word, those who are the real friends of the Union" were those who favored republican policy as being "the only *cement* for the Union." [19]

Madison's argument, that since some device for order was needed, the Union was an experiment to ascertain the nature of both ends and means, was also the view of President Washington's Farewell Address. This Address is an excellent portrait of the Union as a means; the President called it "a main prop of your liberty." To any reflecting mind, he contended, "the continuance of the UNION as a primary object of patriotic desire" should be obvious. This being so, said Washington, if there were any doubts as to whether Union and liberty were compatible, "let experience solve it." To discard this view of Union as a flexible means and to "listen to mere speculation in such a case were criminal." [20] Washington's advice was to be increasingly ignored during the next fifty years.

A subtle change soon affected this ideology. The Union remained for many a means to secure liberty, but the experimental character of the technique withered. William H. Seward saw Experiment's demise when, in 1856, he told the North, "We inherited a fear of the dissolution of the Union, which can only be unwholesome when it ceases equally to affect the conduct of all the great parties to that sacred compact." The New York

Senator insisted that his section had allowed its "love for the Union to be abused so as to make us tolerate the evils that more than all others endanger it." Comparing the North to a man who built a splendid edifice and then refused all duty and enterprise lest he incur enemies who might destroy the building, Seward argued that, while the American people ought to preserve the Union, they also had to keep it a means of advancing "justice and humanity." Neglect in this respect "involves the chief peril to which the Union itself is exposed." [21] Nevertheless, Seward would be found leading in the support of Union as an Ultimate.

America never quite forgot the persisting opinion which opposed a Union Absolute by using the Experiment idea. Typical of those who saw unity a means was Josiah Quincy. In an 1811 speech he dismissed the widening adulation of Union by insisting upon analyzing its nature: "There is in it nothing of mystery. It depends upon the qualities of that Union, and it results from its effects upon our and our country's happiness." Revering Massachusetts, Quincy cherished Union as "the best external hope" for his state's peace and prosperity.[22] Less sanguine was Timothy Pickering, who warned against being deluded "by a word." Said this Federalist, "there is no magic in the sound of Union. If the great objects of union are utterly abandoned . . . let the Union be severed. Such a severance presents no Terrors for me." [23] Where a lingering sense of Experiment allowed Pickering to speak easily of Union's dissolution, a generation later Seward would have to approach the crisis of ends and means more cautiously.

Joining Pickering was his Southern counterpart, John Randolph of Roanoke, who combined vigor with more precision, as when he called Union "the *means* of securing the safety, liberty, and welfare of the confederacy and not itself an end to which these should be sacrificed." Ten years later, in 1824, Randolph persisted, actually falling into Pickering's own idiom: "There is no magic in this word *union*. I value it as the means of preserving the liberty and happiness of the people." The bachelor Randolph found Union, like marriage, less than inevitably good.[24] Even the young Daniel Webster accepted such conclusions.

Long before he embraced the Absolute concept which troubled
Seward, Webster warned that Union was valid only where certain
principles were safe. He even saw these principles gravely menaced
in the name of saving Union. Borrowing a leaf from Washington,
as was his habit, Webster thundered: "Those who cry out that the
Union is in danger are themselves the authors of that danger. . . .
They alone, sir, are friends to the Union . . . who endeavor to
maintain the principles of civil liberty . . . and to preserve the
spirit in which the Union was framed." [25] Webster's rival, William Pinkney, who was no less an orator, was more succinct during the Missouri debates: "The Union is a *means* not an *end*. By
requiring greater sacrifices of domestic power, the end is sacrificed
to the means." [26] And the New York *Examiner* bluntly asked: "Is
it certain that the union and liberty are inseparable? Is it certain
that they are compatible?" [27]

This equivocal Union, hovering between roles of Experiment
and Ultimate, supported by such spokesmen as Webster and Calhoun, tarried for another generation. Calhoun contended, in his
Address of 1831 to fellow South Carolinians who had been aroused
by the high tariff bill of 1828, that their struggle would disclose
if a free government could be widely extended. He insisted that
he still saw in "Union, as ordained by the Constitution, the means,
if wisely used," of establishing justice and security.[28] Repeatedly
he emphasized Union's role as Providence's method of bringing
power and renown, as long as members of the Union recalled the
distinction between means and goals.

By 1830, Daniel Webster seemed to allow this contrast to entice
him from his position of 1814. Scorning those "words of delusion
and folly, 'Liberty first and Union afterwards,' " he offered the
memorable contribution to Union piety, one which defied the rich
tradition of experiment and means: "Liberty *and* Union, now and
forever, one and inseparable." [29] Earlier, in first answering Robert
Hayne during their debate in the Senate, Webster had chastised
those who sought "to bring the Union into discussion, as a mere
question of present and temporary expediency; nothing more than
a mere matter of profit and loss." This view simply entitled its
holders to keep Union "while it suits local and temporary pur-

poses." [30] Such proponents, said Webster to the Pickering devotees, deemed Union "hardly a good. It is regarded as a possible means of good."

Even so, Webster remained somewhat ambiguous, which may help explain why the semblance of Experiment continued to attract his friend Justice Joseph Story, whose *Commentaries* observed that if Union "has become more deeply an object of regard and reverence, of attachment and pride, it is, because it is felt to be the parental guardian of our public and private rights." Story explained that this meant Union was "beloved, not for its power, but for its beneficence; not because it commands, but because it protects; not because it controls, but because it sustains the common interests, and the common liberties, and the common rights of the people." Twenty years later, an Indiana politician, Cyrus L. Dunham, was among those who echoed Story by saying: "I love this Union, not for itself, but as a means of securing and preserving what I hold dearer than aught else on earth—the liberties of the American people." [31]

Nevertheless, the Experiment version grew more awkward, thanks to the tempting view of Union as more than a means of perpetuating liberty. Did it not offer the only hope for liberty? Thus, the concept of means receded before an insistence that Union was divinely ordained to guarantee freedom. Webster had wrought his work well. Outside the South, the shade of Pickering was less often seen, although it did move through the pages of John Carrington's *New Englander*. The latter reproached those who prayed for Union's preservation, "whatever sacrifice of principle on our part may be needed." Instead, prayer was proposed, "*first* for the preservation of the law and the prophets, and *secondly* for the Union." [32] As for Webster, he now seemed oblivious to this plea. In a message regretting his inability to attend the seventy-fifth anniversary celebration at the Bunker Hill memorial, Webster hoped that the monument would be reduced to dust before it should behold a disgraced and ruined nation sacrilegiously breaking up "that UNION which has secured its liberty, fostered its prosperity, and spread its glory and renown throughout the world." [33]

The continued confusion of Union as means with Union as embodiment of liberty was well illustrated by an 1851 article in the *North American Review,* replete with the Websterian overtone: "Foremost among the questions of the day is that which relates to the preservation of the Union." All save the selfish believed that Union was the "absolute and fundamental condition" for welfare and rights. However, this plea held to the experimental guise by observing cautiously that America must "consider the relations which liberty, law, and Union sustain to each other." [34]

Even Abraham Lincoln was affected by this moment of transition for Union's ideology. In an 1845 statement, Lincoln mingled Union and liberty: "I hold it to be a paramount duty of us in the free states, due to the Union of the states, and perhaps to liberty itself (paradox though it may seem) to let the slavery of the other states alone." Talking in New York City on the eve of his inauguration, when Union hardly seemed an experiment, Lincoln still felt affected by this version. He judiciously conceded that he would never consent to destroy the Union under which the country had acquired its greatness, unless obliged by "that thing for which the Union itself was made." [35]

Others, like George William Curtis, made the same point by using ridicule. Speaking in 1859, Curtis demanded a real Union, not one "which good old gentlemen must coddle and pat and dandle, and declare wheedlingly is the dearest Union that ever was, so it is; and naughty, ugly old fanatics sha'n't frighten the pretty precious, no they sha'n't." Deploring how many persons still felt Union had to be saved through liberty's holding its tongue, Curtis said that these victims of the Absolute Union were telling the South, " 'if you'll really consent to stay in the Union, we'll see if we can't turn Plymouth Rock into a lump of dough.' " [36] This, for men like Curtis, allowed the means to destroy the end—a gross perversion of Union's character.

II

If the Union was an experiment in political technique, then surely it was modifiable and even dissoluble. Indeed, a casual approach to Union was widespread.[37] Union sentiment made A. C. Hanson, a generation after the Revolution, quite disgusted. "For my part," he wrote in 1810, "I say without reserve *the Union was long ago dissolved*," adding that it had never been criminal to argue for disunion. Now, despite current efforts to pretend to the contrary, Hanson announced that he would outlive the Union even in his feeble condition.[38]

Ten years later, John Quincy Adams and John C. Calhoun solemnly wondered if Union might survive. Although Calhoun considered the current Missouri Compromise controversy incapable of destroying unity, Adams nevertheless found his colleague musing aloud over Southern tactics should the Union collapse. Adams himself argued that the eradication of slavery's foul stain would necessitate "a dissolution, at least temporary, of the Union as now constituted," whereupon "the Union might then be reorganized on the fundamental principle of emancipation." Since there was no solution "but a new organization of the Union," Adams calmly explored methods toward this end. A constitutional convention might create "a new Union of thirteen or fourteen states" which could rally other states to the banner of emancipation. Although he would not always take this experimental approach, Adams was certain of one matter at that moment: "If the Union must be dissolved, slavery is precisely the question upon which it ought to break." Another national conclave could then "remedy the great imperfection of the present system." [39]

What made this disunionism strikingly different from the approach familiar after 1840 is that it lacked despair or finality. Those who so talked of dismemberment reflected the experimental mood; usually they planned simply to wipe the slate clean, beginning afresh with more insight. This relatively genial view soon disappeared, leaving the belief that dismemberment would be a desperate last act, with gloomy overtones not only for national unity but also for the nature of man. This development, however, had to await the wider acceptance of Union in its Absolute design.

An intermediate position was taken by Maryland's Robert Goldsborough. In accepting the virtue of disunion, he urged that eastern states combine with those north of the Ohio River to rule until disunion came. Denying that any person "dreads a Dispoliation of the Union" more than he did, Goldsborough considered it obvious that the collapse of the experiment was at hand. Therefore, "common prudence and common sense wd. say choose you the safest side of the Wreck." [40] More public and memorable was Thomas Cooper's candid 1827 speech at Columbia, South Carolina. Emphasizing that the principles of equality had been destroyed, Cooper said, "We shall 'ere long be compelled to calculate the value of our Union; and to enquire of what use to us is this most unequal alliance." [41] At the height of the Jacksonian tariff controversy, a letter in the Columbia *Telescope* insisted that dissolution had already occurred because the Union had been destroyed where it could really only exist, "in the hearts of the people." Talking of a bitterness so extreme between North and South that the passage of a century would not erase it, the writer said simply, "It is vain to cry out for the preservation of the Union." Samuel L. Southard, a New Jersey man, said in agreement that, with the day ruled by madness, wisdom and prudence necessary for saving Union could not be expected.[42]

The lingering acceptance of dissolution as an unexciting, logical result for experimental Union forced Daniel Webster to tell the Senate that many believed "our Union is nothing but a jumble of different and discordant interests, which must, ere long, be all resolved into their original state of separate existence." For the moment, he admitted that Union was a matter of mind. If the public accepted that it was merely a bundle of diverse interests, "our Union can hereafter be nothing." It had to be more than "a bond without affection." [43] Speaking a half-century after the Constitution's ratification, Webster and the nation now could discard the Union's role as Experiment in safety. America was secure in the Atlantic community. But Webster still hinted at the

Union's plasticity, an attribute remaining from the experimental role.

As late as 1844, while addressing Amherst's Literary Society, William H. Seward pictured the Union as in a state of becoming, "not yet absolutely centralized or consolidated." The crucial point remained, said he, whether the Union "so simple in principle, yet so complex in organization, and resting so much on consent" could endure. Seward seemed sanguine, even predicting that the secession of "one or more" states would not destroy the Union "as it might have done formerly." For "disunion is no longer a real terror, but is sinking into an antiquated superstition, haunting only minds which court the enervating spell." Momentarily falling beneath his own spell, Seward predicted that populous centers might exist on the western coast. Should Union not survive this challenge, he assumed that it could be dissolved amiably, teaching the world yet another lesson, "that of dividing without violence, and reconstructing without loss of liberty." [44]

This view proposed that time disclose whether Union was logical. For Benjamin Lincoln in 1786, Union was "little more than a name," the states "are really not embarked in the same bottom." Economic differences alone were "fountains . . . from which streams are constantly issuing of such different and discordant qualities that they may not be united without producing violent fermentations." This might be otherwise, said Lincoln, if Union extended from east to west. For him, unity between slave and shipping areas seemed foolish, convincing him that reason dictated a division.[45]

Similarly taken aback by this unnatural linking of North and South, George Clinton wrote in the New York *Journal* that a Union made up of elements "opposite and dissimilar in their nature" would "be like a house divided against itself." Clinton's foe, Alexander Hamilton, who believed that the public could be persuaded of almost anything, seemed happy to use the story of Clinton's insistence on Union's "inutility" against him.[46] The point was, however, well taken. Throughout the states people repeated Melancton Smith's insistence in the New York conven-

tion of ratification in 1788 that such a Union defied knowledge
and experience. Timothy Pickering of course used logic to batter
Union. A Northern league would be much more sensible and
promising, for it would "unite congenial characters." [47] In reply,
the more numerous ardent Unionists like Hezekiah Niles begged
that these skeptics recall Washington's refusal to admit "that the
south and the north are 'natural enemies.' " [48]

Later, with Absolute Union triumphing amidst the confusion
between ends and means, Ralph Waldo Emerson brought another
indictment based on logic. He observed in 1839 that it seemed
fashionable to join in the Websterian proclamation of Union as
sacred, with men subordinated to it, and commented: "I never
can forgive a great man who succumbs so far to the mere forms of
his day." Nor would nature forgive this distortion of itself, since
"man exists for his sake and not to add a laborer to the State."
Or, as Emerson put it in 1851, when he condemned Edward
Everett's support of the Fugitive Slave act, "Union is a delectable
thing, and so is wealth, and so is life, but they may all cost too
much, if they cost honour." [49]

The record justified Emerson in believing the Experiment concept had been forgotten. Few in 1861 harbored the sentiment in
Samuel Osgood's 1784 remark to John Adams, "Time will discover whether our Union is natural; or rather whether the Dispositions and Views of the several parts of the Continent are so
similar as that they can and will be happy under the same form
of government." [50] In suspending judgment on Union's logic,
Osgood used perhaps the basic quality of Experiment, that Union
was malleable. By the time Emerson chafed, this attribute, too,
had been overwhelmed by the Absolutists, who dismissed any
notion of Union being plastic or changeable. Despite some who
viewed America's search for Union as "chimerical," Nathan Dane
felt the past encouraged the experiment; with so fine a start, to
dissolve the Union now would be "worse than annihilation." [51]

While George Washington was hardly so sanguine, he did see
Union's future depending upon its flexibility, saying: "We have
errors to correct, we have probably too good an opinion of human
nature." Some kind of broad government was needed to make

Union effective, it could not rely upon Spirit alone. However, wrangling over new forms of Union left it "like a house on fire, whilst the most regular mode of extinguishing it is contended for, the building is reduced to ashes." Washington believed Union's final design to be far distant. Before achieving it, he was certain that the experiment "will yet be much troubled and tossed, and possibly wrecked altogether." [52]

A shattered Union was a real possibility to Washington. As the experiment's latest phase began in the Philadelphia Convention, he wondered if the theory of Union outstripped man's capacity for implementation. "Notwithstanding the boasted virtue of America," said the General to John Jay, "it is more than probable we shall exhibit the last melancholy proof that mankind are not competent to their own Government." [53] But not long after hearing these dour views, Jay received a surprisingly hopeful expression from John Adams. Still in England, Adams felt "that the union has great weight in the minds of the people. It is, indeed, an object of such magnitude that great sacrifices ought to be made to its preservation." But he agreed that the future form of Union "cannot be foreseen, fully, perhaps, by any man." [54]

Perhaps the chief beneficiary of the ratification era was the role of a popular spirit in a plastic Union. As Pierce Butler expressed it in 1788, "Our System is little better than matter of experiment, and that much must depend on the morals and manners of the People at large." Since Union covered "a large and wide Extended Empire," no matter how perfect its machinery might seem to be, its stability in Butler's view still relied on the "Patriotism of the Citizen." [55] The strength of such sentiment gratified Madison who ventured optimistically that now "the importance of the Union is justly estimated by all its parts," therefore "it may become perpetual." [56]

Young Oliver Wolcott viewed these efforts differently. Despite his new appointment as Auditor in Hamilton's Treasury, he called Union "an experiment of doubtful success." An assured future could come only with "steady operation," and Wolcott found that Southern participants in the experiment lacked this maturity in political science required for success.[57] Another New Englander,

Timothy Dwight, felt that reason would in time operate against the Union. "The limited powers of the human mind seem, hitherto, to have been incompetent to direct with success the internal affairs of a great empire." The Union was designed to promote public safety and prosperity. "How far it will answer this is yet to be proved." But Dwight willingly conceded that "for aught which man can foresee, other divisions, and other unions may be unnecessary." [58]

The elder Oliver Wolcott, then Governor of Connecticut, simply refused to rely on reason. He was convinced that the emotions accompanying Washington's retirement would "ascertain whether our present system and union can be preserved," and that Union's life "will be but of short duration." [59] Certainly President Washington's farewell message could not escape this uneasiness. The endeavor at unity was "well worth a fair and full experiment. With such powerful and obvious motives to Union, affecting all parts of our country, while experience shall not have demonstrated its impracticality, there will always be reason, to distrust the patriotism of those, who in any quarter may endeavor to weaken its bands."

At this point in his remarks, Washington planned to rebuke all skeptics by stressing the thoughtlessness of saying that diversity would ultimately bring the Union to ruin. But this statement was removed from the galley sheet, as was the further reminder, "To teach the minds of men to consider the Union as precarious—as an object to which they ought not to attach their hopes and fortunes" would thereby "chill the sentiment in its favor." The retiring President, seeking to avoid the excesses of experimentation, suggested: "It will be much wiser to habituate ourselves to reverence the Union as the palladium of our national happiness." [60]

The start of a new century saw Union's plastic nature nevertheless still popular. New York Congressman John Van Ness spoke typically of the experimental design: "We have opened a new road to ourselves, and are traveling on it without knowing to a certainty, what dangers may await us by the way." [61] Neither an election victory nor success in acquiring the Louisiana region persuaded Thomas Jefferson of Union's certainty. He told Dr.

Joseph Priestley in 1804 that it was actually of little importance to the happiness of the American people whether the Union remained unchanged, or whether "Atlantic and Mississippi confederacies" were formed. Jefferson, in fact, proposed to be quite noble about prospective disunion, for he reminded Priestley that the people "of the western confederacy will be as much our children & descendants as those of the eastern, and I feel myself as much identified with that country, in future time, as with this." [62] Not everyone understood or accepted Jefferson's attitude. Amidst New England's chilly displeasure at the Union's interior growth, Fisher Ames thought Jefferson's policy supposed that "our political probation was over." The belief that Union could emerge out of a constitution engrossed in parchment Ames called absurd and presumptuous. [63]

Tensions in 1820 seemed for some to confirm the tentative nature of Union. Richard Peters, who considered the Union unwieldy, predicted its evolution into "three or four governments, republican or monarchical" in the continent's vast interior. Until this transformation occurred, Peters advised doing "the best we can in our day; and leave future events to time or chance; or rather to the decrees of heaven, which we can neither foresee nor control." [64] The aged Jefferson now rejected such stoicism as Peters recommended. No longer comfortable with a plastic Union, Jefferson warned his old friend, Maine's John Holmes, of the blessings to be lost if an unwise generation failed to see that all principles were advanced more "by Union than by scission." Proclaiming that he would die believing the effort of 1776 was in vain, the Virginian still saluted Holmes "as the faithful advocate of the Union." [65]

Occasionally even Henry Clay's certainty was shaken. Not long after his defeat by Jackson, Clay doubted that reason would guide the experiment after all. Said the Kentuckian: "We have no past, no future. After forty-five years of existence under the present Constitution, what single principle is fixed?" Clay felt the Union's career was "as much afloat at sea as the day when the Constitution went into operation." He told Vice President Martin Van Buren that if the people persisted in their behavior, "I shall begin to fear that our experiment . . . had failed." This meant to Clay a prospect of "a few years of lingering and fretful existence," whereafter "we should end in dissolution of the Union, or in despotism." [66]

Amidst these Whiggish misgivings appeared a surprising note of confidence from James Fenimore Cooper in his *Notions of the Americans*. He seemed convinced of success for the Experiment of Union based on reason, drawing his confidence from the fact that the old confederate ideal was dying. For Cooper, the Union was "a superstructure regularly reared on a solid foundation, and not a tower from which a number of heavy and ill-balanced dependents are suspended." He added, "as to prognostics of its dissolution, they are founded on theories that are getting to be a little obsolete." The most discouraging thing to be said about Union was its short life. Yet even this had to be discounted, said Cooper, since hope for Union's continuance was brightened by the fact that now a life of less than 50 years contained progress enough to represent what would once have necessitated 300 years.[67]

Long after Cooper and Clay had seen in Union an Experiment, the semblance still lingered as voices in both North and South pronounced malleableness to be Union's redeeming quality. During the heyday of Union Absolute, in 1856, a *Democratic Review* author regretted that esteem for the intelligence of the people encouraged belief that the Union was firmly in place. This belief created the delusion that "the most awful earthquake could not shake, or the severest thunderbolt shiver this Union to pieces." All this proved that Washington's misgivings in his Farewell Address still were relevant and accurate.[68]

Emphasis upon the tentative Union entailed renewed pressure to distinguish between the functions of means and end. One detached observer, James Russell Lowell, bewildered by the "posture" of Union's development, attributed the confusion of 1860 to the nation's lack of political experience. Consequently, America's "experiment of democracy" was obliged to operate without basic principles. He added: "We have been running long enough by dead-reckoning . . . it is time to take the height of the sun of righteousness." The public needed respect for principle, with which Lowell said, "We shall be saved, even at the cost of dis-union." [69]

Such willingness to restore the Union as a means, and inciden-tally expendable, was endorsed in Wendell Phillips's 1861 oration, "Disunion." He spoke for those who, although become a minority, still embraced the semblance of Experiment. Phillips's words formed a kind of farewell to a now useless Union. "Let us not, however, too anxiously grieve over the Union of 1787. Real Unions are not made, they grow." Phillips added that the dying Union "was made, like an artificial waterfall or a Connecticut nutmeg. . . . It was a wall hastily built, in hard time, of round boulders; the cement has crumbled, and the smooth stones, obey-ing the law of gravity, tumble here and there." Phillips opposed stopping the tumble. Out of the lingering Experiment version he urged new tries at Union building. Since preserving the old would be "only a waste of means and temper," he proposed to "build, like the Pyramids, a fabric which every natural law guar-antees; or, better still, *plant* a Union whose life survives the ages and quietly gives birth to its successor." [70]

Phillips's remarks disclose an important confusion in the con-cepts of Union, one which could not determine whether Union was devised like a compact, or whether it had an organic or evolu-tionary origin. This problem was especially important for another view of Union, that of its role as a Polity.

2: Polity

To the end of his long life, James Madison wrestled with the issues that Wendell Phillips evaded so easily. Madison was dissatisfied with the belief that, unable to create Union themselves, men must await Union's evolution out of nature's mystery. He realized that Union's political career had certain physical engenderments. The same realization later encouraged both Jackson and Lincoln in their legalism. Yet the questions about Union as an organized community which exasperated the old Virginian epitomized the struggle in American thought.

Although Madison's concise mind resented it, he was baffled by the difficulty of cataloguing Union as a Polity. The problem was to distinguish between society and government. At first Union was deemed an experiment in governing, but ultimately it became this and more. As the organic thesis thrived, many persons found Union to be society itself. Out of this came more specific features in Union's meaning for America, especially the roles taken by the Constitution, the states, and the citizen. To reconstruct Union's political qualities need not entail reworking ground already turned by students of Constitutional history. The modern scholar, however, has been so preoccupied by the ante-bellum dispute over Constitutional terminology that he overlooks Union's meanings as an organized community. While these representations assuredly involved the Constitution, it was in a peculiar fashion and always as part of a larger complex.[1]

Two ideas of Polity struggled until 1861 to contain the concept of Union. Claims made for Union's constituting a system of government asserted either that such a Polity was grounded on a compact or that it had emerged organically. Yet these versions were vexed by an ambiguity which itself reflected the inexplicit history of the Union. Long before Hegel's immense influence, many Americans, heeding such advocates as Alexander Hamilton and James Wilson, accepted a Union arising from process rather than from human mandate. This role preferred a vague past for a Union clearly antedating both states and Constitution. Yet a confusion of terms sometimes made "organic" and "compact" synonymous and allowed those who invested these states with indivisible sovereignty to support the idea of an organic Union.

Conversely, the bond or compact idea usually found Union born from deliberate action. What proved impossible was to secure agreement over the identity of Union's maker—was it the states themselves, or could it have been the citizens of the states? To talk of Union as a compact raised inquiries about sovereignty's location and divisibility. Here, again, a semantic pitfall caused disorder, since some organicists made their case rather inconsistently on a mystically tinged compact, while the legalists employed the more precise contract.

Madison put the problem neatly: "It is so difficult to argue intelligibly concerning the compound nature of Government." This was especially so since "the idea of sovereignty, as divided between the Union and the members composing the Union" forced itself inevitably into the language of "those most strenuously contending for the unity and indivisibility of the *moral* being created by the social compact." Madison, fumbling with this concept, escaped by announcing that the Union's political character was unique and needed always to be so judged.[2]

To the eve of the Civil War the nation generally disregarded Madison's plea, permitting the Union as Polity to invoke ideologies never fully clarified. Finally, in behalf of the majority, Lincoln dismissed Union's theoretical character as irrelevant, thus

closing an astonishing tale. Where geographical challenge made
the early Union necessarily a metaphysical being, so a victory
over this challenge eventually swept aside the Union's appeal as
abstraction. Lincoln hardly deserves his repute as the great Mystic
of Union, for technological advance allowed him to accept majoritarianism as feasible. Lincoln actually broke with the mysticism
of Daniel Webster and Rufus Choate, which was rooted in the
fear of localism's erratic nature. Consequently, Union as Polity
was no longer debatable. Its Absolute quality could abandon the
docile status held uneasily since the time of Washington.

I

Union seen as a compact or a contract carried several implications. Had not the states served as contract-makers? Or, was
Union not built upon a compact among citizens? Was Union a
compact between the popular mind and the states, or did it arise
between states and the federal agency itself? Even more puzzling
was Benjamin Huger's analysis in 1803, when Congress found its
discussion of the electoral amendment often turning upon the
nature of the Union. Huger insisted that the Union was "in its
essence, a compact, a bargain, a perfect compromise of the interests, powers, influence, and rights of a number of independent
societies, who have united for their common advantage." Arguing that Union participants were no more bound than "by the
articles and conditions in the written contract," Huger rejected
the notion that state inhabitants had formed the Union "in mass
as one people." For him the Union was a compact, but not with
respect to the federal government itself, for such application
would combine all citizens "into one common mass." To avoid
this, Huger reiterated that the "one great Union" was compact
among the states themselves.[3]

Huger's troubles with the compact idea were often matched.
When the Massachusetts legislature criticized the 1812 War, it
insisted, "the States, as well as the individuals composing them,
are parties to the national compact." All states must avoid
measures failing "to cement that Union, which ought to be the

permanent aim of the General Government." Greed for more
territory was especially dangerous since it had "a direct tendency
to destroy the obligations of that compact, by which alone our
Union is maintained." Soon a Tennessean, John Rhea, argued
that the unique Union Polity found every citizen bound to every
other citizen by a "solemn obligation, either express or implied."
Put more directly, it was "that bond of Union that unites the
social compact and collects in one integrity the sovereign people
of the United States of America." [4]

Such bewildering references to Union as compact Polity spread
beyond Congress, as James Madison's struggle shows. During the
writing of the Constitution, Madison had said that similarity between the federal Union and the theoreticians' fundamental compact meant that one party was absolved from Union, should the
contract be breached by another. Similarly, in 1812, Madison told
the state rights extremist, Spencer Roane, that Union was "established by compact, not between the Government of the U. States,
and the State Governments; but between the States as sovereign
communities." Yet Madison also pleaded that in any collision
between the federal and state powers: "If the knot cannot be
untied by the text of the Constitution it ought not, certainly, to
be cut by any Political Alexander." Van Buren soon had Madison's word that if there proved no provision for deciding questions "between the Union & its members, but that of negotiation,
this failing, but that of war," then no actual Union Polity existed,
but merely a league. Worse, said Madison, it was a league, "with
too many Parties, to be uniformly observed or effectively maintained." [5]

A blurring, if not a change, of Madison's version of Union as
compact was apparent. Early in the South Carolina crisis, Madison tried for clarification. He conceded in 1829 that if Union
were "a mere league, each of the parties would have an equal
right to insist on the bargain as in another to renounce it." But
Madison now beheld a constitutional Union built upon a compact whose nature the participants as a Union must judge, yet
one where oppression might warrant a member's departure. "But
until such justifications can be pleaded, the compact is obliga-

tory." Even in his more elaborate statement to Nicholas Trist in 1830, Madison allowed renunciation, for since Union was a compact "among individuals as embodied into States, no State can at pleasure release itself therefrom. . . . The compact can only be dissolved by the consent of the other parties, or by usurpations or abuse of power justly having that effect."

Here Madison introduced a new insight. American Union grew from two compacts, he said. The first or "original compact is the one implied or presumed but nowhere reduced to writing, by which a people agree to form one society." The other was the written compact stemming from a people's creation of a government. Madison felt both the social and political compacts were blended, for the Union was first recognized and formalized in the Constitution.[6] Madison ignored the tantalizing implications of a Union rooted in the mystical realm of unwritten agreement. Another Virginian, John Taylor, was similarly smitten by this vague sense, as when he asserted, "The Union is a compact between two distinct minds, state and popular." [7]

Andrew Jackson long preferred Union as a compact, but without the ambiguities of the Virginians. He told Andrew Donelson in 1823 that Kentucky's printing of paper money violated the "compact," insisting: "Kentucky being a party to the social compact of the Union cannot pass laws inconsistent with the fundamental terms of that compact." Nullification was for Jackson an abomination which struck at "the social compact." It had to be met, he informed Van Buren, "or our Union is gone, and our liberties with it forever." The Union was designed to be perpetual, and Virginia's peculiar ideas of the compact failed here. Jackson compared Madisonian interpretations of Union's Polity to "a bag of sand with both ends opened, the moment the least pressure is upon it, the sand flows out at each end." [8]

A Kentucky senator, John Rowan, braved the mysteries of Madison's synthesis, by calling each state the locus of a social compact, thereby making each anterior to the Union. In the Union's creation, the aggregate people "absolved from the social compacts" surely had no role, since the new compact would entail majority rule. This meant that the Union as Polity was created by "the People of the States in their corporate capacity which is inseparable from civil society—which can be conferred by the social compact alone, and which alone exalts the People of that society into citizens, and enables them to act as a moral agent— as a unit—as a State." The compact for Union could never entail a national government.[9]

No matter what peculiar role the compact semblance was assigned, the implication never varied. Union as compact was a Polity out of deliberate association by explicit terms. Thus President John Tyler gloried in a national future resting upon "a love of union" which required "a sacred observance" and "a rigid and close adherence to the terms of our political compact." [10] While Tyler exulted, the governors of New York and Virginia debated the refusal of New York to surrender Negro seamen who were fugitive slaves. Virginia's acting governor, John Rutherfoord, challenged New York to decide if "the compact which binds together in peace and harmony the confederated states of our glorious and happy Union shall remain inviolate." Governor William H. Seward retorted that New York would ever "adhere to that Union with persevering fidelity and with unchanging affection even toward those who shall attempt to overthrow the sacred compact." [11]

It was this emotional foundation for compact that Webster rejected during his debate with Robert Hayne: "What is such a state of things but a mere connection during pleasure, or, to use the phraseology of the times, during feeling?" Even worse, it was not the feeling of the people who actually originated the relationship, but that of the state governments.[12] Yet, as Webster himself would show, the organicists relied on a Polity which suffered from the same ambiguity plaguing the contract idea. The fact that public opinion in America was concerned with property and order favored a Union superior to the whims of confederate policy or non-policy.

As a matter of course, James Wilson, Pennsylvania's great defender of order, insisted upon a Polity stemming from no state or states, "but resulting from the union of the whole." Consequently, in many respects the United States had to be "considered as one undivided, independent nation," possessing all the rights and powers provided by the great "law of nations." [13] This same sentiment embellished the Constitutional Convention, especially in the proposition that the United States "shall be for ever considered as one Body—corporate and politic in law, and entitled to all the rights, privileges and immunities which to Bodies Corporate do, or ought to appertain." [14]

Wilson's view was widely attacked, forcing Alexander Hamilton to assert that the overly compact-minded states would menace the happiness of the nation by too readily becoming "so many eccentric powers." Hamilton, of course, stressed that before the federal system was formed a Union Polity prevailed, and "therefore the idea of sovereignty in the Union is not incompatible with it." [15] Obviously, in an era dominated by a sense of experiment, the organic idea moved uneasily. The generation after Hamilton and Wilson found help in the common law traditions. For example, an 1825 essay in the *North American Review* said that 1776 had found the Americans "one people" clinging to the legacy of English common law, since the Revolution "did not dissolve the bonds of society, nor reduce us to a state of nature." The essay featured Peter S. Du Ponceau, Provost of Philadelphia's Law Academy, who maintained that a general legal system was spread over America long before the Constitution was drafted. Yet Du Ponceau himself confused the issue by embracing a contract semblance, saying that Union owed its nature to enduring fundamentals of the pre-existing social order.[16]

Alexis de Tocqueville, who listened to all sides in this controversy over Union's Polity, uneasily adopted the Madisonian equivocation. Although he set Union's birth in 1789, Tocqueville insisted that within its sovereignty the Union intended to "form one and the same people." Tocqueville acknowledged that this was "a singular position," and admitted that, while Union in some matters meant one people, "in relation to all the rest it is a nonentity." [17] Even John Quincy Adams, who often excelled Webster in advocating the organic Polity, was victimized by this paradox; he told Henry Clay that neither the Union government nor those of the states could lawfully interfere with each other.

Adams had to find the concept he could live with. He argued that the people's congress in 1776 had proclaimed the Union, which made the Constitution simply Union's "commission of government," so that "the Union is and necessarily must be, the judge of the extent of its own powers." Yet so were the states, and the resulting misunderstandings were "the more portentous of evil to the Union." Men "have all been nullifiers when in a passion." [18]

To make Union as Polity firmer than mere association or contract was encouraged by a staunch endorser, Daniel Webster. His reply in 1833 to Calhoun's Senate resolutions on Union was a significant move toward organicism. As Webster saw it, Calhoun's Union allowed members the right of withdrawal; whereas the true Union, antedating the Constitution, could not be left except by revolution. Nullification and secession were equally destructive, for they struck "a deadly blow at the vital principle of the whole Union." To this he added, "The Union is not a temporary partnership of States. It is the association of the people, under a constitution of government, uniting their power, joining together their highest interests, cementing their present enjoyments, and blending into one indivisible mass, all their hopes for the future." Thus Webster proclaimed himself bound to Union by indissoluble ties of affection and duty, and he felt all the "PEOPLE" agreed with him.[19]

In time, Webster would move closer to the more mystical implications of organic development, far beyond deliberative acts of creation. At the moment, he used the ambiguities of contract and compact. Compact, for him, meant organic development. Not so for South Carolina's Congressman Joseph A. Woodward, who insisted that Union had been a "remedial measure," arising from "no views of positive good or advantage." It "lay in the apprehensions of momentous evils—discord, turmoil, anarchy." Thus, "our fathers summed up in the word disunion" the epitome of evil. This position, in which Union could not confront its own death, contained surprisingly organic emphasis. Woodward's Union was an idea prevailing eternally among participants. It carried a force that was "an extra-governmental power relating to no function, office, or faculty," depending upon "those primordeal causes from which the Union itself sprang." [20]

This view of Union, evolving out of remote immutables, gained in appeal as the sectional crisis worsened. It provided President Franklin Pierce with material for his first message, which held that a return "to those principles, which constitute the organic basis of Union" actually revealed that "the substantive power, the popular force, and the large capacities for social and material development exist in the representative States." These, being "well-constituted republics," said Pierce, "alone are capable of maintaining and perpetuating the American Union." Thus, cultivated men would look to the states for the "vital essence" of Union's "being and greatness." [21]

To the unabashed organicist, Pierce's view was absurd. In his *Political Grammar of the United States,* Edward Mansfield insisted that Union stemmed from *"the whole people!"* To make the states sovereign would preclude "a close Union." But what puzzled Mansfield was the public's change of mind. In Washington's day, *"the consolidation of our union was the great end."* All else had been of "inferior magnitude." With the close of the Mexican War, it was Mansfield's opinion that "consolidation, whether of the union, of laws, or of government is the great object of fear and danger to a class of men, who either think or assert themselves to be the purest of patriots." [22] George Ticknor Curtis challenged this "class of men," and accused them of discarding all valid concepts of nationality. The South's "darling doctrine was that the Union was a contract." For Curtis, the only element of contract in the nature of the Union was in the honor of the participants—and, in his opinion, the South had lost all honor.[23]

Typical of the South's opinion, so despised by Curtis and Mansfield, was an editorial in the New Orleans *Bee,* which denounced the "intensely Unionish" nature of the Republican party. The editorial charged that the Republican party's "dogma of the perpetuity and imperishability of the Union carries with it the right to coercion for its enforcement." It further condemned Republican unawareness "that the very term 'Union' implies voluntary association, and that if any of the parties should be forced to maintain a compulsory compact, it would cease to be a Union, and would become a despotism." [24]

A more vigorous impatience was expressed early in 1861 by Illinois Congressman John A. McClernand. He found that history proved "the idea of *nationality* of the American people is as old as the Revolution itself," and he considered any debate over Union's organic or contractual nature "a complete dissipation of the misty and frivolous disquisitions that have taken place upon a mere philological question." Such inquiry had "no practical or useful application" unless the nature of the Union as Polity was "perverted to the conditions of an arbitrary and illogical definition." [25]

This judgment was overly harsh, for many contributors to Union ideology were genuinely interested in clarifying the political aspect of unity. Unfortunately, neither semantics nor history would co-operate. But controversy over the Union as Polity soon moved into more appealing areas: the relationships between the Union and three familiar segments of the body politic—the federal Constitution, the states, and the citizens. These discussions revolved around five exciting issues: the transcendent Union, the Constitution as Union's embodiment, the Union as balancing technique, the fraternal Union of states, and the Union of citizen-fellowship.

II

The idea of a transcendent Union, one not to be understood in terms of form, one which loomed as paternal figure above the states, had its function mostly in a matter of time. The argument was that Union preceded the Constitution, an important contention in the discussion of Polity. Rarely was there a question about Union pre-dating the Constitution, even Calhoun usually conceded this; rather, was there anything inherent and commanding about the historical presence of a Union? This hint of transcendence not only aided the campaign for contract, but organicists also found it a peculiarly satisfying appearance for Union.

Ideas of Union certainly flourished before 1787.[26] Late in 1775, Thomas Jefferson observed hopefully in Philadelphia that Canada would join the Congress, and thus "complete the American Union as far as we wish to have it completed." The Virginian also noted that independence could not exist until undecided colonies had acted favorably within their own assemblies. A premature declaration would mean that some colonies "might secede from the Union." [27] Many persons recognized the disastrous nature of such a split even at that time. John Adams brushed aside those who saw Union as simply "independent individuals making a bargain together." The question must never be "what we are now, but what we ought to be when our bargain shall be made." This, said Adams, was "to make us one individual only, it is to form us, like separate parcels of metal, into one common mass. We shall no longer retain our separate individuality, but become a single individual. . . ." Similar sentiment brought Henry Laurens to write that it was both the power and the duty "of the People . . . to establish the Honour of the American Union, without regard to private considerations." [28]

While the idea of Union evidently flourished in the 1770's, the political connotation was rarely clear. A Union in sentiment and action there was, but what of a formal design for Union? From the outset the response found two Unions to be present, a Union of thought and spirit as well as one of a formal body politic. George Washington's comments are a good example, as he put Union in the dual role of broad association and formal political bond. This appeared in his 1783 *Circular to the States,* which told the governors that American success depended first upon providing "An indissoluble Union of the States under one Federal Head." Ceaselessly stressing the weakness of the flesh, Washington reiterated "that without an entire conformity to the Spirit of the Union, we cannot exist as an Independent Power." An effective political design for Union could come through a proper "Disposition." [29]

But the fear was that this might be delayed until, as Richard Peters put it, "Some great Calamity must happen." Must the inspiration to translate Union into Polity await a sobering disaster? In such an atmosphere of experiment, the calamity might itself be suicidal. State selfishness was especially ominous, to "be pushed I fear 'till the Band is broken." Peters could only hope that Union still abided with "the good sense of the People." Ultimately this had to be put to use; otherwise, he said, "We shall be despised abroad and convulsed at Home if something is not speedily done to support our tottering Union." [30]

The dread crisis seemed at hand to the Virginia legislature in 1786. Now "the good people of America are to decide the solemn question whether they will by wise and magnanimous Efforts reap the just fruits . . . of that Union which they have cemented with so much of their common Blood." Virginia instructed her delegates to the Philadelphia conclave to contemplate "Alterations and further Provisions" necessary to make the Constitution "adequate to the Exigencies of the Union." These now famous admonitions were virtually copied by the other states in advising their representatives.[31]

Generally, the Convention members assumed the existence of a Union surpassing the merely political device of the hour. When several delegates contended that the word "perpetual" in the Articles meant that all states should meet in council upon equal terms as sovereigns, Butler of South Carolina replied for the prevailing mood that the reference meant "only the constant existence of our Union, and not the particular words which compose the Articles of the Union." [32] Jay and Madison supported this in their post-convention labors. Jay's second *Federalist* said that "a strong sense of the value and blessings of Union induced the people, at a very early period, to institute a federal government to preserve and protect it." In that same series, Madison later wrote how changes proposed by the new Constitution consisted "much less in the addition of NEW POWERS to the Union than in the invigoration of its ORIGINAL POWERS." [33]

While he agreed, Washington also feared that citizens might not always recognize this transcendent Union. During the ratification controversy he said, "The truth is men . . . cannot extend their ideas to the general welfare of the Union." To overcome this, Washington made the Farewell Address a blending of the mysticism and pragmatism so desirable in Union's early career. He warned: "To the efficacy and permanency of Your Union a

Government for the whole is indispensable." Washington praised the public for agreeing and acting: "Sensible of this momentous truth you have improved upon your first essay, by the adoption of a Constitution of Government, better calculated than your former for an intimate Union." Lest he seem to be advancing the Constitution as a powerful means of strengthening Union, Washington added that, whatever government did exist at any time "is sacredly obligatory upon all" until it might be "changed by an explicit and authentic act of the whole People." [34]

Union's transcendent version caused debate well into the nineteenth century, especially in contending that Union, being older than the Constitution, might somehow elude the constraining effect of the written word. The eminent lawyer, William Pinkney, closely paraphrased Madison and Butler in defending the Bank of the United States. Pinkney denied that the states possessed more original power than did the Union. He said that the Union's 1787 change of character "consisted much less in the addition of new powers to the Union than in the invigoration of the original powers." These were drawn from the people, "who are the fountain and source of all political powers." [35] Pinkney cherished Washington's Union, one fundamentally apart from any form of polity. A generation after Pinkney, the *Whig Review* discovered the same idea. Admitting that there may have been no "*Nation*— at least by a formal instrument," when the Continental Congress labored, yet there had been "one nation—more completely one than any in the world," thanks to "unity of territory, language, religion, and *interests*." Formal measures later "only confirmed this unity," so that the Constitution simply gave the Union a means "by which its powers should be ascertained and confirmed." [36]

But if Union's political essence surpassed any statute or document, then how could one define resistance against it? Pinkney sought an answer, arguing in Cohens v. Virginia that the Union's constitutional power "knows no locality. . . . Its march is through the Union, or it is nothing but a name." [37] Here appeared a fatherly Union, tenderly shepherding the states, a concept employed in William Rawle's famous study of the Constitution.

After noting that the Union was an association of the "people of republics," Rawle said that upon Union depended the states' republicanism. If the latter were menaced, "the paternal power of the Union could thus be called forth." [38]

Abraham Lincoln relied on this concept in rebuking those Union-lovers who disliked such federal prerogatives as holding forts. To them, "the Union, as a family relation, could not be anything like a regular marriage at all, but only a sort of free-love arrangement—to be maintained on what that sect calls passionate attraction." Asserting that states had their identity because of Union itself, Lincoln asked how a state could "carry with it out of the Union that which it holds in sacredness by virtue of its connection with the Union?" [39]

Lincoln was certainly not the first to contend that Union's transcendence gave it enduring reality. Andrew Jackson said in his South Carolina Proclamation that a sense of Union had prevailed even before independence was declared. When the Constitution became involved in the struggle for more perfect Union, it should have destroyed at least for all men "of plain, unsophisticated understanding" any lingering notions of a Union reliant upon local interests.[40] A month later, the North Carolina legislature affirmed that the Revolutionary watchword had been "liberty and union, now and forever, one and inseparable." So devoted were the American people to this ancient Union that its dissolution would "be accompanied by deeds of violence and scenes of blood, at the sight of which valor may stand appalled." [41]

Also during this time, Alexander H. Everett wrote that the central concern was not whether a Union would carry on. Any dissolution would be temporary, for the states could not remain politically apart, since America was one family, "bound together by the million various indissoluble ties of personal relationship." Americans "are in fact and in feeling *one people*. They were united, before they framed the Constitution, by the high and paramount device of the great Law giver of the Union: and whom God hath joined, man *cannot* put asunder." Enlarging this version of the fundamental Union, Everett said that, in defying England, colonists found that a *"substantial* Union naturally existed

among them." But the refinements in the Constitution made it
clear that Union's authority proceeded from and acted upon the
individual citizen, "and has little or no concern with the States." [42]
Even Webster agreed, telling the New-York Historical Society
shortly before he died, "No doubt the assembly of the first Continental Congress may be regarded as the era at which the union
of these States commenced." [43]

Among the great figures, however, the most revealing debate
over the Union's political transcendence ran between John Quincy
Adams and John C. Calhoun. Ex-President Adams vigorously
endorsed such a Union in orations of 1831 and 1839, insisting
that the people proclaimed Union prefatory to decreeing independence. "Their Union preceded their independence; nor was
their independence, nor has it ever since, been separable from
their union." The colonies never became sovereign states; they
had their being only in the transcendent Union. "Without Union
the covenant contains no pledge of freedom or independence."
Consequently, Adams scolded South Carolina for exploiting an
error emanating from the Confederation. The Confederation was
anti-Union, said Adams, built as it was upon an alliance of states.
The Declaration had studiously avoided designating the states as
sovereign, so that Union's soul was actually in this great popular
mandate. To see Union elsewhere was to distort its true nature.[44]

For Adams, America's great moment came with the decision to
retrace its steps "from the irresponsible depotism of state sovereignty to the self-evident truths of the Declaration of Independence." While state rights fostered discredited power, the true
Union was founded upon universal rights. It triumphed despite
the aberration of the Confederacy. The Constitution on the other
hand was a "work in which the people of the North American
Union . . . achieved the most transcendent act of power that social
man in his mental condition can perform." [45]

While Adams placed Union in an organic setting of human
fraternity, stronger and more enduring than any mere govern-
mental device, Calhoun was busily predicting calamity if the
Union's Constitution was defined as the act of the American
people "considered in the aggregate." For then, "the States at

once sink into mere geographical divisions—bearing the same relationship to the whole, as counties do to the States." In fact, said he, reassuringly, "the very idea of an *American People,* as constituting a single community, is a mere chimera. Such a community never, for a single moment, existed,—neither before nor since the Declaration of Independence." Calhoun admitted that some persons believed the Union preceded even the Declaration, and "that the Government is derived from the Union and not the Union from the Government." These confused minds, he observed, forgot "that the real question relates to the *character* of the Union, and not to the *time* of its commencement." With this baffling point, Calhoun immediately affirmed the Union's origin from a body of pre-existing groups, leaving it a Union "of communities," not "of individuals." While he acknowledged an "informal union" existed before independence was asserted, for him it was a union of the colonies as "political communities." [46]

Calhoun modified little of this 1831 position in his later *Discourse;* to him the Union remained "a government of States united in a political union in contra-distinction to a government of individuals socially united." While willing for Union to antedate the Constitution, Calhoun was appalled by the thought of a popular Union transcending government. It was gruesome enough to behold a Polity of individuals, since this might usher in the dreaded control by numerical majorities. But a transcendent Union, actually an organic one, was even more to be dreaded. Thus, Calhoun arrived at his version of Union's changeless Polity: the men of 1787 may have adopted a new government, but "their Union rested . . . on the same basis, as under the confederacy and the revolutionary government," a Union of separate communities.[47]

Young Congressman John Bell of Tennessee, a famous pacifier, made one of his early efforts in commenting on the clash between the Adams-Calhoun positions. He asserted that confidence in Union inevitably lagged as "the value of the Union itself, its date, and the consequences of its disruption, begin to be tolerated and canvassed in private discourse—nay in public debate." For the moment, Bell could believe that the controversy was not hostile "to the Union, for both parties, I verily believe, are equally friendly to the Union, but to a Union upon their own terms." [48]

As late as 1860, Union's transcendent version still encouraged the belief that trivial local and private considerations would be put aside. The Reverend James Craik observed that all real patriots loved their state, but they loved their country more, "and the whole Union is that country." Craik emphasized that "the Union is coeval with the colonization of the country. The Federal Government is but the present conventional expression of the previous Union, and the instrument by which the Union accomplishes its beneficent purpose." Craik distilled the transcendent Unionist's cry: "The UNION, therefore, is a FACT before and above the new form of government which is its *present practical expression.*" [49] It was thus a familiar context in which Lincoln set his First Inaugural Address. First asserting, "the Union is perpetual, confirmed by the history of the Union itself," Lincoln then emphasized Union's precedence over the corpus of Polity.[50] In so doing, he brought into focus another political aspect of Union closely allied with the transcendent version.

III

Those who accepted the organic Polity, like Lincoln, readily saw the Union as a vast fellowship. By investing Union's strength in the citizen himself, this idea happily countered the state rights view. George Washington wrote in 1783 that progress could come only with unity, and unity could arise only when counties and states would submerge themselves before "the general Interest." Until the nation accepted the pre-eminence of "the whole," Washington added, "I think we may properly be asked for what purpose do we farcically pretend to be united." [51] In endorsing a Union of citizens, James Wilson early told the Continental Congress that "the objects of its care are all the individuals of the states," and that the new Polity was "not so many states; we are one large state." At the Philadelphia Convention, Rufus King, in deploring the confusion over such terms as sovereignty, national, and federal, described the states as deaf and dumb political beings.

Although he admitted that the "Union of the States comprises the idea of a confederation," King insisted, "it comprises that also of consolidation." It had to be a "Union of the men comprising them [the states], from whence a *national* character results to the whole." [52]

It was apparent to James Madison that Wilson and King's version prevailed at the Philadelphia meeting; he told Jefferson that the Convention had "embraced the alternative of a Government which instead of operating on the States, should operate without their intervention on the individuals composing them." Although seeing men generally agreed that "Union could not be secured by any system founded on the principle of a Confederation of Sovereign States," Madison later repudiated this view. There would be no fraternal Union, for "each State, in ratifying the Constitution, is considered a sovereign body, independent of all others, and only to be bound by its voluntary act." [53] Possibly Madison spoke reassuringly to counteract Hamilton's insistence that the authority of the Union had to be extended to the "persons of the Citizens."

Of course Madison's equivocations revealed little about Union's design once the states had performed the precious "voluntary act." Perhaps James Wilson was correct, that the revised Union would indeed rely upon the *"majesty of the people."* In so urging, Wilson described history as irrelevant, for the experience of former leagues and unions offered little help. If Union were set upon a "representation of the *whole* Union," was it not "reasonable to suppose that the counsels of the whole will embrace the interest of every part?" [54]

Two generations later, Ralph Waldo Emerson sought to answer Wilson's question, which had continually recurred in national thought. Emerson envisioned America leading all mankind to the true Union, one of world-wide human fellowship. He wrote in his journal of "the destiny of America, the Union,—yes, great things, dear to the heart and imagination, and not to be put at risk by every young ranter." But there was "a larger state, a prior Union, still dearer to heart and imagination, and much longer to be our country," which of course was "the World." Against this implication of the American Union of human fellowship, said Emerson, "we will not levy war . . . to please this New Hampshire strapper nor the Carolinas." [55]

Between these expressions of Wilson and Emerson the Union's fellowship role pursued a varied career, while it steadily encouraged the organicist impression of Union. Something of it entered Justice James Iredell's 1796 charge that every citizen must see himself as a member of the Union community, "his individual interest, when it comes into competition, must yield to that of the State in which he resides"; and the state itself "when it stands in competition with that [interest] of the United States, must yield to this as a superior interest also, since a real and effective Union can be founded on no other basis." [56] Even such a doubter as Fisher Ames was struck by this idea. Ames told John Ward Fenno that, while "the mass of the nation are, of course, little affected by theories," nor hardly by events; nevertheless, a few ideas were deeply rooted in the citizens' minds. Said Ames: "I hope love of Union is one, and when the crisis arrives that will oblige them to choose, I flatter myself they will choose right." [57]

A more formal endorsement of this concept appeared in the 1823 House report on elections, which called for a popular attachment to Union, "this great palladium of our security and happiness." Consequently, state pride and sectional prejudice must recede before awareness that the citizens "are one people." Being "born to a common inheritance, purchased by the toils, the sacrifices, and the blood of their common ancestors," obviously "they should be united, not less by the ties of common sympathy and kindred feeling." [58]

Meanwhile, rising sectionalism dismayed many, including the Carolinian, George McDuffie, who said: "It seems to me that a new reading of State Rights is now, for the first time introduced. . . . Now the rights of the *States* are brought out in array against the rights of the *People*." [59] This battle made the fellowship Union even more prominent, and it encouraged William Pinkney to salute "the unsophisticated good sense and noble spirit" of the people. The citizen body, he said, would never countenance principles which would "not only shake the goodly fabric of the Union to its foundation, but reduce it to a melancholy ruin." The people know the Union as "the single pledge and guarantee of power and peace. Their warm and pious affections will cling to it as their only hope of prosperity and happiness, in defiance of pernicious abstractions." [60]

On the idea of a fellowship Union, Justice Joseph Story's pessimism was reminiscent of Fisher Ames. Story said, "The great difficulty is to make the mass of the people see their true interests." Awareness of Union as fellowship was kept from many citizens, because "so many political demagogues and so many party presses," were "in league to deceive them." [61] Story stressed a popular corollary of the fellowship version: Union was the people's, but it was always endangered by evil men who might pervert this natural relationship.

The often inconsistent Tocqueville lingered over this ingredient of fellowship Union, the citizen's awareness. Agreeing that "the subjects of the Union are not states, but private citizens," the Frenchman insisted that, where the old Confederation had presided over communities, now "the Union presides over individuals. Its force is not borrowed, but self-derived." Although the Union not only imposed law but actually governed, Tocqueville said that individuals, "each one of whom finding that he confronts the Union alone and isolated, cannot contemplate resistance." [62] Or, as Governor Levi Lincoln told the Massachusetts Legislature, "Let none be deceived. Resistance to the Union is treason against the people. . . . They who say nullification may be made consistent with the preservation of the Union, are unsafe guardians of the public weal." [63]

One of these "unsafe guardians," Calhoun, recently resigned as Vice President, found himself the recipient of an elaborately patient explanation from Webster. Calhoun's position, argued Webster, had the mistaken view that the "people of their own authority, can make but one government; or that the people of all the States have not united and cannot unite . . . together, directly as individuals, united under one government." Put simply, said Webster, Calhoun sought to resist the power of the popular will which could and had united the American people. Francis

C. Gray later said, during a ceremony honoring Webster, the Union was one "of the people . . . and it behooves the people . . . to maintain the Union as it is, in all its integrity." [64]

The fellowship or family image had a special appeal during the Nullification quarrel. For instance, the *American Quarterly Review* rejoiced that, while American society "composed of one people," might be divided into communities, still the people were "bound by a perpetual bond of Union." Americans had always been "one family." Deeming it absurd to think that separation of residence could dissever "the fraternal feeling that united them," the *Review* went back to the 1643 Boston association of the New England colonies to locate the beginnings of perpetual Union in America. "This Union, which may be considered as the germ of the American political system," clearly contained "the doctrine of the Unity of the American family." [65]

A *Whig Review* writer in 1849 rebuked those consolidationists who created a family Union into a "false god, or national idol," which had "drawn off so many worshippers from that sacred Federal Shrine." Such an idea was inherently ridiculous. "That the government is an *union* of some sort, will not be denied;" but "an union of the people *with themselves* is a manifest absurdity." Yet such was the family argument, said the *Review,* leaving the states which actually formed the Union nothing "but twinkling satellites," while the people as "a mass" were given vast power.[66]

In spite of many similar demurrers, acceptance of the fellowship Union grew; it reached its climax in Lincoln's reminder that the nation belonged to the people.[67] Lincoln surely knew the familiarity of this insistence that a state's concerns hardly compared to "the interests of the whole American Union." This comment was made by Charles H. Larrabee, who boasted of being not a Wisconsin citizen but an American citizen.[68] In the final days of crisis, politicians like Larrabee and Lincoln were joined by such authors as James Craik and George T. Curtis in urging the Union of fellowship. In his monumental constitutional history, Curtis pleaded for the "fundamental idea" upon which the Constitution rested—"the political union of the *people* of the

United States, as distinguished from a Union of the States." Craik hoped that the crisis might "arouse the people to their duty. . . . Let them take care that neither the commonwealth nor the Union shall be harmed. The power they possess is held in trust for the preservation of the Union, and not for its destruction." [69]

The fellowship concept was obviously advantageous for occasions when legalistic approaches were awkward. Since this proved often, the Union's supra-political semblance flourished accordingly, lending itself especially to organicism's cause. Not everyone, of course, could accept the resort to Spirit, especially if it suggested a Union whose political basis had all the dubious formality of a brotherhood. Thus, while many persons beheld the citizen body as the repository of Union, others looked to the Constitution as unity's bond.

IV

For some people the Constitution had become much more than simply a means of facilitating Union; Union itself became a way of preserving the Constitution. The Constitution had become the bastion for beleaguered sections and interests and a defense against the majoritarian attack. Even in the 1820's, and more especially with the labors of Webster, Calhoun, and Jefferson Davis, the Constitution became the incarnation of the Union. Calhoun put it majestically in his last public utterance: "It is in vain for a man to say he loves the Union if he does not protect the Constitution; for that is the bond that made the Union." [70]

Calhoun's view contained a principle superfluous earlier in the Union's life, when it luxuriated as an abstract ultimate or, paradoxically, as a means. The sense of Experiment was vivid enough to forestall any glorification of the Constitution during New England's uneasiness in the age of Jefferson and Madison. In fact, people were more concerned with how ineffective it was. Even so, the place of the Constitution in the political dimension of Union was discussed in the pre-Jackson period. Typically, Jay said simply that Union's only salvation was the Constitution. Anything else meant that " 'to your tents, O Israel!' would be the word. Then every band of union would be severed.... Then farewell to fraternal affections." Madison insisted "that the question on which the proposed Constitution must turn, is the simple one whether the Union shall or shall not be continued. There is in my opinion no middle ground to be taken." [71]

Hardly had the new federal Congress begun when the Pennsylvania legislature sent it a petition filled with pious Unionism which called the Constitution, "that compact... providing for the dignity and honor of the Union." During the same session, other voices, notably Theodore Sedgwick of Massachusetts, spoke of the Constitutional Convention as "forming the Union." [72] Perhaps the first great proclamation of the idea of Constitutional bond, however, came from Thomas Jefferson, newly inaugurated Vice President, when he told the Senate: "I consider the Union of these States as the first of blessings, and as the first of duties the preservation of that Constitution which secures it." [73] In his Inaugural Address, Madison listed among his intentions: "To hold the Union of the States as the basis of their peace and happiness; to support the Constitution, which is the cement of the Union, as well in its limitations as in its authorities." [74]

During the Monroe era, many people invoked the Constitution as a means of smoothing over divisive issues which had arisen. The inquiry of Virginia's Congressman Alexander Smyth in 1820 was typical: "What forms the Union of the United States?" His answer: "The Constitution," and therefore, "to become incorporated in the Union of the United States is to become a party to the Constitution." [75] By the time John Quincy Adams became President, Union ideology was so restless that it hastened Union's entombment within the Constitution.

Georgia's redoubtable Governor George Troup told his legislature that Georgia, far from being hostile to the Union, actually labored "to cement and perpetuate that Union, by bringing it back to the principles of the Constitution." By this, said Troup, "we mean a union of definite signification—a Constitutional union for all constitutional objects—a union for safety, for security of life, liberty, and property." Stressing Union's role as a method, Troup spoke of craving "a Union which means something, and which we love and cherish as a blessing." Instead, there arose "a Union for absorption and consolidation," one which "claims supremacy and exacts obedience—which construes that Constitution for itself." For Troup, "Such a union is not the union adopted by the states, and is not such a one as the states will support." In South Carolina, Governor John Taylor pleaded for "the instrument which binds the Union together." Eulogizing the Constitution as the embodiment of fairness and guardian of right, Taylor asked all to *"venerate the instrument"* and to "hold fast to it as the rock of our safety." [76] South Carolina swiftly followed this advice, as she understood it. Before an Independence Day gathering in Charleston, Robert Hayne announced his "sincere and ardent devotion to the Union," and his willingness to "lay down my life" if that would preserve Union "inviolate." Then he came to the point: "But the Union which I revere, and which is dear to my heart, is founded on the Constitution of my country. It is a constitutional union, which we are sworn to 'preserve, protect, and defend.' " To clarify the Union as Polity meant basing Union upon the Constitution, allowing James Hamilton to assail men who "could cry disunion against those who mean nothing more, than such a reform in the Constitution as will prevent disunion." To save the Union, one must save the Constitution.[77]

With this in mind, Justice Joseph Story's influential *Commentaries* opened with the hope that all men would realize that the Constitution was "the truest security of the Union." Without its guarantees, Story saw fears persisting that must "forever preserve the elements of doubt and discord, and bring into inquiry among many minds, the question of the value of the Union." [78]

Where Story accepted the constitutional bond with modest realism, Daniel Webster turned to passionate oratory. He told a New Hampshire crowd that when he beheld the Constitution, "I feel a burning zeal which prompts me to pour out my whole heart." Webster depicted the Constitution as "the band which binds together twelve million of brothers . . . the nearest approach of mortal to supreme wisdom." He declared to those who purchased liberty with blood "that without organization, freedom was not a blessing." Four years later, Webster confessed that the Union he served required that he "move off under no banner not known to the whole American people," who were united "in every thing in regard to which the Constitution has decreed their Union." No wonder Governor Edward Everett hailed Webster as a knight, "with the banner of the Union above his head, and the flaming cimeter of the Constitution in his hand." [79]

While some Boston citizens toasted the marriage of the Union and the Constitution, others attacked the abolitionists as marriage-wreckers. A meeting in 1835 condemned as "sinister" any provocation of "disaffection to our happy Union." This was a reference to the abolitionists' attack on the Constitution because it recognized slavery. People were not to forget that it was also "that sacred compact which constitutes the American union one nation." [80] In the Senate, James Buchanan said Constitutional Union was possible only because slavery was a matter left to the states. Consequently, the Constitution brought innumerable blessings to flow "from our happy Union" instead of "anarchy, jealousy, and civil war." If Congress acted against slavery to please the petitioners, "the Union will be dissolved, and incalculable evils will rise from its ashes." [81]

In the mid-forties, this version of Union as Polity was perfectly expressed in the chant of the *Southern Quarterly Review:* "To preserve the Constitution is to preserve the Union." Wilson Lumpkin said that scars upon the Union had come from attacks on the Constitution, a matter to be taken personally, for Lumpkin wanted the "continuance of no Union which degrades me." He predicted that, if the Union "cannot be brought back to the Constitution, this generation will not pass away before the glory of our Confederacy will have departed." By then, the *Democratic Review* was also in vehement agreement that David Wilmot's notorious proposal to ban slaves from any region acquired from Mexico would dissolve the Union by destroying the Constitution, "that sacred instrument of our common faith." [82]

Into the ensuing crisis stepped two figures, Daniel Webster and Jefferson Davis. The Massachusetts Senator's efforts in behalf of the Compromise of 1850 included the concession that American Polity was a Union "established, defined, and sanctioned by the

Constitution." [83] Then, a year before the 1852 election campaign, Webster announced that, if the Constitution and the Union endured, "they must stand together; if they fall, they must fall together. They are the images which present to every American his surest reliance and his brightest hopes." But as an organicist, Webster could not tarry here. Constitutional dispute should be set aside, he said, since the basic question merited neither ingenious disquisition nor theoretical or fanatical criticism. Repeatedly, Webster stressed that "the support of the Union is a great practical subject, involving the prosperity and glory of the whole country;" it affected "the prosperity of every individual in it." The only question was, "Are you a Union man?" Yet in his uninspired conclusion, Webster fell back: "To maintain that Union, we must observe, in good faith, the Constitution and all its parts." [84]

Emotionalism was indispensable to Webster. He held to the Constitution as bond of an absolute Union, while pleading that uncritical faith rather than alert scrutiny be the tie between citizen and Union. Even Washington was called from the tomb and made to relinquish his pragmatic Unionism in favor of Websterian Constitutionalism. Webster described how from the "abodes of the blessed," Washington cried out: "Hold fast by that Constitution which is the only security for the liberty which cost me and my associates seven years of war, of fire, and blood." [85]

There was a mild similarity between Webster and his fellow-Unionist, Jefferson Davis, in their reactions to the Constitution. Davis promised in 1850 that the Southern people would "preserve our constitutional Union; but the Union without the Constitution they hold to be a curse. With the Constitution, they will never abandon it." Thus, said he, one could be party "to this Union only under the Constitution." Rejecting the term "disunionist" as "odious," Davis described the essential quality of "our Union" to be a compact whose terms in "the Federal Constitution, form the bond of its connection, and breathed into it the breath of its existence." While touring the Northeast with President Pierce in 1853, Davis added, "I cannot conceive of the day when that bond can be broken." Five years later, he told cheering Bostonians in Faneuil Hall: "We became a nation by the Constitution; whatever is national springs from the Constitution; and national and constitutional are convertible terms." [86]

Writers in the leading political journals of the day offered ecstatic expressions over a Union bonded in the Constitution. The *Whig Review* stated that "our Union is but the symbol of Constitutional freedom;" and, "The Union, without a living, vital Constitution, is but a vain and empty name." If the original qualities were lost, the Union "is but a body powerless for good, strong for evil." Here was a challenge to a community torn between a devotion to rights and "an almost superstitious veneration for this Union." The *Democratic Review* assented: "The Constitution of the United States is the Union and the only Union known to the American people." Sacrifice founded the Union and the same would maintain it.[87] In the Lincoln-Douglas debates, Douglas called for "all Union-loving men," regardless of party designation, to "rally under the stars and stripes in defense of the Constitution, as our fathers made it, and of the Union as it has existed under the Constitution." [88]

It is difficult to select from the vast amount of material available the expression best conveying the bond concept of Union's Polity on the eve of the war. Congressman Eli Sims Shorter of Alabama asserted: "I love the Union. I am no disunionist *per se*. . . . I wish it to last as long as the sun shines or the water runs. Its 'music' has a charm to my ear; but I can never 'keep step to it' unless I am marching under *the banner of the Constitution*." Representative Muscoe Garnett of Virginia insisted upon a Union governed "by no visible embodiment of the law, but by the silent omnipotence of one great grand thought—the Constitution of the United States." Amidst House applause, Garnett proclaimed the Union's life and soul to be the Constitution.[89] The significant quality in this idea was that time had brought many organic implications to the Constitutional compact-bond version. This semblance, however, as shown by the Webster-Davis views, was useful to more than one position, an ambiguity which leads to another political design.

V

While the simplest and most manageable political position for Union was incorporation into the Constitution, it implied a more complex semblance, the Union seen as a technique in balance. Webster, in particular, had usually sought to avoid the idea that Union's structure was balanced between order and liberty—an exacting challenge in so broad a domain. Despite Webster's insistence that only as a remote abstraction could Union be mutually manifest, the balance function became a significant part of Unionist ideology. It apparently was the most useful transcription of the contract idea.

Insistence on the idea of preserving balance usually proceeded from a determination to prove that sovereignty could be successfully divided. This concept promised that it was possible to eat one's cake and have it too. Elbridge Gerry saw this when he announced that most men joined him in a devout prayer that the Confederation be "bound together by the most indissoluble union, but without renouncing their separate sovereignties and independence." [90] Gerry denied in 1790 that the Administration's efforts to strengthen the public credit would "raise the importance of the Union, and tend to depress the States." He said, "the constitutional balance between the Union and the States ought to be preserved," which left Union "a great political machine, in which the small wheels are as essential as the large; and if the former are deranged, the system must be destroyed." Vice President John Adams joined Gerry in this concern. Adams was convinced that "the rivalry between the State governments and the National government, is growing daily more active and ardent. Thirteen strong men embracing thirteen pillars at once, and bowing themselves in concert, will easily pull down a frail edifice." Balance could be achieved, in Adams' opinion, by clarifying the strength of the national government.[91]

John Quincy Adams sought for his generation to make manifest an inference from his father's views. The son wrote his elder: "In that *Union* is to me what the *balance* is to you." He asked his father to agree that, without these ideas, "there can be no good government among the people of North America." Both father and son did, however, remain disturbed by the widespread power-hunger among the states. The 1809 resolution of the Connecticut General Assembly expressed this attitude in the states when it urged them "vigilantly to watch over, and vigorously to maintain" the powers given them rather than the Union.[92]

In state assemblies and in the national legislature this balance was endlessly examined. Representative John Rowan of Kentucky pleaded that Congress do its utmost to invigorate the "sovereignty of the Union," which "should be retained to itself, and should not be encroached upon by the State authorities. As the whole to a part, so was the National existence to that of the State authorities." In the Union, said Rowan, "each sovereignty was politically, though not physically, of equal power." Thus, "that sovereignty, whether of the States or the Union, had an equal bias to self-extension." The nation must guard against menace to state powers, but it also "must not let them encroach on the sovereignty of the Union." [93]

Virginia's John Taylor ridiculed such fears and scoffed at the notion "that the Union is endangered by the ambition of the States." Taylor called this "a broad grin at common sense." All wise men knew from the Federalists' error that the way to damage the balance within Union was not through broad consolidation but "to assail the States in detail." He emphasized that "as the Federal government is designed to operate generally upon all the States for the sake of union, its partial operation upon one or a few, dismembers the intended combination and reinstates separate inimical interests." Then, offering a charming picture of balanced Union, Taylor asked: "May not the Federal government preserve the Union, though the States shall exercise their powers? Why then should the Federal government fish for the minnows reserved to the State Governments? Why should the strong David covet the poor Uriah's ewe lambs? If he gets them, will he love Uriah the better, or kill him through fear of his resentment? Is this the way to preserve the Union?" [94]

William Pinkney supported Rowan's position when he ex-

pressed alarm lest the haste to rescue the states' rights might ruin
the Union's power and so make it "a mere phantom . . . to deceive
and mock us," through "a pageant of mimic sovereignty, calculated to raise up hopes that it may leave them to perish." Pinkney demanded that a sense of balanced sovereignty save the Union
from becoming "a Creature half made up, without heart or brain,
or nerve or muscle." A generation later, the disillusioned Calhoun
ruefully noted how the North's desire to pull these nerves and
muscles had meant that the Union "instead of tending toward
dissolution from weakness tends strongly toward consolidation
from exuberance of strength." [95]

Persons in or near the presidency were especially prone to
depict Union's Polity as one hovering between sovereign polar-
ities. Andrew Jackson, seeking that high office in 1824, asserted:
"To keep the sovereignty of the States and the general government properly and harmoniously poised, is the pivot on which
must rest the freedom and happiness of this Country." Struggling
to please as many political supporters as he could, Old Hickory
praised the balance existing within the Union; too much power
for the Union "would bring despotism," while too small a share
would "introduce amongst the States anarchy, rivalry, and disunion." Keeping this balance was not easy, Jackson had to confess
after a year as President. In the Maysville Road veto message, he
acknowledged: "What is properly national in its character or
otherwise is an inquiry which is often extremely difficult of solution." [96]

Another Chief Executive, William Henry Harrison, said, "Our
Confederacy is perfectly illustrated by the terms and principles
governing a common copartnership. There is a fund of power to
be exercised under the direction of the joint councils of the allied
members, but that which has been reserved by the individual
members is intangible by the Common Government." [97] Even
Webster, lured by Presidential ambition, briefly seemed to accept
division of authority within Union. He advised the New York
Pilgrim Association, "this united system is held together by strong
tendencies to union, at the same time that it is kept from too
much leaning toward consolidation by a strong tendency in the

several States to support each its own power and consideration."
Thus the Constitution was, "for certain purposes, to make us *one
people,* though surely not for all purposes." Webster extolled the
beauty of this balanced system on his sojourns through the South.
The Union was "not an amalgamation of the whole people . . .
not an extinguishment of the State sovereignties. That would
have been an extinction, not a union of existing States." [98]

What politicians described so glibly, the earnest observer, Tocqueville, struggled to clarify. He noted how nearly all the plain
folk he met in America had an amazing grasp of the Union's complexity. The Union, said he, "consists of two distinct social struc-
tures, connected, and, as it were, encased one within the other."
In short, "there are twenty-four small sovereign nations, whose
agglomeration constitutes the body of the Union," although "the
sovereignty of the Union is so involved in that of the states that
it is impossible to distinguish its boundaries at the first glance.
The whole structure of the government is artificial."

The essence here was divided sovereignty, which "must always
be weaker than an entire one." Tocqueville did not hesitate to
point to Union's precariousness if it quarreled with a state, for
"fiction would give way to reality." The balance would be destroyed, since "the sovereignty of the Union is an abstract being,
which is connected with but few external objects; the sovereignty
of the states is perceptible by the senses, easily understood and
constantly active." [99]

The journals also took notice of this role for Union. During
the Nullification era, the *North American Review* righteously
asserted that for those accepting the general government as real
and rightful, whether Union originated in the will of the state
governments or from the people as a whole "is a point of no importance." Only those who "wish to establish the proposition that
the Union is a confederacy of independent States *subject to no
common government,*" found the question of Union's origin
vital.[100] Fifteen years later, the *Whig Review* spurned as "an idle
question" of political dawdlers, "the relative *dignity* of the State
governments, as compared with the Union." It would be about
as reasonable to have a "contest of pride between the human body

and its members," and it might help to remember that Union was in one sense a spirit and in another sense a government. The challenge was to have Union's mental and spiritual development keep pace with the "stupendous growth" of the political Union.[101]

This moderate position, seeking escape through appeals to both process and spirit, grew troubled when pressure after 1850 encouraged the proponents of more dramatic versions of Union's Polity. As late as 1860 in Louisville, however, the Reverend James Craik published a last justification for the idea of balance. In a pamphlet appropriately called, *The Union, National and State Sovereignty Alike Essential to American Liberty,* he urged that America recall the "forgotten but vital feature of Union," the element "which gives to the system its real character and its only chance of success and permanency." This was that "STATE SOVEREIGNTY AND NATIONAL SOVEREIGNTY CO-EXIST, AND ARE THE HEALTHFUL EQUIVALENTS OF EACH OTHER." For this ideal, Craik urged that rational men everywhere defend the dual nature in a Union of balance. Let the cry be: " 'We intend to preserve our rights and this Union together. You shall not touch the one, you shall not destroy the other.' " Craik feared that "little men" in Congress were incapable of seeing that dissolving Union or annihilating State sovereignty were each treasonable ventures against liberty, social order, humanity, and God. Craik was convinced that the "little" souls who prated about dissolving the Union simply did not or could not understand this divinely-balanced Polity.[102]

VI

Many of those castigated by Craik beheld Union as a fraternity among sovereign states. This political role has been made familiar through its association with the doctrine of state sovereignty. We need only acknowledge this concept, pointing to features about it that have been often ignored. A sense of fraternity arose from the fact that Union was a combination of states who were both creator and assurance of an uncorrupted Union. There was an implicit realization of the need to defend the states against rising majoritarianism in the Union.

Ultimately, this view had each state stand simultaneously in and out of the Union. States could not be more autonomous unless they embraced secession itself. Jefferson's Kentucky Resolutions, with their talk of "co-States," had encouraged this attitude. The first and key resolution called the Union a compact, in which "each State acceded as a State, and is an integral party, its Co-States forming, as to itself, the other party." Proceeding, "the government created by this compact" was not the judge of power delegated to itself, but rather, each state "has an equal right to judge for itself, as well of infractions as of the mode and measure of redress." [103]

Moving only slightly apart from such sentiment, President Monroe contended that the Union "contains two separate and independent governments"—the state for local and the other for national purposes. Struck by the unprecedented nature of this association, Monroe added that these two polities were linked by "a band altogether different and much stronger than . . . any league that was ever known before." This was the marvelous tie of similar ancestry, language, religion, birth, hazards, and history, which allowed sovereign states to blend, although Monroe cautiously remembered that Union had not arisen from an aggregate people. Although people could have devised a Union incorporating "themselves into one community, under one government," if they so desired, Monroe pointed out that "they wisely stopped, however." [104]

What Monroe approached circumspectly, the South Carolinians, tutored by Calhoun, confronted more directly in 1831. A report prepared for the legislature advised of the necessity "for a State to be both *in* and *out* of the Union at the same time." A member was "*in,* for all constitutional purposes,—and *out,* for all others; *in* to the extent of the delegated powers, and *out,* to that of the reserved." [105] Therefore, when South Carolina replied to Jackson's Proclamation against Nullification, it emphasized that each state had the right "whenever it may deem such a course necessary for the preservation of its liberties or vital interests, to secede peaceably from the Union." Nothing in the compact idea allowed the forcible retention of any state in the Union. During the crisis,

Calhoun wrote that the Union was ruined unless some method could make the Union's parts "just to *each other*." As he saw the design, the states "were intended to perform this high and conservative function, through the power of interposition." [106]

This portrait containing a fraternal Union of equals grew more fixed in Southern thought and inspired Democratic party doctrine until 1860. The *Democratic Review* affirmed in 1843 that "the Union can hold together" even if a population of 240 million spread within a century across the continent. The only condition to the continuance of fraternity was that "the theory of the State Rights doctrine be but fully and fairly carried out into practice." Nine months later, the *Review* was arguing that, for the friends of Union and the harmony of the states, the states' rights had to be preserved. "They present the only certain means" by which Union could be secured "to the lasting glory and happiness of our people." Such rights encouraged the *Review* to praise the "beautiful and well-ordered system of government which our fathers have given us and woe to the man who shall lay unhallowed hands upon it." [107]

This emphasis was often coupled with a warning that the Union's power, in evil hands, might menace the family. The *Southern Quarterly Review* reminded its readers that it was early feared Union would collapse from encroachments upon the federal government by the states. But half a century had proved the reverse to be quite likely. "Every State," said this journal, "that has a proper respect for itself as a sovereign and independent member of the Union," must not fail to guard its rights.[108] In the face of such continuous alarm, President Franklin Pierce urged Congress to avoid measures subversive to the true theory of the Union. He asked: "Are we not too prone to forget that the Federal Union is the creature of the States, not they of the Federal Union?" [109]

Southerners continued to warn against what one called "that school of politicians who believe that the Union is paramount to everything else." Senator Albert G. Brown of Mississippi said, "I put the rights of the States above the Union; I put the sovereignty of the States above the Union." For Brown, all these had been above Union "in the beginning." Consequently, he felt "a proper degree of devotion to the Union without feeling that all power is concentrated in the Union." Warning that "I shall sing no paeans to the Union," Brown re-emphasized that the rights of the states were undoubtedly superior, "and if that is to be disunion, let it be so." [110]

The strain of defending the fraternal view took its toll of Brown's usually urbane colleague, Jefferson Davis. Davis said in Maine that true Union spirit required the North to rejoice at the South's great agricultural advances. Such respect for local interests was unique and crucial, and Davis fretted at what might happen if America stepped into the tragic train of history. "Were ours a central consolidated government, instead of a Union of sovereign States, our fate might be learned from the history of other nations." [111] Later, in the Senate chamber, Davis remarked that William H. Seward was incapable of understanding "our doctrine of State rights," and attacked the New Yorker's Union simile, wherein the fathers built a temple, only to be stopped by a quarrel over whether the marble should be white or varied in hue. For Davis, this ignored the fact that the fathers simply were "providing a common agent for the States. . . . The States remained each its own temple. They made an agent." Union's citizens rested beneath the state government, sitting "as under our own vine and fig tree, secure in our power to maintain our rights." [112]

Before the South made this concept of Union's Polity largely her own, it had thrived elsewhere. The New England community, of course, once accepted the idea. The statement of the Connecticut General Assembly in 1812 was typical: "It must not be forgotten that the state of Connecticut is a FREE SOVEREIGN and INDEPENDENT state." But New England was far from alone. Alarmed at the prospect in 1811 of renewing the charter of the Bank of the United States, Pennsylvania's General Assembly insisted the Union's political nature was "to all intents and purposes a treaty between sovereign states." [113]

Soon after the Missouri Compromise struggle the idea of fraternal Union received ardent support from Missouri's Thomas H. Benton, who denounced majoritarianism within the Union. Benton preceded Calhoun in warning that, should both elements of Congress come under majority rule, consolidation would be "false and ruinous" to the Union's Polity. "The Union could not have been formed in that principle, nor could it now exist under it if introduced. The federative principle yielded all that can be yielded in . . . 1787." Explaining that any further concession would jeopardize the voice of the small states, Benton called their guaranteed identity the essence of the fraternal Union.[114] Another spokesman, Ralph Ingersoll of Connecticut, said: "The federative power is about all we have left to remind us what we once were." Now with this menaced, how could men be indifferent as the Union, "the old family mansion," was being destroyed? Assuredly, he said, the little states would fight rather than submit.

Small states' anguish encouraged Southern spokesmen to voice their own fears. The problem, according to Andrew Stevenson, was that so many minds had been deluded to see the Union "for all purposes, as one People." Stevenson suggested that foreign policy diminished the fact that "internally, and for other objects, we are distinct and independent Societies of Freemen." When a stand against the world was needed, this version of Union offered status as "one, and indivisible," but "amongst ourselves, we are many!" Although this seemed obvious, Stevenson described thirty years of disagreement over whether the states were parties to the Union in their sovereign and political character or whether the Union was formed by the people of America as "one Nation."[115] Tocqueville recorded John McLean's opinion: "What seems to me most favourable with us for the institution and maintenance of Republican institutions is our division by states." It would be impossible long to govern the Union democratically, he felt, if it were "composed of but a single people." Thus, under a Union of states, "we have the happiness of small people and the strength of a great nation."[116]

Typical of the rising editorial plea for this concept of Union was the Lynchburg *Jeffersonian Republican*'s insistence that the Union was one of states, "not a union of all the people of the states, as one great and indistinguished mass, but *a union of the several states,* each considered as individual bodies politic." To betray this role through consolidation would inevitably bring such a disaster.[117] The *Republican* felt it better that dissolution come, a view with which William Rawle had earlier agreed. Certainly states could withdraw from the Union, Rawle said, since "government of dissimilar forms and principles cannot long maintain a binding coalition." And when the cleavage did appear, Rawle asserted that "the secession of a state from the Union depends on the will of the people of such state." [118]

Rawle's outlook, like others cited here, suggests that Union's political semblances forced men to consider even more fundamental its spiritual roles. Tocqueville had trenchantly observed that Union's power was as an abstraction. In the end, this quality was considered by many people to hold more security than any consideration of Polity.

3: *Spirit*

The Union's role as Spirit represented its greatest triumph as well as its deepest failure. As Spirit, the Union was approachable from two vantages. One of these visualized Union as inherently a sense of fraternity, a zeal of mystic origin; in short, the Union was a matter of intuition. There were strongly organic overtones in this Romantic view. Union here was made to emanate from instinctual association on the part of participants. The other vantage found Union arising from rational choice. Here the Union as Spirit was seen stemming from a sense of interest, of practical necessity. In such a setting, Union's appeal waxed in direct proportion to the adversity felt by participants. This spirit of felt need, of deliberateness, also resembled a form of contract.

In its spiritual character, Union blended the two great intellectual traditions of the early nineteenth century, the Romantic and the Rationalist. When Lincoln had to abandon the Union as intuitive spirit, it was the Romantic cause suffering another defeat. When a tangible, absolute Union was called forth by the circumstances of the mid-century, it marked victory for a side fundamentally Hobbesian at heart.

Hermann von Holst, the historian, sensed this spiritual design when he spoke of America's venturing "to outdo the mystery of the Trinity by endeavoring to make thirteen one while leaving the one thirteen." He added: "The sovereignty of the Union was an abstraction, an artificial idea which could be made a reality only inasmuch as the circumstances which had made this idea a necessity should imperatively demand it." [1] Here, von Holst could not see how Union's ideology was influenced by technology. Where, in the age of Jefferson, Union was seen as a pious hope for a shared sense of unity, in 1860 the New America created by technology decreed a Union which must be endorsed rationally. With physical consolidation, the idea of Union abandoned John Taylor's agrarianism to accept the fact and responsibility of unity necessary and absolute.

I

Union as intuition had two strong supporters, George Washington and James Wilson. Gloomily noting the chaos in 1785, Washington put into two remarkable letters his conclusion that no Union would succeed until a spiritual awareness was born in the public heart. The retired hero contended that, with wisdom absent in American politics, Union must wait until the citizens sensed what was appropriate, for "the truth is, the people must feel before they will see." In time, even the mercantile interests would somehow grasp the concept of the *"whole* Union," for Washington predicted that, while the awakening might be slow, "the people will be right at last." To aid in hastening an awareness of Union's merit, Washington proposed some central seat of learning. Young Americans, though from all parts of the nation, would here discover "the true interests and policy of their Country," thus helping "to do away with local attachments, and State prejudices." [2] Washington's dream of a national university had wide appeal through the next generation, although some people, like Thomas Jefferson, thought that simply attending Congress might teach young men "the importance of the Union." Those who remained at home found it easy to see human affairs merely as "a system of jealousy and self-interest," views which Jefferson found corrosive to the idea of Union.[3]

Overcoming this "system" often seemed discouraging to Washington, who wondered if citizens could respond to such an abstraction as the "general welfare of the Union." Men could not realize "that those very things which they gave up operate to their advantage through the medium of the general interest." Repeatedly Washington called upon citizens to create Union by embracing its essence, "a spirit of accomodation," or as a pattern of "temporizing yieldings." In talking of the intuitive grasp which to him was Union's core, Washington always recognized American circumstance. Given the political and physical facts of a dispersed community, exalted sentiment was all that advocates of Union could use.[4]

The views of James Wilson were much more elaborate. In Philadelphia during the winter of 1790-91, President Washington and other leaders heard Wilson argue in a group of lectures that Union's hope rested in its being accepted on a spiritual basis. If confederation were to survive on the American continent, a "union of councils and interests" would not be adequate. To provide the "very life and soul," Wilson called for "A Union of hearts and affections." He knew that "to embrace the whole, requires an expansion of mind, of talents, and of temper," a disposition threatened by excessive moderation and prudence. By these, "the patriotic emanations of the soul, which would otherwise be diffused over the whole Union, will be refracted and converted to a very narrow and inconsiderable part of it." [5]

The concept of a spiritual Union, intuitively perceived, rising from a concept of sublime human fraternity, and ardently espoused by Washington and Wilson, was popular from the beginning. It thrived especially among those opposing Union's transformation into a mundane absolute, those like James Buchanan who were not in favor of a formal Union. Warning a later Philadelphia audience that "The Union cannot long endure, if it be bound together only by paper bonds," Buchanan invoked Washington's majestic vision by saying simply that Union could be "firmly cemented alone by the affections of the people of the different States for each other." What had to be rekindled, he insisted, was the "fraternal affection" of the noble Founding Fathers who understood the true character of Union.[6]

The careers of Wilson and Buchanan, both Pennsylvania missionaries for a Union built upon the capacity of man to surpass himself, span Union's history as an idea. Their cause was evident in 1774, when John Trumbull offered verse to this shadowy semblance. Clearly hoping for a spirit Union, he wrote:

> Fraternal bands with vows accordant join,
> One guardian genius, one pervading soul
> Nerves the bold arm, inspires the just design,
> Combines, enlivens, and illumines the whole.[7]

But was this guardian soul simply an exercise in the idea that thinking might well make it so? There was a hint of this in Dr. John Witherspoon's fear that, unless the idea of Union remained uppermost, citizens would be distracted by petty quarreling. Indeed, he predicted: "Should the idea get abroad that there is likely to be no union among us, it will damp the mind of the people, diminish the glory of our struggle, and lessen its importance." [8]

Need for a proper attitude was emphasized during the days of constitutional revamping. Edmund Pendleton suggested no one ever believed that, mechanically, the Articles of Confederation had maintained Union. The credit went to the "spirit of America"; this was the bond of Union, "not that insignificant paper." Pendleton deplored how many now turned from that Union spirit, preferring "to catch at feathers." [9] Although the revitalized Union encouraged a scramble over economic mandate between central and local authority, Pendleton was convinced that only a superior Union spirit would produce an economic program palatable to all.

In this there was wide agreement. Congressman Thomas T. Tucker of South Carolina emphasized that no tariff must hinder the critical presence of "mutual deference and accommodation." [10] James Madison, equally distressed by excursions into economic legislation, insisted that local material needs did not stimulate his opposition, but did cause him to fear that they menaced "the existence of the Union." Imprudence would lead to "detestation" of the Union, so that "the language of complaint will circulate universally, and change the favorable opinion now entertained to dislike and clamor." Later, in pleading that patriots see Union's complexity, Madison asked that all men help "to erect over the whole, one paramount Empire of reason, benevolence, and brotherly affection." [11]

But a new century seemed to discourage this view by heaping high our domestic and international tribulations. Many people became even more dependent on the belief that Union could prevail in spite of enormous physical and political harassment if only the proper chords be struck in men's minds. It became no easier, however, to define this spirit. Josiah Quincy asked: "What is it that constitutes the moral tie of our nation?" In reply, he rejected "that paper contract called the Constitution," pointing to "that moral sentiment which pervades all, and is precious to all, of having shared common dangers for the attainment of common blessings. The strong ties of every people are those which spring from the heart and twine through the affections." This, Quincy said, was the essence of the Union, that "family compact" whereby "in the temple of patriotism all have the same worship." [12] On this basis, twenty-two-year-old Robert Y. Hayne chastised New England, lamenting: "The benefits of our UNION have been questioned, and we are called upon, to establish by reasoning, what once rested upon the basis of universal public feeling." [13]

The Jeffersonian group was similarly inclined to urge the Spirit Union. Commenting on the folly of the Hartford Convention, where New England states debated Union's advantage, Jefferson himself observed, "The cement of this Union is in the heart-blood of every American." [14] Albert Gallatin felt that the War of 1812 had "renewed and reinstated the national feelings and character which the Revolution had given." Now Union's citizens possessed "more general objects of attachment with which their pride and political opinions are connected. They are more Americans; they feel and act as a nation; and I hope that the permanency of the Union is thereby better secured." [15]

However common were such evocations of the Spirit Union, physical and political realities still threatened to undo this intuitive system. A rising generation, confronted by the controversies of Monroe's era, had to hope that a Spirit appeal might perpetu-ally assuage and sublimate Union's irksome material disagree-ments. These controversies involved questions as to what the Union as Polity might do, sharpening the contrast between a Union of action and Union as intuitive fraternity. Some, like Henry Clay, saw little difference. But Congressman James Pindall of Virginia told Clay that the affirmation of Union by consolidat-ing the states would be disastrous. While agreeing that America was one family, Pindall stressed that "we are a family by affinity, and in habit." This did not mean that the family dwelt in a common room. Another Virginian, Philip P. Barbour, conceded that more association between the sections might diminish the alarming prejudices and jealousies, thus allowing Union to "be knit together by a sympathy of feelings, by a community of habits and manners." Barbour was only one of many who spoke of spirit, of brotherhood, of harmonious reciprocity, as the very Union itself.[16]

Under these circumstances it was appropriate that *Niles' Reg-ister* should offer an editorial on American sentiment. Marking the close of the century's second decade, the journal praised national feeling as "the bond of social compact, the centre point of social virtue." No one without this sense could be respected, although even Niles conceded that another generation would be required before the citizens of the Union "would believe and act [as] if they belonged to and had a country for themselves." [17]

Niles sensed that Union ideology could not elude the tangible considerations that were obvious by Monroe's time. These changes brought a more complex maturation than the national mind might find convenient, for treasured localism was being overcome. The improvement of transportation, commerce, and industry meant a revolutionized setting not to everyone's liking. Conse-quently, devotees of the Spirit Union grew more ardent, hoping to avoid an impersonal or structured design. The moment dreaded was that when disillusioned men would cease intuitively to reach for Union, recoiling instead into provincialism. A Spirit concept thus steadied those who hoped that the world of Jefferson might somehow be spared the pain of growing with the nineteenth century.

The difficulty, obviously, was deciding the character as well as the nurture of a fellowship Union. A group from Virginia, aroused by the bitter tariff and Missouri struggles, chose in 1820 to reiterate, "identity of feeling and interest is the cement of our Union." The Virginians threw down the gauntlet: "In the nature of man, it cannot be expected that the agricultural and commercial portions of the Union could experience any other feeling than that of the bitterest hatred toward the manufacturing interest." If the manufacturing interest made impossible demands upon the fraternity, men of Union "would cease to feel as members of one great family." [18]

Equally moving was the semblance pictured in 1826 by Edward Everett: "The Union, comparatively speaking, is the metaphysical and theoretical thing." The real beings, the states, find that "the family feeling binds their parts together. The seat of power is in their bosoms." New Yorkers petitioned that new issues be judged by whether they "promote those feelings of common interest and mutual kindness on which this Union was founded, and which are its strongest cement." [19]

Such views always stressed the delicacy of the Spirit Union, thereby revealing its tentative aspect. In 1824, South Carolinians were begging that Congress devise ways of encouraging "national character and national sentiment." According to one, George McDuffie, these required "some great monuments of the enterprise of the nation, which the people of the Union will contemplate with a common pride." But such, McDuffie admitted, would not guarantee to "make this Union perpetual; for the frailty and imperfection of everything human forbids us to indulge that hope." [20] In the North, Daniel Webster urged a Bunker Hill throng: "Let us cultivate a true spirit of Union. . . . Let us act under a settled conviction, and an habitual feeling, that these twenty-four States are one country. Let our conceptions be enlarged to the circle of our duties. Let us extend our ideas over the whole of the vast field in which we are called to act." [21]

A marvelous coincidence spurred these advocates. In 1826, the simultaneous passing of two great Founding Fathers, Jefferson and Adams, was so awesome as to be a contemporary fable. Now indeed, said one eulogist, ought America to bring her divisive sentiments under "this sublime symbol of Union." The moment was an important one for the Union of faith.[22] It was also appropriate, for Jefferson himself had fought the nation's growing cynicism before his death. He implored Edward Livingston to use his lifetime "in cherishing every measure which may foster our brotherly Union," although this was possible only by "much compromise of opinion." All of which meant "that things even salutary should not be crammed down the throats of dissenting brethren, especially when they may be put into a form to be willingly swallowed." Jefferson's mature advice foreshadowed the intuitive Unionist program: "a great deal of indulgence is necessary to strengthen habits of harmony and fraternity." [23]

Even those most alarmed at sins in the name of Union turned repeatedly to its muse. The staunch foe of majoritarianism, James H. Hammond, insisted that all nullifiers "love and venerate the American Union. We have a holy, all-but a superstitious reverence for it." There was no doubt, said Hammond, "that an Union, such as it ought to be, will be incalculably beneficial to us." But such unity arose from a sense not only of "future blessings," but "from the events of the past." [24] Robert Y. Hayne agreed the states were "restrained by a sincere love of the Union. The people of the United States cherish a devotion to the Union so pure, so ardent, that nothing short of intolerable oppression can ever tempt them to do anything that may possibly endanger it." [25]

Hayne's remarks reveal an important change in the Spirit design, for the Union was becoming less a spirit than an entity about which spiritual responses formed. This distinction meant trouble, for such a semblance could not represent an autonomous Union to which individuals necessarily had to respond. In time, the body and the spirit were rent, despite the pretense of men like Webster and Buchanan that the dichotomy either was non-existent or else of no consequence.

Such a split bothered Livingston as he pursued the charge given him by Jefferson. Asking "if the people are taught to believe in a permanent hostility of one part of the Union towards another," he urged that disunion instead should be deemed degrading, and banished from men's minds. Yet while endorsing right-thinking, Livingston himself could not resist Union's material dimension, saying that, were Jefferson present, he might join in likening the Union to the Capitol's columns. Where once their elements were "worthless heaps of unconnected sand and pebbles, washed apart by every wave," now they were "bound together by the indissoluble cement of nature." These lofty columns were "symbols of the Union and strength on which alone, our Government can rest; solid within, polished without." [26]

Struck by this dualism, Tocqueville caught the issue which men like Hayne and Livingston sought to resolve. Said he, "the Union is an ideal nation which exists, so to speak, only in the mind, and whose limits and extent can only be discerned by the understanding." From this came a federal system, built "upon a theory which is complicated at the best, and which demands the daily exercise of a considerable share of discretion on the part of those it governs." Nothing so astonished the European traveling in the United States as the absence of government. "Written laws exist in America, and one sees the daily execution of them; but although everything moves regularly, the mover can nowhere be discovered. The hand that directs the social machine is invisible." Tocqueville received a good explanation of this from Timothy Walker, a Harvard-trained lawyer in Cincinnati. "Up to now everything prospers," said Walker, for "at the bottom of men's hearts there is even a strong instinct that attaches all to the Union." Even so, Walker had to add, "I am not without uneasiness as to its duration." [27]

It was caution well founded, since the Spirit concept was soon sorely tested by the Nullification issue. Once this crisis had passed, the Spirit's defenders breathed easily. William Ellery Channing could boast: "Our Union is not so weak as our alarmists imagine. It has stood many storms, and will stand many more. It is not, as many think, a creature of a day." In fact, said Channing, the Americans' "whole history was silently preparing them to become

one great people." These knew that "Union does not rest only on
the clear perception of the good it confers. It rests on sentiment
as well as interest, and on a higher sentiment than binds any
other people." [28]

Such sentiment was the topic of letters between Andrew Jackson
and Nathaniel Macon. Macon found the Union to be an opinion
emanating from the people. Should this attitude flag among the
citizens of a state, the latter could not morally remain in the
Union. In fact, Macon argued a state had actually left the Union
when the spirit disappeared. Relentlessly facing the dilemma of a
spiritual Union which found "unfit" both South Carolina's policy
and Jackson's ideas about compulsion, Macon concluded: "the
word Union has a force more powerful than fleets or armies," but
when this spiritually compelling quality had fled, the Union was
gone.

Jackson seized Macon's vulnerable point, that the Union was
"a matter of choice," although the President admitted the Union
to be one of opinion. But the Spirit Union needed law to imple-
ment it. Enforcement was possible, since when the Union was
formed, the states had surrendered any recourse to secession. Jackson obviously sought to play both sides of the street, a tactic of many
who had to administer the Union as Polity. It allowed the comfort
and ready appeal of the Spirit idea, while evading the lurking
majoritarian implication. Jackson, of course, finally said that if
the Spirit Union vanished taking obedience with it, a condition
of revolution resulted. Once more there was an ominous hint that
an instinctual Union could not always be relied upon.[29]

Certainly slavery was the gravest threat to Union as Spirit.
Agitators like John Greenleaf Whittier now demanded that reverence for Union not blind the nation to the harsh fact that
justice was left undone. This was a danger far advanced, since
"geographically and politically united, we are already, in a moral
point of view, a divided people." [30] To this, the endorsers of Spirit
only replied with more ardent proposals that Union be preserved
by belief in Union. Sumner L. Fairfield, editor of the *North
American Magazine,* used verse in replying to Whittier. In "My
Fatherland," were these lines:

Wild rage (they say) shall sunder the great bond
    Of Union—and proud oligarchs arise,
Bringing dismay and death—and so beyond
    The veil of thy bright power, prophetic eyes
Behold what ages never shall reveal,
    As Heaven forefend! for to thy mighty breast
Ten thousand heartstrings, quick to throb and feel,
    Bind all the freeborn Nations of the West.[31]

Another journal praised Daniel Webster, and saw in his thought confirmation of the transitory nature of America's internal divisions. If America embraced the triune precept, "love the Union, reverence the Constitution, study and aim to promote the great interests of the country," there would result a feeling of "compatriotism." The possessor of this Union spirit found that "his prejudices subside; his national instinct rises." [32] Webster himself advised against material lusts in a tone reminiscent of Hamilton: "The spirit of Union is particularly liable to temptation and seduction in moments of peace and prosperity." Conversely, war, with its recall of past glory and presence of common danger, strengthened Union's posture. If this essential spirit were desecrated, America's statesmen "will cherish no common object of patriotic love," leaving a similar language as the only bond. Union's "vital principle exhausted and gone, its power of doing good terminated, the Union itself," predicted Webster, would "become productive only of strife and contention." When the Spirit essence weakened, the Union "must ultimately fall dishonored and unlamented." [33] Even John Quincy Adams agreed, telling citizens of New York City that "the indissoluble link of Union between the people ... is, after all, not in the sight, but in the heart." He added: "*Union! Union!* was the instinctive and simultaneous cry throughout the land." [34]

The exhortation of these two utterly different Massachusetts sons echoed as the question of admitting Texas entered the debate over Union's nature. The Spirit concept again proved useful. Knowing this, William Henry Harrison in his inaugural remarks asked the nation to avoid thinking of divisive issues. Union could draw all men beyond themselves. The President appealed for "the careful culture of those feelings of confidence and affection which are the effective bonds to Union." This had to be thoroughly done, he warned, for men blinded by errant passion had been known to stray beyond Union's call. Harrison's solution, which showed the influence of Webster, was "to destroy or keep down a bad passion by creating or fostering a good one." It was certain that Union's perpetuation could only arise from "the affectionate attachment between all its members." [35]

Yet the Wilmot Proviso, controversial for its proposal to exclude slavery from regions gained by the Mexican War, unleashed in some those baser passions so feared by Harrison. According to William F. Giles, a Marylander, the Proviso menaced that "feeling of brotherhood which has ever made us one people," as well as "all that was calm, all that was elevated, all that was purifying in reference to our common country." Significantly, observers now tied "that community of feeling" more frequently to the past. Spirit and legend were typically combined in Giles's assertion: "So long as there is among the American people that respect and love for their common ancestry," then "no disunion will ever be permitted to take place. The Union will be dear to them [the people]; they will stand by it and die, if need be, in its defence." [36]

An interesting variation was William H. Seward's 1848 effort to translate reverence for Union into a matter of American morality. Seward advised a Cleveland audience, "the first principle of our duty as American citizens is to preserve the integrity of the Union." Without the Union, only catastrophe lay ahead. Yet, warned the New Yorker, "this Union must be a voluntary one, and not compulsory. A Union upheld by force would be despotism." Again in Ohio, five years later, Seward happily observed how technical advances served to strengthen both the "physical and moral centralism" inherent to Union. Mindful, though, of the Union's roots in public intuition, Seward exulted: "Loyalty to the Union is . . . in all the states, the strongest of all public passions. It is stronger . . . than the love of justice or even the love of equality." [37]

While men like Seward spoke confidently, behind the scenes an elder Unionist statesman, Henry Clay, felt that the flesh needed encouragement to keep the spirit willing. He wrote in 1849 that intemperate Southerners threatened the Union's majesty more than he had anticipated. Although the masses still venerated Union, Clay feared "they may become influenced and perverted." So he called for arranged Unionism, contending that Union Spirit was best "to be derived from popular expressions of public meetings of the people." He ordered an associate to arrange such mass demonstrations for Lexington, Louisville, and elsewhere, so that both parties could "express in strong language" their devotion to Union.[38]

While Clay suggested fighting the territorial question with as much Union idealism as possible, his Southern opposition contended that by embroiling the Union with this issue, "the fraternal feeling which gives the Union all its value may be destroyed." Alabama's Congressman Henry W. Hilliard predicted the expiration of that "lofty patriotism" which made all Americans feel at home in any region of the nation. Robert Toombs of Georgia took an additional step, declaring that the continual cry of "Union, Union" was merely a distraction with little meaning. To this Edward D. Baker of Illinois replied that such a shout for Union would soon be "taken up by the masses" until it "becomes a perpetual anthem of hope and joy," swelling across all America to "be repeated by a thousand advancing generations." Baker's was an extreme optimism; he contended that no Union failure was possible "as long as an American heart beats in an American bosom." [39]

Such hope obviously drew on a sense of the past. George Bancroft's study of history proclaimed American triumph as much as did his public utterances. In commemorating the death of Andrew Jackson, he stressed that all the influence of the past joined in the great refrain, "The Union: it must be preserved." The saga of Jackson's time taught that "the Union, which was constituted by consent, must be preserved by love." [40] A North Carolinian concurred; Representative Thomas L. Clingman told the Congress that instead of material advantage, the key element to Union was the "historic associations and the recollections of common ancestral struggles and triumphs." But in the Senate chamber, John Bell dissented, saying that should the "mutual confidence" and "fraternal regard" which made "that noble sentiment of loyalty" fail, the pursuit of Union "will cease to inspire a rational interest," and not "all the sacred associations or traditionary references derived from its early history" could save it.[41] In fact, Bell suggested that not even the most venerated names could keep life in the Union's body after the spirit was gone.

The efforts of Calhoun and Webster were linked in protecting this spirit. Now, however, such ardent supporters, faced by internal controversy, could not easily portray Union as rising naturally from a mystical American instinct. Instead, the spirit had either to be contrived, as Clay suggested, or to be joined by some more substantial form, such as the Constitution. Modification of the Constitution, Calhoun said, would "make the Union a union in truth,—a bond of mutual affection and brotherhood, and not a mere connection." [42] While similarly tempted to rely on a corporal Constitutional presence, Webster did confess that his Union "is not merely a union of law, of constitution, of compact, but while it is that, it is a union of brotherly regard, of fraternal feeling." No person should feel bound simply by a legal corporation, but should see Union as "those unseen, soft, easy-sitting chains that result from generous affections and from a sense of common interest and common pride." Surrounded by tumult, Webster doubted "whether we have the true patriotism, the Americanism, necessary" to maintain the real Union.[43] Already Union was hastening toward an external Absolute.

Rufus Choate explored this problem, warning a Faneuil Hall audience "that while the people sleep, politicians and philanthropists of the legislative hall—the stump, and the press—will talk and write us out of our Union." The Union was so vulnerable that "the anger of a fool—or the laughter of a fool—may bring it down in an hour . . . a beautiful, yet fragile creation, which a breath can unmake, as a breath has made it." Choate's description of the Union's spiritual essence obviously emanated from his disillusion, for the 1850 debates persuaded him that Union would no longer be preserved "by stereotyped declamation." Somehow there had to be kindled a new spirit for Union, a great resolve "to leave the Union, when we die, stronger than we found it," for "here is the field of our grandest duties and highest reward." [44]

Choate's struggle to be realistic portended a rising demand that the apparent contradiction between spirit and fact be settled. Gradually a Union in Spirit, emerging from Americans' instinctual qualities, retreated before ineluctable forces. The prospect forced many to see the dilemma, as James Brooks did. While Union had to be preserved even with force, still what "is a Union worth without love, without loyalty, without pride in it, and only protected by arms?" Would some "mad men" be impervious to the Spirit? Brooks's Union of brotherhood hearkened to a dead past, for the technological and centralist trends aided those seeing Union as Absolute.[45]

Sympathy for the Brooks quandary entered the memorable 1851 address by Thomas Starr King: "Patriotism has learned to pronounce with emphasis the word Union. It is a hallowed word to it. It does not like to hesitate in uttering it." Yet there was danger, he warned, that a preoccupation with eulogy would cause men to "overlook or too slightly estimate the conditions of Union." By this he meant its basically ideal character. America's whole natural structure was made "for the home of an idea," and her glory could not come "from vast extent, populousness, power and wealth," but "from the unquestioned dominion of an idea." If there was truly to be a Union, insisted King, "we must have great undying sentiment," which for him proved to be the Websterian chant about inseparability of Union and liberty. This was the Union's "marriage vow," and King sternly urged the realization that "no political unity, no charter however wisely concocted" could survive a confrontation of antithetical principles. Such an event would destroy the Union's vital "feeling of brotherhood." Once intellectualization of principles crowded men's instinct for brotherly Union, it destroyed "the ideal beauty of our nation," and "its hovering genius will flee." [46] Here was one of the last great Romantic appeals, aimed at a nationalism which King deplored.

Inevitably some looked to the past for a haven for the Spirit. Jefferson Davis, Secretary of War, warned that "we shall be untrue to the great principles which our fathers bequeathed as a legacy to us if we should attempt to bind our Union together by other than the bonds of fraternity...." [47] With Jeffersonian localism more and more a relic, Davis and others fought centralism by calling further upon mysticism. While mysticism had been the hope of Washington's generation, now the spiritual guise of Union became dissemblance. Leander M. Cox, among others, asserted that Union would be "a monument of political wisdom" just so long as memories of the hallowed past inspired "a just appreciation of the cognate ties of Union." If "devotion to abstract notions of morality" should stifle the Union's true spirit, then "the preservation of the Union will neither be practicable nor important." [48]

Abraham Lincoln's comments show how confused he, like most descendants of Clay, became in seeking haven for Union's harassed Spirit role. Attacking the Kansas-Nebraska bill as "an aggravation, rather, of the only thing which will ever endanger the Union," Lincoln asked men to restore the sacredness of compromise. Otherwise, he asked, who would ever again trust the "spirit of mutual concession," which "has thrice saved the Union?" By confirming compromise in its symbolical Missouri status, "we thereby restore the national faith, the national confidence, the national feeling of brotherhood," all of which made up the essential nature of the Union.

Lincoln then reversed his position by calling for the spiritual cleansing of the soiled "republican robe." He advised: "Let us turn and wash it white, in the spirit, if not the blood of the Revolution." With the Declaration's principles reaffirmed, said Lincoln, more reminiscent of John Quincy Adams than of Henry Clay, "We shall not only have saved the Union; but we shall have so saved it, as to make, and to keep it, forever worthy of the saving." [49] Lincoln's demand that the spirit show itself was

echoed in Whittier's poem, "The Panorama," which predicted
that, when the errant South:

> Resumes her old attire, and seeks to smooth
> Her unkempt tresses at the glass of Truth,
> Her early faith shall find a tongue again,
> New Wythes and Pinckneys swell the old refrain,
> Her sons with yours renew the ancient pact
> The myth of Union prove at last a fact!
> Then if one murmur mars the wide content,
> Some Northern lip will draw the last dissent,
> Some Union-saving patriot of your own,
> Lament to find his occupation gone.[50]

Rufus Choate, however, continued to defend the mystical view.
He told another Faneuil Hall audience to recall "the grand and
unalterable conditions and peculiarities of the American national
life," of which the "capital fact" was that historically, legally, and
practically, the Union was "a mere neighborhood of separate and
sovereign States." The essence of Union could be nothing but the
"moral ties of blood and race, a common flag, the memory of common dangers, the heritage of a common glory." Choate wove
Union itself from "that subtle essence of nationality, the consciousness of unity, the pride of unity," matters "requiring still
to be solicited, to be reinforced, to be diffused." [51]

Unheeding, Amos Kendall told President Buchanan, "Let it be
understood that no man who *talks* about a dissolution of the
Union ... is to be considered a friend of the Administration. In
short," he said, "let the Union sentiment, in the spirit of the
Constitution, be embodied as the leading element in the Administration." [52] Like others, Kendall bound Spirit to the Constitution, while at the same time he invited all newspapers to join in
a chant for Union's perpetuity in an effort to invoke the mythology of Union to save the Union itself. Another Democrat,
Stephen A. Douglas, who was less friendly to Buchanan, also
looked beyond Spirit. Debating with Lincoln, Douglas said his
party's great mission "is to unite the fraternal feeling of the whole
country," for the purpose of "carrying out the Constitution as our

fathers made it, and thus to preserve the Union and render it perpetual in all time to come." Despite his own attempt to anchor Union's spirit to a political device, Douglas nevertheless scolded Lincoln and the Republicans for doing the same thing. Theirs was no scheme endorsed "wherever the American flag waves over American soil." So long as the Union prevailed, "any political creed is radically wrong which cannot be proclaimed in every State and every section of the Union alike." [53] The mysticism was obvious, for Douglas wanted to believe that the crucial universal creed would arise from the instincts for Union.

The Illinois Democrat counted upon a mounting Congressional affirmation of Union's claims upon men's hearts. He was not disappointed. Tennessee's Thomas A. R. Nelson predicted the supremacy of a national love—love for country, for mountains, for "church-going bells," for the star-spangled banner, for the memory of "the world's only Washington," and so the list ran until the supreme affection was revealed. Nelson believed that, above all, "we love this glorious Union, purchased by the blood and treasure, and consecrated by the prayers of our fathers, and preserved by the valor of their children." With this came a determination to live under Union, "one in mind, one in heart, one in interest, one in feeling, one in all that makes a nation great, one in all that makes a people happy." While the galleries applauded, the Tennessean implored surrender to "an abstract question." [54]

Virginia's R. M. T. Hunter could not, however, forget James Brooks's dilemma. Were there actually a "natural" hostility between the Union's sections, then "there ought to be no Union between them; for this Union can only promote the happiness of the people when they entertain fraternal feelings toward each other; it can only succeed when it is founded on the affection of the people." But, like so many others, Hunter now had to add that true Spirit could prevail only if "this Union were properly administered." Union was made akin to marriage, a scornful union if it were "kept together by the compulsion of law, and not by the ties of mutual respect and affection." [55]

The paradox gave President Buchanan peculiar satisfaction. How could one wage war against a state to preserve the Union? he asked. There could never be a reconciliation, no matter how much blood and treasure were spent, because "the fact is that our Union rests upon public opinion and can never be cemented by the blood of its citizens shed in civil war. If it can not live in the affections of the people it must one day perish." [56] So also spoke Jefferson Davis in the dying days of 1860, insisting that the Union was "not the less sacred to me because it was not sealed with blood." It was a mystical achievement by the states, "the farewell offering of men who chose to live together." Davis pledged: "I cling not merely to the name and the form, but to the spirit and purpose of the Union which our fathers made." Shaming those who would "idolize the name of Union, when its blessings are lost, after its spirit has fled," Davis wondered, "Who would keep a flower which has lost its beauty and its fragrance, and in their stead had formed a seed-vessel containing the deadliest poison?" His analogy nicely showed how he favored the ethereal over the vilely physical.[57]

As if in reply, Lincoln's first inaugural message showed his choice. While saluting the Spirit Union as an ideal, he gave allegiance to the Union Absolute. Addressing the South, Lincoln said: "I am loth to close. We are not enemies, but friends. We must not be enemies. Though passion may have strained, it must not break our bonds of affection. The mystic chords of memory, stretching from every battlefield, and patriot grave, to every living heart and hearthstone, all over this broad land, will yet swell the chorus of the Union." Invoking the Union of instinct, he predicted that the bonds of affection would surely again be touched "by the better angels of our nature." [58] Nevertheless, Lincoln abandoned as insufficient a Spirit semblance devised from mystery and instinct.

II

Spokesman like Lincoln and Seward, who leaned toward a mystical source for the Union of spirit, nevertheless came to rely upon a version incorporating mundane impulses. This reliance, ultimately part of an Absolute Union's triumph, embodied material advantages and concerns. While Seward could join Lincoln in beseeching the nation's angelic spirit in 1860, ten years earlier he had asserted: "The Union stands ... upon enduring physical, social, and political necessities, which will survive all the questions and commotions and alarms of this day." Rebuking his colleagues: "Even senators speak of the Union as if it existed only by consent;" Seward begged to differ: "On the contrary, the Union was not founded by voluntary choice, nor does it exist by voluntary consent." Instead, the Union was "the creature of necessities, physical, moral, social, and political," and it "endures by virtue of the same necessities" which were now stronger than when it emerged.[59]

Seward's wavering between mystical and material positions did not escape notice. It was seen with special clarity by Wendell Phillips, who centered much of his 1860 election lecture in Boston's Tremont Temple on what he described as the notable change in Union's quality which lately had become discernible. He found Seward merely one of many who hid their embarrassment by continuing the mysticism which so long characterized the Spirit Unionists. Speaking of the New Yorker, Phillips remarked: "I recollect a striking picture he drew in 1850 of the value of the Union, and every line was *dollars!*" Phillips described Seward's thesis now as: "Whoever says trade is the cement of the Union, libels the idea of American civilization." Leaving aside the motives of Seward, Phillips lamented generally: "The saddest thing in the Union meetings of last year was the constant presence, in all of them, of the clink of coin—the whir of spindles,—the dust of trade." When principle was menaced, Everett and others were, in Phillips' sardonic eye, mindful only of loss of commerce, of tariff hostility, and danger to the Navy.[60]

What Phillips saw was hardly new. A Union born of material need had been as familiar as the Romantic theories. While the Romantic theories fell at Fort Sumter, the material need carried on in Union's presentation as an Absolute. Technology gave Lincoln an advantage Washington lacked. While this materialism is best linked with a triumphant Absolute Union, it is useful here to see why some Spirit adherents claimed a mundane footing, especially since the Union's early role as expedience was increasingly plagued by material and moral considerations.

Actually Wendell Phillips himself retreated into oversimplification when he observed, following Lincoln's election, "I must confess, these pictures of the mere industrial value of the Union made me profoundly sad. . . . Is this all? Where are the noble elements of national purpose and life? Is this the whole fruit of ages of toil, sacrifice, and thought—those cunning fingers, the overflowing lap, labor vocal on every hillside, and commerce whitening every sea,—all the dower of one haughty, overbearing race?" Should men see that the glorious records of American history "result only in a workshop?" [61] What Phillips chose to ignore was America's insistence that virtue's proof was in material progress. It was therefore logical that Union's essential spirit was discerned in a healthy vineyard. Here, the weakness was that, like its instinctual companion, this concept was predicated upon an ambiguity which Lincoln's generation need not tolerate. When commerce and technology afforded genuine unification, it meant disaster for any intuition-based system.[62]

Material considerations about the Union sharpened the discussion over adopting the Articles of Confederation. John Witherspoon observed that Union's decline "will open to our view future prospects of war & dissension among ourselves." [63] Here, in contrast to the Romantic's Union of instinctual association, was a spirit of Union steeped in worldly necessity, one that was calmly rational. Frequently in the troubled days under the Confederation, observers felt that the Union had been wrought too well in spirit. In 1784 an anonymous essayist wrote that this "perpetual" Union actually gave "so much of the appearance of permanency" that it led the people into error "by building their expectations too much on it." The deception rested in this Union's failure to rally vital material interests, the only way states could "become perfectly united." A wishful Union without the practical foundations was frail and fleeting.[64]

This theme carried into the Philadelphia federal debates. There Edward Rutledge brushed aside "religion and humanity" as having little relevance to the great considerations over Union,

"Interest alone is the governing principle with nations." A common variant of this was uttered in the Massachusetts ratification discussion by Reverend Thacker: "While we were at war with Britain, common danger produced a common union, but the cause being removed, the effect ceased also." [65] When Benjamin Rush watched Philadelphia's parade honoring ratification, he thought a float representing the "manufactory" of cotton was emblematic of Union's continued wealth and independence. Foreseeing what the next generation would call the American System, Rush spoke of cotton's southern growth and eastern manufacture as a productive alliance so promising that "Hence will arise a bond of union to the states more powerful than any article of the new Constitution." [66]

Shortly, this material appeal acquired more intriguing qualities. The early nationalist, New York's Peter B. Porter, spoke of Union's internal potential, condemning the popular notion that America was "divided, by a geographical line, into two great and distinct sections," the Alleghany range being the demarcation point. Porter vehemently disagreed with those who emphasized a contrast "of interest and pursuit between the people of these two great divisions . . . and the difference of character to which these occupations give rise." This concept not only invited an early death to Union, Porter said, but it failed to see that "this very diversity of interest will, if skillfully managed, be the means of producing a closer and more intimate Union of the States." He then insisted that federally-financed roads and canals were means not merely of enriching all segments of the Union, but were also a way "to subdue local jealousies and to bind the Union together with the indissoluble ties of interest and friendship." [67]

During the War of 1812, Union's mundane dependence was especially relevant. Said Josiah Quincy, "the only sure and permanent bond of Union is interest. And the vital interest of States, although they may sometimes be obscured, can never for a very long time, be misapprehended." If any section of the Union was conscious of unfulfilled needs, discontent would result. Should this uneasiness combine with a region's "great physical power, and with acknowledged portions of sovereignty, the inbred ties of nature will be too strong for the artificial ties of parchment compact." Repeatedly, Quincy returned to his point—the Union had a contrived character, and its statesmen needed constantly to be guided by the interests of regions. For Union's career, these materialist motives were far more important than "theories and speculations of the closet." [68]

Supporting Quincy, Massachusetts citizens in a petition to Congress said that Bay Staters had entered the Union chiefly from "the expectation that their commerce would be better protected by the General Government." Then, haughtily: "The hardy people of the North stood in no need of the aid of the South, to protect them in their liberties." Put bluntly, the Union was a matter of prosperity.[69] However, the war's end did not diminish the Northeast's economic uncertainty. With protection succeeding the embargo as a malevolent force in Union's hands, Connecticut citizens requested Congressional action in a petition which stated that in any "hour of danger, a safe reliance cannot be placed on the mere love of native soil." Binding the people required "the paternal encouragement of all the various classes and of all the useful occupations in the community," since "mutual interest is the most indissoluble bond of union." [70]

Others found internal improvements to be the welder of a substantial Union. A New York celebration for the completion of the Erie Canal acclaimed a "proud day . . . for the Union," since the route "will long serve as a chain" to bind otherwise discordant interests. William Bayard, one of the speakers, said the canal's commerce would "secure and consolidate the union of these states," thus preserving for all the Union's republican institutions. Another orator said the canal had such "grandeur of conception" that it revealed an "intelligence and wisdom that cemented the Union of different republics" at a time when consolidated interests were desperately needed. The canal allowed "the states to be united by ties stronger than that of national compact." The toasts featured Cadwallader Colden's tribute: "The canals of the United States, links in the great chain; they will be the bond of our Union." [71]

Yet the House of Representatives, to the disgust of many, hesitated before using federal funds to repair the Cumberland Road. Young James Buchanan insisted: "The truth is, we are still all so connected together by our interest, as to place us in a state of mutual dependence upon each other." Consequently, "the prosperity of all the States depends as much upon their Union as the human life depends upon that of the soul and the body." An assenting voice explained this very simply: "The Union cannot be preserved, except by commercial intercourse, and a free and easy commerce will always keep us united." [72]

Such enthusiasm for the materialist concept in the Northeast startled the South, driving Virginia's William S. Archer to proclaim that Union would not be saved "by the parchment of the Constitution—for, who regarded that but a few Virginians, who had cried Wolf till they were no longer regarded, now that the fold was invaded." Rather, "the bases of the Union are the sense of its equal benefits, and the belief of the justice of the Administration of its government." Once these were sapped, the Union would crumble.[73] Much more famous was Dr. Thomas Cooper's 1827 address rallying the Southern materialists. Cooper's words were an echo of New England's previous sentiments, especially the warning "we shall before long, be compelled to calculate the value of our Union; and to inquire of what use to us is this most unequal alliance by which the south has always been the loser and the north always the gainer?" [74]

Obediently, Robert J. Turnbull issued a peculiar command in his 1827 "Brutus" essays: "Away, then, away with all this unmeaning cant and jargon of Union, which at all times, and under all circumstances, are in the mouths of some self-constituted patriots. We all know, and feel the necessity of Union. We all desire Union." But it must be a "proper Union." Turnbull's position would become famous: a federal Union meant health to Southern material requirements, while a national Union would mean Southern disaster at the hands of, at best, an indifferent majority. He blamed Southern apathy for encouraging this seizure of Union's discretion by a region whose material views were so alien. "Brutus" concluded: "Apathy, in a word, must ultimately lead to events, that will dissolve the Union: but firmness and constant jealousy in the South will preserve it." [75]

Any reply to Turnbull had to glorify the indistinguishability of a state's true interest from the Union's. The Clay-Webster Unionists took just such a tack. In an 1831 New York address, Webster asserted that no alternative existed but for New York and the Union to live and die together. "Every blow aimed at the Union," he said, "strikes on the tenderest nerve of her [New York's] interest and her happiness." Surely his audience could not be "forgetful of the past and blind to the present," for this would mean sickness of existence. [76] But Webster ignored the fact that the Jacksonian era saw there was no longer need to fear external danger. Now internal material interests could monopolize attention.

William Ellery Channing sensed this new province of unity on interest. "The great good of the Union," he announced, "we may express almost in a word. It preserves us from wasting and destroying one another." Noting the peculiarly bold nature of Americans, Channing said Union was necessary to keep the spirit from breaking into inner turmoil. Union would be superfluous if Americans were a "quiet, cold, phlegmatic race," but under the circumstances Union was necessarily a negative force designed to remove evil, just as liberty was negative in implying the removal of obstructions. He did not hesitate to portray "the saddest page yet written in human history," when the Union stumbled, thereby allowing Americans to descend to internecine war. [77] While Channing chided American nature, lending Union an even more Hobbesian character, Tocqueville was similarly concerned. Nothing about Union's citizens, he reported in his notebook, "betrays an appearance of order or stability," which explained why one of Union's assets "is that all the powerful men and all the great political passions have an interest in maintaining it." [78]

This opinion was softened in the Frenchman's published analysis: "in defending the Union" every citizen "defends the increasing prosperity of his own state or country . . . which may be favorable to his own interests." While Tocqueville admitted that "these

are motives that are wont to stir men more than the general interests of the country and the glory of the nation," he added that,
while Americans talked much of their attachment to the Union,
"I do not rely upon that calculating patriotism which is founded
upon interest and which a change in interest may destroy." Nor
did Tocqueville take seriously the Americans' repeated pledge
to preserve their fathers' Union, for he believed the Union's effective power was steadily declining. Born in an international
crisis, Union had lived in spite of the dread and hatred it aroused,
because "it satisfied an imperious want." For Tocqueville this
meant that in creating such a Union, the people "had risen, to
some extent, above itself." But with America's achievement of
security in the world, her citizens' basic nature more and more
would assert itself.[79]

Among those rejecting the pessimism of Tocqueville and
Channing was a commentator for the *American Quarterly Review*.
In discussing the Frenchman's first volume, the reviewer said that,
as far as Union was concerned, the past was unhelpful, for "we
are but a link in the chain—lying midway between the two eter-
nities." With Union, Americans "have dared to venture farther
from the lesson and examples of those who have preceded us,
than any other people." After rejecting history, the reviewer embraced material determinism: "Our interest united us, and it has
proved, thus far, too strong for fear or ambition." This interest
would be eternal no matter what happened—it would "always
bring us together again, not perhaps under circumstances so
favourable as the present to our rapid development, but sufficiently so to preserve the essential interest of freedom." [80]

Even Webster occasionally forgot his more complex imagery to
plead the all-sufficient material spirit, saying there was "nothing
more cementing, nothing that makes more cohesive, nothing
that more repels all tendencies to separation and dismemberment,
than . . . this overwhelming interest of one commerce." He asked:
"Who ever hears of any American enterprise of a commercial
character that does not bear the impression of the American
Union with it?" [81] Representative Samuel F. Vinton, an Ohioan,
told the House how important were "the brute facts of geography,"

which revealed that "the united West would rally to the rescue of the Union." They also indicated that "this law of necessity, this bond of Union will every day accumulate new force and gain new strength." Here he invoked the legendary role of his region, recalling that Providence itself asked the West "to preserve this Union, to make its existence immortal." The role's physical significance recalled the material essence of Union.[82]

Despite this optimism, widespread in the 1840's, many still felt that unreason, rampant emotion, might prevail over the sober facts of physical Union. George Ticknor predicted to a London friend that, while the Union was too crucial for the moment to be broken, whenever it was severed "it will be because, as so often happens, the passions of men triumph over their interests." [83] Nahum Capen, writing at the close of the Mexican War, said that Union's history showed that wise Founders made Ticknor's gloom baseless. Union's earliest experience disclosed that if one depended merely on instinct or voluntarism, then indeed diversities of interests would "soon sever the ties of a common attachment." Fortunately, the Founding Fathers strengthened the Union, otherwise hostilities might well have led Americans to subvert their own "paramount interest." [84]

Generally, it became old-fashioned to picture a Union of interest, whose effectiveness depended upon an inner acceptance of that fact among the participants. There was a rear-guard defense, of course, including efforts by Joseph Bradley, who later sat on the Supreme Court. Lecturing in 1849 at Rutgers, Bradley asked, "What constitutes the indissoluble band which unites and keeps us together as one nation, and one people?" His own reply was an echo from past decades: "what but the mutuality of interests produced by the great variety of our industrial productions and the consequent exchange which the mutual supply of wants requires." [85]

Thus, the semblance of interest, once so simple, was absorbed by the vast proportions and more subtle appeals of the Absolute version. Except, of course, in the South. While Webster and Clay usually assisted in interest's metamorphosis, Calhoun defended the earlier concept which long before had migrated from New

England. He said that, while Southerners "love and cherish the Union; we remember with the kindest feelings our common origin, with pride our common achievements, and fondly anticipate the common greatness and glory that seems to await us," they now faced issues involving "not only our liberty, but, what is greater, (if to freeman anything can be) , existence itself." With the old Spirit fleeing, it obliged the South "to turn our eyes on ourselves." Calhoun was almost jauntily confident: "It is not we, but the Union which is in danger." [86]

There was a more sober tone in Alexander H. Stephens's insistence that "the Union was formed for the benefit of all." When one area took advantage of another, "this Union is dissolved." He chose to ignore the awkward economic questions thus raised, stressing instead another sort of realism: "if gentlemen supposed that by singing paeans to this Union it is to be preserved, they will find themselves mistaken." Since "the Union was founded upon justice—immutable justice—and right," it meant the weak were never to be despoiled by the strong. By this reasoning, Southerners had no choice but to accept even death rather than degradation under a Union whose essence had been so perverted.[87]

Some of President Buchanan's anguish came from his conviction that events, particularly the John Brown episode, had convinced the South not merely that Union had material disadvantages, but that these events threatened extinction of the region. Buchanan told Congress that should men's firesides be disturbed, "it would be vain to recount . . . the political benefits . . . from the Union." Self-preservation was nature's first instinct, and the Union's material appeal was nothing if alien to it.[88]

Had Buchanan found acceptable a Clay hypothesis ten years before, he would have had a path out of Union's maze of conflicting interests. Clay's argument, proposed during the 1850 crisis, was the logical climax for the troubled career of a spiritual design seeking both material and mystical attributes. Pleading for "the reunion of this Union," the Kentuckian demanded from all men a selfless spirit filled with thoughts of God and "our glorious Union." Then, exalting Union's appeal, he asked what was man, and promptly replied: "An atom . . . A mere speck . . . a drop of water in the great deep." Should such a being, "so small, so petty, so fleeting," hinder the Union's progress? Clay's organic Union was such that his final question could be rhetorical: "What if, in the march of this nation to greatness and power, we should be buried beneath the wheels that propel it onward?" [89]

III

With this exhortation, Clay brought the Union's role as Spirit to its final confrontation. Contained in this organic concept were demands for obedience and fidelity. But could a Union, more often seen in Romantic terms, incorporate a requirement for submission and obedience? Although the effort proved fatal to the tradition of Spirit, there were attempts to adjudicate between the coaxings of spirit and the dictates of complex reality. Henry Clay's life was largely such an effort, as he watched the nation's physical transformation make a Union enrobed in Absolute character credible. When Clay accepted unity as unquestionable, he led a significant part of the community slowly away from Union's Romantic presence. At first this departure was reluctant, since a last hope remained for those who believed Union was a sentiment. This rested on the endurance of James Wilson's belief that American unity arose from a diverse people adhering to one body of principles.[90] Here was the ultimate spiritual appeal. It fused principle with instinct, much like Clay's attempts for his American System. This last bastion for the Spirit Union warrants attention.

Union mysticism was skillfully used by Fisher Ames in eulogizing the deceased Washington. He recalled how at the close of the Revolution the hero had retired to Mount Vernon, when "Union was a name that still commanded reverence, though not obedience." Washington's glory, said Ames, was the triumph of his conviction that the Union's life was "in the breath of the people's nostrils," as they inhaled a common acceptance of its great precepts.[91]

This idea, that spiritual Union could anticipate effectiveness by the universal appeal of its principles, moved easily from Ames to his foe, Thomas Jefferson. Upon becoming President, Jefferson

said that differences of opinion did not mean differences in principle. Were not all Republicans, were not all Federalists? Thus,
for those "who would wish to dissolve this Union or to change its
republican form, let them stand undisturbed as monuments of the
safety with which error of opinion may be tolerated where reason
is left free to combat it." If the Union's spiritual appeal could
rely on this consensus, then fidelity and obedience would issue
endlessly from the citizen body. The Union as Spirit must persist
as the supreme rationalization or idealization of man's collective
requisites.

Such a view, of course, assumed that Union's fundamentals
would never provoke serious disagreement upon essences or application. At the century's start, Jefferson's exaltation of Union as
a precept seemed safely inclusive. It simply required that disciples
of Union should support "the State governments in all their
rights, as the most competent administrations for our domestic
concerns and the surest bulwarks against anti-republican tendencies." Then Unionists should seek "the preservation of the
General Government in its whole constitutional vigor, as the
sheet anchor of our peace at home and safety abroad." [92]

But maintaining a commanding quality about this lofty appeal
proved difficult. Henry W. Desaussure, Chancellor of the University of South Carolina, reviewed Jefferson's reign and pronounced
Union's plea a failure. Desaussure, a leading Federalist, described
his fear that, "in opposing the weak and wild policy of our Virginia
masters," the northern people would be driven by enmity and
jealousy, to break the tie binding them to the South. "In that
moment of resentment," he predicted, "all the counsels of moderation, all the considerations of interest drawn from the infinite and
indeed inappreciable value of the Union would be forgotten by
the people." Further, any leader who pleaded for Union would
lose his influence, should the breach between Union and popular
principle widen.

Desaussure urged that the masses be managed by demonstrating
the tie between Union and interest. "I beg, then, that our Eastern
friends would pause, and avoid stirring up those passions among
their own people which may become too strong to be controlled,

and may lead to measures destructive to the Union and ruinous to the country." [93] The ambiguity of the early Union's essentially spiritual form here forced the contention, startling for a Federalist, that Union's effectiveness depended upon the public's response to its symbolical role as purveyor of both lofty precept and crucial interest.

Many sharing the Jeffersonian opinion believed that there would always be such a response. Philip B. Key put it clearly in saying, "whatever difference of opinion may exist among ourselves, there can be none as to the propriety of supporting the integrity of the Union." [94] As Key spoke, New England's determination to equate Union with her interest found expression in demands emanating from the Hartford Convention. Should interest and principle no longer bask together in the sun of Union, then which visage of a schizoid Union must be accepted? In praising New England's self-concern, Reverend Joseph Lyman insisted that "a Union preserved by timidity and submission would be the greatest infamy and curse.... A Union founded upon submission is the Union of slaves." The only way to make the Union worth preserving, said Lyman, was through "fearless and upright measures" designed to give New England "our just rights." [95]

Lyman merely reflected the first great failure of the Jeffersonian insistence that principle, interest, and Union were as one. After the War of 1812, however, Massachusetts' Governor John Brooks could discuss the Union in a way suggesting that Jefferson's portrayal of perfect fusion might, in spite of past anguish, achieve an enthralling quality. Brooks observed how at first Union had relied upon "courtesy," but in time "national interests" had demanded that it be "one of efficiency and coercion." Here he meant that a government worthy of citizens' confidence had emerged from a cautious discernment of "the just mean between a too limited and an indefinite grant of power." The result was a system designed to preserve "the true spirit of the Union," which throve when men knew that the Union's "several parts... are so well proportioned and adapted to each other as to render the mighty movements of the whole equable, salutary, and lasting." [96]

Henry Clay, of course, generously supported the evolution of a

Union implicit in the nature of things. He told his fellow Representatives, before leaving to become Secretary of State, that it was "the solemn duty of this House to strengthen, by every means in its power, the principles of cohesion which bind us together—to perpetuate the union of these states." The significant trend in this design for Union found the Union so vital that its dictates must be met. John W. Taylor of New York, who hoped to exclude slavery from Missouri, felt confident of this appeal, for he scoffed at predictions that slavery restriction would weaken the Union. He saw the Union so strongly cemented both by interest and history that its preservation had become "the first lesson of lisping infancy, and the last prayer of expiring age." [97] But in the South men were unsure that Union was so imbued with all men's interest. Its support was less than Clay's innate American response.

So might Dr. Thomas Cooper, after acknowledging his reverence and affection for Union, say: "I am so 'ineffably stupid' that I would not choose to be bound to an union, such as Mr. J. Q. Adams and Mr. H. Clay would impose." [98] An editor of the *Georgia Journal* added, "that whatever may be our religious veneration for the Union, you are compelling us to ask ourselves when you strike at our bread, to which we owe the highest obligation, the law of God, the law of nature, the law of necessity, or that of artificial and political association?" Here was a premature use of a "higher law" doctrine, one which rejected any Union envisioned as the embodiment of material wisdom blessed by fraternal ties. The Georgia commentator preferred a more subjective approach to this creeping absolutism: "We tell you that we love this union, that we have sacrificed not a little to it, and that nothing but your injustice and unkindness can drive us out of it." [99]

This issue entered a curious congressional exchange in 1832. When ex-President Adams requested to be relieved as chairman of the Committee on Manufactures, he was proclaimed the only umpire for the impending tariff struggle. James Bates of Maine spoke for many in describing Adams as "the only man who would possess the power of preventing that dire catastrophe which seemed to be impending." But some feared for Union's mystical appeal, should a mortal be so significantly endowed. Edward Everett asserted: "I will not allow that the preservation of the Union is to depend upon his [Adams's] individual services, or those of any other one man." Instead, Union's endurance must look to "the intelligence and the patriotism of the people at large." [100]

Such a role did require the wise affection of the people. Robert J. Walker of Mississippi spoke in 1836 of drawing hope from the great public. They "established and maintained, and will perpetuate this Union. It is they who will come to the rescue when the Union is in danger. . . . From the humblest cottage they will come forward, with American hearts and American feelings." Webster, too, moved toward the all-encompassing view which Clay would adopt in 1850. He told a Boston audience to cherish "the Union under which we live, which we respect, which we love, under which we mean to die, which we will defend with all our power to the last gasp." So also did James K. Polk affirm in his Inaugural Address the existence "among the great mass of our people a devotion to the Union of the States which will shield and protect it against the moral treason of any who would seriously contemplate its destruction." [101]

Although Polk added the thoroughly Jeffersonian reminder that all citizens should recall "that they are members of the same political family, having a common destiny," [102] his mysticism came no closer to resolving the dilemma of authority than did any previous spiritual effort. The challenge from reason grew stronger. Jefferson Davis suggested in 1850 that reason was more than ever the guide for Union. First admitting, "If I have a superstition, sir, which governs my mind and holds it captive, it is a superstitious reverence for the Union," Davis attributed this to his revolutionary father. The son, however, feared this spirit had become an autonomous power which he found menacing. Said he: "It is past the age to which the Union should have lived," for this majoritarian Union was not the one which "I was taught from my cradle to revere." The implication for Davis was obvious—"even that deep attachment and habitual reverence for the Union, common to all—even that, it may become necessary to try by the touchstone of reason." [103]

Two days after Davis denied the Spirit Union, Henry Clay was dead. Within a few months the *Democratic Review* featured an essay by New York's A. B. Johnson, "The Philosophy of the American Union," which rejected the concepts of intuitive fraternity and material necessity. Instead, the Union was "the result of consummate art to unite those whom God separated." In spite of differences between states, there still was Union. But Union would continue only if the states were free from compulsions. Johnson said, "no mathematical proposition can be more certain, than that we diminish the cause of disunion, in proportion as we circumscribe the number of occasions in which the action of the general government can legally conflict with any local special interest." For all men to be "Union-men in an intelligent, pervading, and enduring sense," would require construing Union's powers narrowly.[104] However, *The New Englander* accused the North of betraying the real Union by the Kansas-Nebraska bill, which showed "that the love of Union at the north has been employed so basely to induce its [the North's] consent to the practice and extension of national wrong." In freedom's land, "weakheaded, deluded, or mercenary representatives" had used "their regard for the dear, the glorious Union" as "plea and justification for whatever abandonment of human rights they have been cajoled, or alarmed, or tempted into." [105]

Obviously, the Spirit Union's transcendent shimmer could no longer obscure the material and moral disparity which appeared to divide the nation. In a significant 1856 statement, Senator Ben Wade of Ohio challenged his Southern colleagues to prove that Union actually threatened their region. Wade was stung by the Southerners speaking "as though it were a peculiar condescension on their part that they permitted the Union to stand at all." Nodding to the materialist, Wade conceded that no region could be blamed for leaving the Union if ever it threatened security. Under such circumstance, said he, "You will not then find me backward in being the advocate of disunion; but that contingency never having come, I have never yet opened my mouth in opposition of the Union." Although he found Union spiritually and materially feasible, Wade added, "You cannot forcibly hold men in this Union; for the attempt to do so, it seems to me, would subvert the first principles of the Government under which we live." [106]

Wade's disquisition summarized the disease afflicting the Spirit concept. The Union's equivocal essence was overwhelmed as the nation's consolidation routed the regional autonomy enjoyed in Jefferson's age. Once Federalist and Republican had shared a Union of Spirit, laced with prospects of material bliss. But when the Republicans of Lincoln's time stood on principle, the Union of mystical communion was already an anachronism. This was the point Lincoln illustrated with his analogy of the divided house. Accepting an Absolute concept, Lincoln predicted that the Union would survive the transformation into a monolith. One faction must succeed in imposing its view of Union's body and soul upon the other. "It will become all one thing or all the other." [107]

Lincoln's remarks might be construed as a death sentence for the Union of Spirit. Reality demanded no less. Neither the mystical nor material charms of a past buried with Jefferson and Clay could now persuade a torn nation to live as one. There was no longer an alternative to a semblance of absolute proportions. Here was the Union's tragedy. Clay's Union of commanding spirit failed to enlist all beholders, even though it had implied quaintly that there was perfect safety in thus surrendering. The totality which Lincoln proposed asked surrender of a nature which could not be brushed aside by appeals to the Jeffersonian image. Now there was a Union whose demands seemed absolute, mirroring the needs of an America caught in the century's frenetic change. Thus, the Union seen as Spirit, an emotional unification out of need and instinct, had lost its relevance. Time had grown restless with a vague fraternity whose being was no more than its mystical or mercenary appeal. The Union's semblance of Spirit declined; its Absolute successor rose.

4: Absolute

Every path through the thicket of Union ideology leads to one destination, the compelling version of an Absolute. Gradually, the Experiment role with its Spirit quality receded before the charm of Union cast as an Ultimate. It was tempting to find an indispensable unity also a perfect Union. Such a Union was easily moved beyond Spirit or sentiment to a corporeal or external dimension that challenged American tradition. The ascendancy of such a concept revealed the effect of three concomitant ideas. It was widely heard that American character required Union. Since it was usually seen as product of the Founding Fathers, Union also developed an aura of immutability, although there proved little agreement as to what was changeless. Finally, many considered such a Union to be an exalted perspective, a view among committed citizens which guaranteed all America's hopes and needs.

These connotations of Union Absolute culminate the story of form and function within Union's ideology. It was a climax that brought von Holst to argue that the old Union debris had to be discarded by 1861; for when the North recognized that blood and iron were necessary to maintain Union, its continuation was assured, though not in its original concepts.[1] What von Holst could not see was that the Northern mind, following the lead of men like Seward, became certain that the South sought a perverted Union, one violating the Absolute, the Immutable.

Beholders of the true, original Union were thus obliged to grasp the sword, so successful had Union been in commanding the American mind. No longer a means, an experiment, a mystery relying upon spiritual response, Union had become a concept of power so compelling and of character so unvarying, that the use of force in its defense was a melancholy but sacred calling.

I

For a representative formulation of Union Absolute William H. Seward's stands as the best example. He seemed called as cleric for the painfully transcribed Webster catechism, whose design was dramatically uncovered by Wendell Phillips the year Webster died. Phillips charged that Webster had originated a new scripture which dismissed the glorification of God as man's chief concern. Volunteering the new dogma's view of human purpose, said Phillips: "—why, it is to save the Union!" [2] Since Seward's achievement is a story of conversion to this Websterian precept, it epitomizes also the transforming of Union ideology. As such, it merits recapitulation.

Once, when the Jackson era faced a dark passage, an alarmed Seward pleaded in a July Fourth address for renewal of the old national "feeling" which had imbued the Founding Fathers. If only the Franklins could return to frown at "Carolina,"—then might the South "throw away her pencil and brush out her figures . . . rashly calculating the value of the Union." Ten years later, while Governor of New York, Seward described his state's unswerving worship of a Union it never questioned. What a contrast to those unfortunate states, said Seward, "whose estimate of the value of the Union is not fully settled." [3]

While eulogizing John Quincy Adams, Seward described how a true sense of Union had required a forty-year wait after 1789 before the "consolidation" of American spirit came with the destruction of "faction." By the latter, Seward meant groups subordinating Union to local concern. With South Carolina's defeat in 1832, he said, "the dangerous heresy had been renounced forever. Since that time there has been no serious project of a combination to resist the laws of the Union, much less of a conspiracy to subvert the Union itself." [4]

This picture of unyielding synthesis as Union's decree characterized Seward's speeches as the final decade before the Civil War began. Union Absolute, certain and incontestable, was obviously his vision. Much clearer and more affirmative than his involvement in the "higher law" idea was Seward's assertion: "The Union was not founded in voluntary choice, nor does it exist by voluntary consent." Physical, moral, social, and political "necessities" had created Union, and "these necessities are stronger than when it was produced." More important, "and stronger than all," were the "now settled habits of veneration and affection" with which Americans viewed "so stupendous and so useful" a thing as Union. This brought Seward to a beautiful summary of the Absolute concept: "The Union, then, *is,* not because merely that men choose that it shall be, but because some Government must exist here, and no other Government than this can." [5]

To recapture this maturation in Union sentiment, we must return to Seward's 1825 Independence Day address. Speaking cautiously of the Union's prevalence, he knelt before "the ashes of WASHINGTON" where "from the silence of his tomb there comes a voice which commands his children to be united and invincible." Seward's theme throughout was the Union as an alternative, as an opportunity, and the people's role as choosers. To the public facing a Union essentially voluntary and spiritual, Seward said: "Let us, then, remember that to us it is given to preserve the Union of these states—the ark of safety in which are deposited the hopes of the world." Stressing the tentative feature, he continued: "If we preserve it, it shall bring down blessings upon us and our posterity. We shall inherit glory more imperishable than Grecian or Roman fame, and shall leave to the world a legacy more valuable than aught but the treasure of inspiration." Then he warned: "Abandon it, and the desolation of tyranny will cover these plains; the curses of posterity will fall upon us, and the last experiment thus ended: for men there will be no more political redemption till the last trumpet shall sound, to call the nations to their last account!" [6]

A quarter century later, Seward had obviously made his choice, telling a Massachusetts Whig convention in 1851: "We are in the Union for richer or poorer, for better or worse, whether in a majority or in a minority, whether in power or powerless, without condition, reservation, qualification, or limitation, for ever and aye." It was incontestable that any state "will be at all times safer under this government when worst administered, than it would be under any other, however wisely administered, or favorably conducted." [7] The contrast between this new and the old version of Union was even more apparent when Seward eulogized Clay, reminding his Senate colleagues that at one time the Union was "little more than an ingenious theory, not yet practically established. The Union of the states was, as yet, only one of compact." This semblance prevailed, he recalled, because the many necessities to which Union "was so marvelously adapted, and which clustering thickly upon it, now render it indissoluble, had not then been broadly disclosed." But Seward did not build his Union Absolute merely on revelations of national political and economic change, those inescapable facts of history. Earlier beholders had lacked another vital quality, he said, "the habits of acquiescence and the sentiments of loyalty, always slow of growth" had not been "fully ripened." But now, "The Union exists in absolute integrity." [8]

On the eve of civil war, Seward put the final touch, telling his fellow senators: "Republicanism, Democracy, every other political name and thing: all are subordinate—and they ought to disappear in the presence of the great question of Union." Seward joined the Clay tradition that man was as nothing before Union. Yet despite such assurance, the idea ironically was not manifest to all, a paradox whose disastrous implication would have been unfathomable in an earlier age whose Union was means and Spirit. Wide acceptance of a certain and perfect Union reveals the gap between Seward's age and the era of George Washington. Thus in 1851 Seward could call the Union a "political anomaly," because "the world has never before seen a state assume a perfect organization in its very beginning." [9] Varying this slightly, George Ticknor Curtis drew a useful analogy in his constitutional history by likening early efforts toward Union to seeds planted for later ripening as "the permanent idea of Union." [10]

We have already examined this seed-time, when Union's character was obscure. The aura of perfection, of course, came later, with the endeavors of Seward, Clay, and Webster. However, there were early suggestions that Union might be an end, not a means, and that it was irreplaceable. In these Curtis thought he discovered seeds of an ultimate. Certainly little time lapsed before the Founding Fathers' concept of Union was proclaimed flawless. Even in the Federalist era, hunger for permanence lent Union an enduring quality. The first President himself suggested that every public thought should be based on the belief that "the Union is considered permanent." [11] But Washington, we know, held a negative Union-sense reflecting the late eighteenth century caution about political adhesion as an absolute good. Yet desperation nurtured hope for a Union so revitalized that it might endure.

Connecticut's poet, Dr. Lemuel Hopkins, pleaded that "pilgrim freedom" not be exiled from "these loved regions," as seemed likely since:

> From ancient habit local powers obey,
> Yet feel no reverence for one general sway,
> For breach of faith no keen compulsion feel,
> And feel no interest in the federal weal.

Out of alarm, Hopkins warned:

> But know, ye favored race, one potent head
> Must rule your states, and strike your foes with dread.

Writing on the eve of the Philadelphia Convention, the poet pleaded:

> Ere death invades, and night's deep curtain falls,
> Through ruin'd realms the voice of Union calls;
> Loud as the trump of heaven through darkness roars,
>
> On you, she calls! attend the warning cry,
> 'Ye live united, or divided die.' [12]

While this despair gives the era an obvious sense of experimentation, Dr. Hopkins' "warning cry" bespoke a hunger for permanent Union which might easily seem indispensable and perfect. A friend wrote Madison as the Philadelphia meeting began that the public now wanted a thorough renovation of Union's basis. Well-conceived, the work "will be done forever," said Edward Carrington, who explained that while he desired a government with "the force of Union," he opposed designing it into "one mass." [13] Doubtful as he was about the proposed Constitution, Virginia's Governor Randolph agreed to Union's indispensable character, saying, "Our very quiet depends upon the duration of the Union. Among the upright and intelligent, few can read without emotion the future fate of the States if severed from each other." [14]

While such views shared George Washington's portrait of Union as means, they also implied that no alternative to Union as method was discernible. An indispensable means became readily a goal or end with an absolute or ultimate quality. Perhaps this transfer brought General William Heath to beseech his associates in Massachusetts' ratification convention to remember: "Everything depends on our union." No state would flourish, said he, if Union fell, for "the strongest-nerved state, even the right arm, if separated from the body, must wither." Heath was unequivocally impatient with talk of experiment: "If the great Union be broken, our country as a nation perishes." [15]

For the moment, of course, Union conceived as ultimate lingered teasingly while experiment held sway in a time when political change was acknowledged desirable. A Philadelphian told James Wilson of the great parade celebrating acceptance of the new Union. So felt was the need and so happy the fact, said Wilson's correspondent, as to make "such an impression on the minds of our young people that 'federal' and 'union' have now become part of the household words of every family in the city." [16] One of the earliest advocates of Absolute Union, John Quincy Adams, took the idea with him to The Hague, where he wrote to his father, then President, that he hoped that stories of disunion plots were unfounded. They should be treated as such, he said,

since men must "consider the Union as the principle paramount
to all others in the policy of every American." [17]

This attitude secured wider support during Monroe's hectic
first administration from certain frantic efforts to prove Union
indispensable and unquestionable. Curiously, no one was more
active than the Chief Executive himself. In his 1817 inaugural
message, Monroe made what was probably the first official announcement that Union's garb of Experiment no longer fitted.
Presidential joy was expressed at the "increased harmony of
opinion which pervades our Union. Discord does not belong to
our system." Indeed, said Monroe, the American people "constitute one great family with a common interest," now growing
more enlightened "on some questions of essential importance."
Admittedly this was a slow process, "dictated by a just reflection
and a faithful regard for every interest connected with it." The
President quickly added that he would "promote this harmony"
essential to "our Union," in which "no essential improvements"
were necessary.[18]

Hardly had Monroe put the cloak of perfection about Union
when new issues threatened. Yet the idea of Absolute Union expanded with the severity of sectional crises. Even old John Adams
joined those who saw an assured Union; he told Jefferson that
these issues would pass "under the ship, and do no harm." It was
now "high treason" to doubt the perpetual duration of Union.[19]
Looking back on this hectic period, Monroe himself had the
faith to insist, "no serious conflict has arisen." The forces guaranteeing Union were "permanent." Soon all the world would admire
and respect the "degree of order and harmony" wrought in
Union.[20] Actually, the acrimony Monroe ignored seemed to add
more credence to Union as an end or ultimate than did his naïve
words. Where tension had taught the previous generation to speak
guardedly of an experimental Union, now these divisive forces
encouraged an image of absolute proportions.

Others, like William Ellery Channing, did not share Monroe's
easy victory for Union. Writing to Webster in 1828 of "my increased solicitude for the preservation of the Union," Channing
said, "I know no public interest so important than this . . . I dep-

recate everything which sows discord and exasperates sectional animosities." [21] The Unitarian leader spoke even more earnestly a few years later: "No one prizes the Union more than myself. Perhaps I may be allowed to say that I am attached to it by no common love." Then, revealing the critical transformation, he announced, "Most men value the Union as a means, to me it is an end. Most would preserve it for the prosperity of which it is the instrument; I love and would preserve it for its own sake."

But as Channing urged Americans to accept Union as the supreme goal, he added in an offhand manner, "So dear to me is Union, Next to liberty, it is our highest national interest." He encountered here the pitfall which all Absolute Unionists confronted; their lofty ideal might become vehicle for a purpose whose cutting edge would threaten its own context. Obviously disturbed by the gag rule in Congress, Channing said that, if Union meant surrendering free speech, "then Union would be bought at too dear a rate; then it would be changed from a virtuous bond into a league of crime and shame." His final statement easily prefaced the travail of Union Absolute: "Language cannot easily do justice to our attachment to the Union. We will yield every thing to it but truth, honor, and liberty. These we can never yield." [22] The idea now had only to await contention that the loftiest verities were inseparable from Union.

Toward this moved William Rawle, whose thesis was the glorious Union, perfect and successful "beyond the warmest dreams of its authors." In the second edition of his constitutional history, issued during Jackson's tumultuous first term, Rawle postulated "a sacred obligation to preserve the Union of our country, we feel our glory, our safety, and our happiness involved in it." This stemmed from an association basically spiritual as well as material, said he, so that disunion must be resisted "with the same feelings that we should avert the dagger of the parricide." [23] The Channings and Rawles brought new appeal in the Absolute concept, just as internal strains seemed ever more severe. It allowed President Jackson to perform Monroe's miracle of bringing good out of evil, asserting that colliding material commitments within the Union would "serve only in the end to foster the spirit of conciliation and patriotism to the preservation of that Union I most devoutly hope is destined to prove imperishable." [24]

A more famous discussion of Union's superior claims was the Webster-Hayne exchange which Chancellor Kent of New York eulogized. It had, he said, destroyed many heresies and false images, so that "the inestimable value of the Union, and the true principles of the Constitution, were explained by clear and accurate reasoning." Now the country could see "the great doctrines of national rights and national Union." No longer were the essentials of unity taught only by some "living oracles of the law." Now the Union had been turned over to the American people.[25] At a dinner honoring a new Governor of Alabama, the leading toast echoed Kent's view: *"The Union of the States.* The only basis on which our federal government can stand—may it be eternal as the everlasting hills." The celebrants then beheld the dread: *"Nullification.* The Trojan horse, carrying within disunion, anarchy, and civil war. If once permitted to enter the temple of our liberty, ruin, devastation, and slavery will inevitably follow." In his brief response, Governor John Gayle reportedly grew rapturous over Union, repeating Jackson's now famous toast to unity which had to be preserved.[26]

The emotionalism of 1832-1833 helped mature the version of an indispensable Union, a distinctly useful quality for those trying to escape contention. In a speech of 1832, Webster said that while the capitol might be rebuilt, the Union certainly could not. He inquired: "Who shall frame together the skillful architecture which unites national sovereignty with State rights, individual security, and public prosperity?" No one would or could, so "if the columns fall, they will be raised not again." [27] This was a view which evidently impressed the touring Tocqueville, who said that if the Union should collapse, "it appears to me to be incontestable that the states of which it is now composed would not return to their original isolated condition, but that several unions would then be formed in a place of one." [28]

In the 1832 campaign, Jackson's lieutenant, Amos Kendall, carried the gospel that Union had to be saved, for, "It is the *only* shield of the people. Its dissolution will soon be followed by the loss of all that is valuable in liberty." Here was a reply to those like Calhoun and Channing who fretted that Union and liberty might part. Disliking ambivalence, Kendall insisted that to escape trouble by disunion was "to rush through the flames of anarchy into the arms of slavery." Never thinking of a free association of men in nature as anything desirable short of Union, Kendall said, "With us, therefore, the Union is *sacred*. Its preservation is the *only* means of preserving our civil liberty. We look upon the enemies of the Union as the enemies of liberty." [29]

Even Mississippi endorsed this view in legislative resolutions speaking against nullification and for the preservation of the "integrity of the Union—that Union, whose value we will never stop to calculate—holding it, as our fathers held it, precious above all price." [30] What this sentiment ignored was the question necessarily entailed by Union's elevation to the status of end or ultimate. Might a prevailing policy of Union be challenged? What means could be used to defend the Union as an end? Webster, during 1833, prudently spoke in generalities, resting in the assurance "that among the political sentiments of this people, the love of Union is still uppermost." But if the spirit failed in part, and scenes of commotion came, Webster admitted that they would be met. "We cannot, we must not, we dare not, omit to do that which, in our judgement, the safety of the Union requires." [31]

President Jackson, who had to exercise such judgment, responded memorably. Jackson told Congress that laws implementing Union had to be enforced. He avoided the experimental idea by insisting that Union owned the means of self-preservation, thus remaining the center of hope for "friends of Civil liberty throughout the world." Later and more simply, "It is no longer a question whether this great country can remain happily united," for the "unerring test of all human undertakings" had proved that only in Union could there be freedom and happiness.[32] Yet by settling for an equivocal entente between the Union and South Carolina, Jackson accepted the older tradition which claimed that common veneration for Union would finally produce accord, so that discord invariably brought a deeper sense of Union. This suggested

that assaults upon the Union merely disclosed Union's indispensability.

The pages of James Bayard's 1834 volume on the Constitution
present such a Union whose dissolution was not only unthinkable,
but unconstitutional. Although he made the usual gesture to revolution as a right against the always vague oppressor, Bayard
preferred to inquire "whether the States are bound to continue
united, without any right to resist the authority of the Union, or
secede from it in case of oppression?" Said he: "The reply must
be that they are." After describing a glowing national future,
Bayard warned that "this truly grand result depends upon our
union; and as we value liberty and independence, we should
cherish the Union." [33]

Bayard's concept contained the familiar switching of ends and
means, inevitable if Union, a Polity, became indispensable to national well-being. Sympathy for this view prevailed in the many
anti-abolitionist meetings scattered across the nation. One of
these, an 1835 Philadelphia gathering, pictured "the Union of this
country as inseparable from its freedom, greatness, and glory."
The group went on: "We consider no sacrifice too great to maintain it [Union], and shrink with horror from all that is calculated
in the most remote degree to endanger or impair it." [34] Senator
Robert J. Walker of Mississippi agreed; he claimed for himself
"the language of a man whose love of this Union is as warm as
the vital blood that gushes from his vital heart." Considering
"life itself as utterly worthless, were this Union dismembered,"
Walker pleaded with Webster and Calhoun, then Whig leaders,
to come forward together "as champions of the Union against
sectional or geographical parties of the South." [35]

Walker's Union was a compelling figure transcending all the
issues dividing the national family. It was a view with appeal.
Daniel Webster, heeding the call, toiled to build the new temple
of Union. Speaking in Bangor, Maine, he described the miracle of
Union, possible "only under the most favorable circumstances,
and only when great men are called on to meet great exigencies,
only once in centuries." This achievement of "unrivalled national
happiness," hinting at supernatural impulses, fitted nicely into

Webster's plea for dedication. Demanding that Americans must practice their Unionism by exhibiting "one harmonious, grand, and magnificent whole, to which the world may be proudly challenged to show an equal," Webster said, "I regard it as the bounden duty of every good citizen . . . to cherish that Union which makes us one people." Taking his gospel west, Webster told a St. Louis audience, "it is our Union which sanctifies all else. What are our magnificent rivers, our rolling inland seas, our mountains, prairies—all!" His response was now familiar: "My soul revolts from them disunited and connected in no gigantic whole. It is our Union which hallows, ennobles, secures all else." He warned, of course, of the virtual impossibility of ever looking upon another Union.[36]

Among the attributes of Union Absolute, the character of irreplaceableness is perhaps most interesting. Since America gloried in human accomplishment, Webster and others had to stress the extraordinary factors responsible for Union. It was awkward to argue that what man had put together could not be taken asunder and reassembled. If the Ultimate concept was to succeed, it needed the lure of uniqueness. Jackson's Farewell Address insisted that no matter how a collapse of Union and resultant civil war might conclude, it undoubtedly meant "an end of the Union and with it an end to the hopes of freedom." Martin Van Buren used much of his second annual message to review the Union's half century of life, concluding that its role and effect were unparalleled. President William Henry Harrison, in his inaugural message, was surprisingly direct: "Of all the great interests which appertain to our country, that of union—cordial, confiding, fraternal union— is by far the most important, since it is the only true and sure guaranty of all others." [37]

These three presidents set a pattern which James K. Polk followed. He acknowledged that Union's "inestimable value" was professed "by all," and that only through it were true freedom and happiness possible. It was a "sacred duty" to preserve this source of indescribable blessing. He asked: "Who shall assign limits to the achievements of free minds and free hands under the protection of this glorious Union?" No one, obviously, so Polk could add: "No treason to mankind since the organization of society would be equal in atrocity to that of him who would lift his hand to destroy it [Union]." He begged that all citizens yield themselves to a Union which "must be sacredly and religiously observed." [38]

Polk's reverent attitude was, if possible, surpassed by President Franklin Pierce's inaugural plea that man prostrate himself before Union. He said, "with the Union my best and dearest earthly hopes are entwined. Without it what are we individually or collectively?" Here was one's only impulse—the "desire for the perpetuation of that Union which has made us what we are, showering upon us blessings and conferring a power and influence which our fathers could hardly have anticipated." Pierce's Union lacked any attribute of means or experiment, it was a pure source of wisdom and strength. Insisting that it was Union "which we are sacredly bound to transmit undiminished to our children," Pierce indicated that Union's character was now immutably fixed. Rejecting any changes in the system, Pierce granted nothing dynamic to his Union. His conservatism made him warn against "experiments where experiments are fraught with such fearful hazard."

Here was a trend which substantiated Monroe and Jackson's belief that the age of experiment had passed. America lived or died with the present Union, and every heart should realize, said Pierce, "that beautiful as our fabric is, no earthly power or wisdom can ever reunite its broken fragments." These words were virtually duplicated by President James Buchanan six years later. He saw in John Brown's raid the occasional salutary experience which gave the people pause, reminding them of the need to resolve anew Union's preservation. Should " 'the silver cord be loosed or the golden bowl be broken . . . at the fountain,' human power could never reunite the broken fragments." [39]

This parade of presidents headed a long procession of opinion deep into the forest of ultimates and absolutes. Moving in near perfect step was Daniel Webster. Far into the South, speaking at Savannah, Georgia, the great Whig attacked those who proposed changing Union's nature. "He must be a presumptuous man indeed who would venture to think he could suggest any new features of improvement, or in any way improve our present form of united government." Webster left with the New-York Historical Society the prediction that Union's dissolution meant the end of its history forever. It was comparable to imagining the chaotic universe should the law of gravitation be overthrown. Once more, Union—like other universals—was indispensable and irreplaceable.[40]

Abraham Lincoln concurred with this in 1856, repeating Webster's identification of liberty with Union. He rebuked the "bugbear disunion" always threatening, and demanded instead remembrance that "the Union must be preserved in the purity of its principles as well as in the integrity of its territorial parts." [41] Many men shared with Lincoln and Webster this Union of perfection and peace, whose charm presumably would banish all fear and conflict. During the Mexican hostilities, Professor Beverly Tucker of Virginia recalled in the *Whig Review* how men once said the weight of George Washington's character alone kept the Union together. After Washington's time, Union's endurance was ascribed to the lingering great men of the Revolutionary age. But these too passed on, leaving the people to discover that Union's health "is indebted to its own inherent *vis medicatrix,* and that strong as it has already proved, it is ever gaining new strength by time." [42]

This idea of a Union whose perfection was continuously disclosed by time and process appeared in an 1848 issue of the *North American Review.* Stressed here were the two centuries of "trying experience" necessary to produce the social and political qualities of an organic Union. Consequently, the Union "may be regarded as placed beyond peril and beyond change," even though "things are not yet adjusted among us, in all respects, according to the pattern at which we aim." While Union had "conflicting elements, that must be removed before order and peace" were perfected, it was comforting to know "that the main body of the structure of our political system may justly claim to be considered as resting on a firm and immovable foundation." Indeed, "if the continuance of the Federal Union were put to a vote, there would be one clear, loud, and unanimous affirmative response." [43]

Two years later, in saluting Calhoun, the *Whig Review* displayed an astonishingly pious Unionism described as the spirit of the late Senator himself. "We never will doubt the virtue of loving the Union, and guarding its inviolability." Union was "beyond all value. No speculation can be indulged as to its worth to posterity and to us . . . no standard of appreciation can be found to designate its relative price." Then followed a new analogy: "It is a sacred heirloom of a family, having higher claims to respect than its age or its parents." In fact, "its worth is at once moral and traditionary. It is full of past glory, of present respect, of future hope. It is the title, the dignity, the birth-record of freedom; the evidence of all that is noble in the history of her noblest contests." [44]

This sentiment permitted Edward Mansfield to argue that the Polity's purpose was perpetuating Union, for "The United States are, therefore, emphatically *one nation*. Politically, socially, morally, they are stamped with one charatcer, and must share the same destiny." Describing the inevitability of progress, Nahum Capen renewed the argument that inner turmoil wrought eventual good. "The combined action of enemies without, and the assaults of party spirit within can have no tendency but to develop new energies and to add new strength." For the Union, "changes can only be those of progress." Even the threats of disunion simply would "increase the knowledge of the indispensable necessity of Union." Capen's final tribute to Union made him especially representative of those beholding an ultimate, for he asserted: "The physical world in its variety, and the mental world in its unity, encircle its [Union's] boundaries and centralize its interests. THE DISSOLUTION OF SUCH A UNION IS A MORAL IMPOSSIBILITY." [45]

The widespread awareness of Union in this role made more agonizing the crisis of 1860-61. To see crumbling an image of timeless greatness and goodness brought a pro-Douglas Chicago newspaper to relate the sorrow of all friends of human happiness who now had to "reckon up the value of the American Union." Its loss was incalculable, for it would leave the nation "utterly bewildered and lost as we gaze into the future," and "ready to pray again and again that this bitter cup may pass from us." It was all a frightful dream, especially if one remembered "the blood and tribulation this Union cost," as well as "its almost miraculous rise and progress." [46] When South Carolina and her associates disavowed the Union, they put aside what for many Americans was no longer a form of human behavior; but rather, was an entity whose power and majesty exceeded the human ken. No wonder the ordeal of 1860-61 had an anguished dimension.

II

A Union indispensable and irreplaceable had three concomitant qualities, of which one was a certainty that American character required Union. This made an apparent necessity into an indisputable imperative, a metamorphosis crucial to the nation's emerging nationalism. America's personality was made to demand Union with more ardor than its practicalities could do. While grim needs dominated post-Revolution years, there was surprising interest in loftier nourishment for Union's roots, seen in John Jay's assertion, "Whenever the dissolution of the Union arrives, America will have reason to exclaim, in the words of the poet: 'FAREWELL! A LONG FAREWELL TO ALL MY GREATNESS.'" Referring to America as "the last Republic on which the sun shines," Silas Stowe of New York said, "Here man enlightened is placed as it were in a second garden, the fruit of life is union, and near it grows the fruit of disunion and death." To bring Americans to consume that fruit would require the power of the devil, said Stowe.[47]

Even the indecisive governor of Virginia, Edmund Randolph, fell under the spell of such a sense, begging the Virginia convention to remember that "the Union is the anchor of our political salvation." He advised: "The American spirit ought to be mixed with American pride, to see the Union magnificently triumphant. Let that glorious pride, which once defied the British thunder, reanimate you again." [48] Writing soon after, Fisher Ames said: "I wish it was a part of the catechism to teach youth that it cannot be [a broken Union] ... I wish to have every American think the Union so indissoluble and integral, that the corn would not grow, nor the pot boil, if it should be broken." [49]

Signs soon appeared that this cause was succeeding. Thomas Wentworth Higginson told Henry Knox in 1790: "The public mind ... has kept pace with the times. ... There seems to be a general conviction, that the Union must be supported, as the alone Source of National Security; and that every burthen necessary to the object must be cheerfully bourne." [50] Toward this end, Justice James Iredell urged upon an Annapolis grand jury the "necessity of maintaining a strong and cordial union," and added that all men felt "an anxiety to promote the real and effective purposes of that Union by the best means calculated to secure it." As for the Constitution, Iredell insisted that its function was "solely the preservation and security of the Union." [51]

In a background of such sentiment, Washington's Farewell admonition becomes simply another fine portrait of Union straddling necessities both spiritual and practical. Here Union took on life out of needs for independence, tranquility, prosperity, and liberty. But a worried Washington could not settle for this version of means. He admonished his fellows: "It is of infinite moment, that you should properly estimate the immense value of your national Union to your collective and individual happiness; that you should cherish a cordial, habitual and immoveable attachment to it." This meant that the American mind must think and speak of Union as "the Palladium" of safety and prosperity. In the first 1796 draft of the message, Washington had hoped that "Our Union may be as lasting as time; for while we are encircled as one band we shall possess the strength of a Giant and there shall be none who can make us afraid." [52]

Washington used an already flourishing concept, that American history and well-being made Union inevitable. Union was therein the fundamental quality of the American character. Federalism's foe, Albert Gallatin, agreed, saying that, whatever differences of party sentiment might exist, there was one supreme issue on which all could agree—"the importance, the necessity of preserving the Union." There was no way, he said, in which the national bond could "be made an instrument to sow divisions of a fatal nature." Even the region-inspired disputes were discounted, for Gallatin emphasized that "The natural bonds of Union . . . will forever counteract the effect of the slight diversity of interests which may exist." [53]

As if in proof, an aggressive spokesman for Massachusetts, Josiah Quincy, forced many fellow congressmen loudly to regret his assertion that disunion had to be achieved, " 'peaceably if we can, forcibly if we must.' " Most joined North Carolina's Nathaniel Macon in amazement that these Federalists had abandoned Washington's plea. This "last advice" was often proffered New England around 1812, along with repetitions of the old maxim, "united we stand, divided we fall." Some, like Representative Thomas Gold of New York, acting on what they called broadly shared sentiment, opposed war because it imperiled Union. While Gold talked of "the imperfect union," and thus "the vulnerable point of the great body politic," he managed to endorse the necessity role: "Holding, as I do, this Union to be the sheet-anchor of our political safety, I cannot consent to any measure which shall jeopardize the Union." [54] Others, like Kentucky's William Duvall, predicted that America's "good sense" would make her realize that Union arose from much more than mere interest, stemming instead from "every tie that can bind society," especially language, common laws, marriage and blood, friendship, and common religion. Duvall in fact found every facet of America's personality requiring Union, so that he might well ask, "how can a stronger connexion exist? Is interest more binding?" [55]

Logically, when President Jackson copied Washington's gesture of farewell, he castigated the ease with which Union's segments quarreled and casually talked of separation. Picturing the unnatural violence that such action would inevitably bring, Jackson asked that all interests defer to Union's majestic dimensions by putting aside any troublesome differences. He considered that an achievement of proper perspective would recognize that the very character of America demanded Union. Jackson cited as Union's essence the memories of battles and victories, the prosperity, the happiness, and the proud name. If these were not enough, he asked, "what tie will hold united the new divisions when these bonds have been broken and this Union dissevered?" Should this Union fall, its successor would employ an alien despotism. The American character would have been altered.[56]

As Jackson penned his celebrated final remarks, another statesman left a death-bed message, but it received scant attention. The aged Madison died in 1836, but not before Mrs. Madison recorded his last admonition to the nation: "The advice nearest to my heart and deepest in my convictions it that the Union of the States be cherished and perpetuated." His tolerance exhausted, Madison no longer saw room for differences over Union. As an ultimate, its enemies should "be regarded as a Pandora with her box opened and the disguised one, as the serpent creeping with his deadly wiles into Paradise." [57] Here was a version with which Daniel Webster could be comfortable, for he often presented Union as the hallmark of American character. In his 1843 Bunker Hill address, he admitted that some slight difference might be noted between the sons of New England and the sons of Virginia, but "only enough to create a pleasing variety in the midst of a general family resemblance." From long before the Revolution, Americans had been bound "to one another by new links of brotherhood." [58]

Facing unbrotherly sentiment in the nation, President Polk spoke of a lapse both of mind and character, for the nearness of national greatness made even more irrational any agitation endangering "the harmony of the glorious Union." It was the latter, said he, "which binds us together as one people, and which for sixty years has been our shield and protection against every danger." Reminiscent of both Jackson and Webster, Polk insisted: "In the eyes of the world and of posterity how trivial and insignificant will be all our internal divisions and struggles compared with the preservation of this Union." Indeed, "No patriot would foment and excite geographical and sectional divisions. No lover of his country would deliberately calculate the value of the Union."

Polk's bequest was thus a familiar one, the very nature of America left each generation a solemn duty to maintain intact the Union in its "vigor and countless blessings." Like Jackson, Polk proposed as the surest manner of cultivating Union the spurning of all divisive issues which threatened it. Rather than allow these issues to torment volatile Congress, let the Courts decide them, and let all of Union's parts cheerfully acquiesce. [59] Polk was neither the first nor the last president who proposed surrender to an ultimate Union of overwhelming proportions. It was reflected in an Indiana assertion, "In the west, we consider the Union our All." [60] Offering a hopeful view in a Peoria speech after the Kansas-Nebraska controversy, Abraham Lincoln observed that "devotion to the Union rightfully inclined men to yield somewhat, in points where nothing else could have so inclined them."

Lincoln, however, then exposed the weakness of Union as Absolute, "I too, go for saving the Union. Much as I hate slavery, I would consent to the extension of it rather than see the Union dissolved, just as I would consent to any *great* evil, to avoid a *greater* one. But when I go to Union saving, I must believe, at least, that the means I employ has some adaptation to the end." [61] For Lincoln, the disputed legislation had no such adaptation, while for Douglas, of course, it did. This left Union to the fate of all human concepts; it would never elude the frailness of subjectivity.

As one who prayed that even this escape might be achieved, Elias Peissner drew strength from history. His volume, *The American Question in its National Aspect,* contrasted the 1860 crisis favorably with the early, fragmented situation when the "principal bond of Union was at first merely a common opposition to a common enemy." In time, "the once separated States blended and grew into each other," so that now "we have all, land and people, grown more and more into a better, united, and more compact body, whose period of epiphysis is almost over." The Union was so intimate "that any separation of its members would leave an open, if not a fatal wound."

The fact that states actually were seceding did not seriously disturb Peissner, for he was convinced that they would be gone only briefly. The Union's recuperative strength was "pointed out to us by Nature." Consequently, "the PEOPLE can not, for any long period of time, remain blind to the immeasurable advantage of a common Union." Their character would force them back from calamitous disunion. Union was thus assured, for "this growing together, this united national life, is ever the very distinguishing characteristic of our present wonderful civilization." [62] In the final analysis, Peissner's organicism seemed confirmed, for the character of change in Western civilization invited cohesion. But the effort to ascribe this to a Union considered as ultimate and indispensable failed. This quality simply would not remain manifest to all who dwelt in Union.

III

Even greater anguish befell another aspect of Union Absolute, the canonization of what must be designated as the "Old Union." Since this stressed the immutable nature of Union, the version was not effective or even very possible until Monroe's era. Thereafter, no matter what the occasion, its argument followed a simple course. Union must stand unchallenged because of the supreme wisdom of the Founding Fathers. To contest it would be to question these Fathers, an act of vile impiety. With this superb conservative appeal, the ideal of a One, True Union inspired some of the moving passages of nationalist literature.

Long before the Fathers had descended to the tomb, their craftsmanship became part of Union sentiment, as the past and original principles were used to design a concept of unity. By the time New England struggled against the Administration, it was an ordinary occasion for someone like Josiah Quincy to urge that Congress return to timeless principles and to assume the wisdom of the Fathers. Quincy said their superior insights were compressed in the "only bond of your Union, the Constitution." What the New England area sought was simply to save the true Union from perversion.[63]

It was quickly obvious that a true Union employing the qualities of ambiguity and subjectiveness would be unsteady. The localism pleaded for by Quincy was attacked by another New Englander, John Quincy Adams, who said that the study of United States history should have as its *"moral"* the "indissoluble union of the North American Continent." This didacticism was necessary because of many "small statesmen" who, said Adams, were hungry for power, "and finding Rome is too large an object for their grasp, would strike off a village where they might aspire to the first station, without exposing themselves to derision." Such small-minded men lacked the broad vision entailed by knowing the genuine Union. In Adams's opinion, the American people generally possessed this awareness, insulating them from the crass disunionists.

In order to perpetuate genuine repose of Union in the people's esteem, Adams called for "historical works, honestly and judiciously executed." He went on: "For if the doctrine of union were a new one, now first to be inculcated, our history would furnish the most decisive arguments in its favor." However, the idea of Union, said Adams, "is no longer the great lesson to be learnt, but the fundamental maxim to be confirmed." In behalf of this truth, "every species of influence should be exerted by all genuine American patriots, to make its importance more highly esteemed and more unquestionably established." So committed was Adams to an ordained and true Union that he condemned John Marshall's biography of George Washington: "Washington was emphatically the man of the whole Union, and I see a little too much of the Virginian in Marshall." [64]

Another early follower of the Union attributed to the Founding Fathers was Hezekiah Niles. As the nation quarreled over Missouri, the Baltimore journalist spoke soothingly of Union's fusion with the integrity of the past. Considering America's highest goal to be perpetuation of "the confederacy in its present super-excellent form," Niles explained that neither consolidation nor annihilation was legitimate. He condemned both the Bank decision's centralism and the Hartford Convention's localism as violations of the Founders' Union. Since modification of the Union "never crosses the mind of a patriot, without a sensation of horror," the editor relied on the people. Having stopped such a move to violate Union once, they must do it again by making the true republican principles prevail.[65]

A brilliant presentation of an immutable Union was made by Senator William Pinkney. After placing Union's ordained character upon divided sovereignty, Pinkney proclaimed: "You cannot recast or new model the Union." [66] While this assertion epitomized the Old Union motif, the idea would be employed for divers purposes, as Niles and Adams discovered. During the latter's presidency, for instance, Virginia Congressman J. S. Barbour condemned a uniform electoral system as an alteration in Union's character. Said he, "the Union of these States rests upon a class of principles, resulting from mutual concession and compromise, which cannot be altered," at least not without subversion. The latter would arise only from "the hand of folly or wickedness," thus being "a thing to be felt, not to be reasoned upon." Barbour's Union was for men to revere. Should the work of the past be warped, "the Union will either dissolve into its primitive elements, or it will be crushed into ruins." [67]

Two years later, South Carolinians were finding new landmarks along the road to the Old Union's shrine. In fighting the tariff and internal improvements, they gave support to the resolutions of a Walterborough meeting proposing action in order "that we may preserve the Union," by restoring it "to its original uncorrupted principles." Resistance was defined as obedience to the true Union. [68] Robert Turnbull's famous alarum, *The Crisis,* hoisted the True Union of 1789, for which "the price we have already paid . . . is more than a fair and sound price." Turnbull added: "Were the bargain to be made over again, I would not give as much." As quickly as he endorsed the Old Union, this Carolinian rejected the new one proposed by manufacturers and the abolition societies. [69]

The debate involving South Carolina and the tariff widely spread the Old Union concept. The famous Jefferson birthday celebration, featuring Jackson's announcement, "Our federal union: *it must be preserved,*" was especially useful. The regular toasts exalted the Union of the Founding Fathers largely by showing what it was not. Said one: "The bane of the Union:—oppression of minorities; unequal taxation; unequal distribution of public benefits." But when Jackson announced his simple principle, there was a rush to define what precisely this Union was supposed to be. For Calhoun, the true Union was one subservient to a lofty ideal, freedom. His famous tribute: "The Union: next to our liberty, the most dear; may we all remember that it can only be preserved by respecting the rights of the states and distributing equally the benefit and burden of the union." Van Buren made an even more obvious appeal to an Old Union, toasting: "Mutual forbearance and reciprocal concessions; through their agency the Union was established.—The patriotic spirit from which they emanated, will forever sustain it." [70]

This dinner, renowned for its revelation of clashing personalities, has not been seen in correct context by later generations. In the story of the Union as a concept, Van Buren's remark becomes the most important. Jackson would later enlarge his Union indisputable. Calhoun's Union confined to the Original Principles was already familiar. It was Van Buren who suggested that, while the true Union indeed appealed to aged verities for its validity, yet it was an absolutism built upon a tactical spirit. This spirit was actually Van Buren's Union, one eternally dependent upon the forebearance which ennobled the Fathers' age. The wily New Yorker sensed the awkwardness in the concepts used by the great protagonists.

Van Buren's affirmation of the past was quickly denied by Georgia's Governor George Troup, who wrote of the mortal danger menacing Calhoun's concept. Seeing "ambition and avarice" making Union a curse, Troup observed how the "many-headed tyrant" vaunted "his love of Union, as if ready to make a burnt offering of his looms and spindles upon the altar of that Union." Yet the past worked for Troup as it did for John Quincy Adams. Despite his alarm, the Georgia Governor did not despair; "the American people will see that the constitution and union can only be preserved by a return to honesty and justice." The true Union, he reiterated, was built upon old precepts still nestling in the American heart. Tying the Union to this popular setting, Troup added cleverly, "The character of the American people is their sufficient warranty that no state would separate from the Union without justifiable cause." [71]

Many, like Troup, relied on the hearts of men who would surely know when Union's ancient and indisputable principles were being twisted. It was a concept widely displayed, especially in South Carolina. Support of this Old Union appeared in

Thomas R. English's cry: "Do you call me a disunionist? You are
guilty of a misnomer. On the contrary, I declare that it is the very
love which I have for the union that induces me to take some
course that will preserve its entirety and integrity." Here was the
concept, built as absolutely as Jackson's Union, which would make
the catastrophe of 1861-65 such an ideological tragedy. English
doubtless was sincere when he confessed: "My mother taught me
to love the union. It certainly entered into the first of all my attachments." In time, he discovered that true devotion to Union
meant constant questioning. Once this would have seemed treasonable, but now, said the South Carolinian, "Thank God,"—"my
eyes have been opened." [72]

The view exemplified by English, allowing as it did for wild
tribute to Union, while preserving a profoundly conservative outlook, continued to flourish. It had to be challenged, of course, and
the Jackson leadership did its best to encourage in South Carolina
a view more in keeping with the simplicity of the President's
toast. On July 4, 1831, Charleston's Union party celebrated by
singing an ode redolent with Van Buren's Union of forebearance,
as its last stanzas suggest:

> By our altars, pure and free
> By our law's deep rooted tree
> By the past's dread memory,
>   By our WASHINGTON:
> By our common present tongue,
> By our hopes, bright, buoyant, young,
> By the tie of country strong—
>   We will still be ONE.
>
> Fathers! have ye bled in vain?
> Ages! Must ye droop again?
> MAKER! Shall we rashly strain
>   Blessings sent by THEE?
> No! receive our solemn vow,
> While before thy throne we bow,
> Ever to maintain, as now
>   'UNION-LIBERTY.' [73]

While praise was heaped upon such a Union, John C. Calhoun retired to his Fort Hill estate to prepare an essay clarifying the issue of what Union should be. Yielding to none in his "deep and sincere attachment" to Union, he noted that "nearly half my life has passed in the service of the Union, and whatever public reputation I have acquired is indissolubly identified with it." His acknowledged reputation of once being "too national" was not a fault, said the Vice President, when Union rested on its true premise of geographically distributed power. Now interposition was needed to preserve "this sacred distribution as originally settled." On this Old Union, "our liberty depends." A year later, Calhoun said that "the Union may be as effectively destroyed by increasing as by diminishing its power—by consolidation, as by disunion itself." [74]

Another voice from South Carolina, Representative Francis Pickens, used this Absolute concept with unusual clarity. It was unnecessary "to talk about the glories and blessings of this Union. These stand recorded in the history of the country." They needed "no feeble voice of mine to hold them up to the admiration of the world," said Pickens, who then explained the danger of uncritical veneration: "Beware! beware! unless in your generous and patriotic attachment to this Union, you should find yourselves finally dragged down and kneeling in idolatrous worship before some idol made by human hands of the *present day*." Seeing this idol in Jackson's Union, Pickens called it a "monster-god," one "begotten in sin and inquity, foul and loathsome," springing from "ambition and fanaticism." To this "bloodshotten and bloated" freak, Pickens shouted, "Give me that Union which springs from truth and virtue, fair and comely in its form," which was the immortal equality precept. Repeating "give me the Union that our *Fathers* gave us," Pickens added, "I will pledge the last drop of blood in my veins to *vindicate* and defend it, but *no other Union*." [75] Thus did Pickens construct an extraordinary version of Union's immutable nature.

After taking the Presidential oath, Van Buren, in clarifying what he had meant at the birthday celebration, brought himself remarkably close to Congressman Pickens. The new President insisted that the half-century just lapsed proved that the perpetuity of our "great experiment" in Union depended entirely upon "an implicit and undeviating adherence to the principles on which we set out." Only these "can carry us prosperously onward." Since slavery was the greatest menace to the Union's harmony, the wise forbearance of the Founding Fathers was exemplary and should prevail, Van Buren insisted, despite recent excitement, for "neither the masses of the people nor sections of the country have been swerved from their devotion to the bond of Union and the principles it has made sacred. It will ever be thus."

Repeatedly he described Union as asking only "an abiding confidence in the stability of our institutions and an entire conviction that if administered in the true form, character, and spirit in which they were formed, they are abundantly adequate to preserve to us and our children the rich blessings already derived from them." Here towered the Absolute, pure and certain; it was man who must keep faith with Union made by the Founding Fathers. It was surely the shepherd making "our beloved land for a thousand generations that chosen spot where happiness springs from a perfect equality of political rights." Van Buren, a professing Jeffersonian, struck by the forces at work within the Union, sought security by casting out Jefferson's dictum that each generation must devise its own Polity. Now Union Absolute demanded the allegiance of unnumbered generations.[76]

Infidelity to the Founders had now become so serious that the ideology could safely argue that men must take the true Union or accept the ghastly fates of disunion or tyranny. As Congressman Thomas F. Marshall of Kentucky expressed it, "if ever this gorgeous, this glorious temple to human freedom should be pulled down, or consumed," absurd talk would do it. For "when Americans spoke of dissolving the Union, they spoke of what they should not—the idea was unnameable." Marshall urged a pilgrimage back to the venerable Union, so that "the North and South could come together as in the olden time, and unite in sustaining and guarding what they had so cordially united to construct! " [77]

Even the South's dread foe, Joshua Giddings, found the Old

Union device useful as the nation argued over Texas. Giddings told how he loved the Union, "sanctuary of American liberty," which was "formed by the wisdom of our fathers." He therefore refused to "surrender this Union, sanctioned and sanctified by half a century of national prosperity, in order to try a new union, and that, too, with slaveholding Texas!" Insisting that every schoolboy recognized annexation "would be, *ipso facto,* a dissolution of our present Union," Giddings invited any who wished to leave the true system for a new arrangement with Texas to do so. All that he asked was candor. It would be the departing Southerners who thus betrayed the Old Union; it would be the North who clung to the Founding Fathers. Giddings enjoyed repeating this distinction: joining with Texas meant the dissolution of the Old Union; refusal to do so meant "to maintain the present Union." [78]

Those who replied to the Giddings position sought to preserve authentic Union from such harbingers of disaster, the tamperers with slavery, who would bring a peculiarly evil desecration of the True Union through servile war. Insurrection's evil germ, according to Virginia's Senator William S. Archer, was already planted "in this garden of our Union." When the harvest was ripe, he saw a willingness to devour the fruit, with inevitable death and "the disappearance of our political Eden, as complete as that of which the tradition remains, that had its position on the Euphrates. So of ours, that had its place on the Potomac." [79]

Did not this garden-Union's creation, however, come from upheaval? A *Whig Review* essay by "A Marylander" admitted that Union itself "was the child of change and cradled in the whirlwind of a stormy revolution." Only the deluded would nevertheless believe "that change is in itself beneficial." The writer was then led to one of the sturdiest expressions of conservatism in Unionist ideology. Change was usually a curse, "Its natural tendency is to weaken and decay." Human nature was so untrustworthy that the wise society kept men in habit's path. But like other advocates of the Old Union, "Marylander" hoped the public would grasp the Truth, for he asserted that a "reverential awe at the voice of a buried world" was "absolutely necessary to the lasting prosperity of a nation." [80]

Such a "voice" infiltrated President Polk's Oregon message to call for the Founding Fathers' wisdom. Had not the Founders always clutched at compromise, thereby making it the essence of Union? Disturbing this spirit, said Polk, in a manner reminiscent of Van Buren's toast at Brown's Hotel, endangered the real Union. The latter's safety required men "to follow the example of those who have gone before us." Making full use of Washington's Farewell, Polk exemplified how far Unionist thought had gone in transforming the past into a guarantor of Union.[81] Certainly the verbal image of the assembled Founders with Washington in its center nicely represented what Polk urged. It was a Union Absolute, but yet one which employed human attributes embodied in the Founders. Trouble came in defining these attributes. While the effort had conservative overtones, the difficulty was that men disagreed on what the Founders did. Veneration for them and for their labors could not prevent diverse stresses upon the concept of Union.

To escape this, defenders of Union Absolute solidified their position by contending that those who brought down the True Union would live forever in infamy, cursed by the rest of mankind who suffered from its destruction. This idea, the menace of an evil few, had a strange career in Union sentiment. Usually it assumed that a demented minority might refuse to accept the True Union. Some contended, however, that a thoughtless majority might be driven into destroying the genuine Union by the goadings of a few. Throughout, there lingered the curious implication that the Old Union could be subverted; it would be done by the wretched few with the mass of men as onlookers. In contrast to John Adams's faith that the multitude supported the True Union, this newly prominent argument warned the public to beware the vicious trifler. Thwarting an evil few led easily to exhortations for changelessness, which made Union into a precious museum piece. Perhaps this explains in part why Americans became so fond of written constitutions, judges, and legalism. Anything was worth treasuring which would discourage the lurking trifler who sought to poison the fountain of security, Union.

But this position invited an embarrassing use of True Union's appeal, as when Congressman David Hubbard recalled that Washington, Franklin, Jefferson, Adams, and all the other Founding Fathers had once been disunionists. During the time of colonial tyranny, they opposed unity with England on the exalted principle of opposing "strong" or "bad" government. The Alabaman observed in a laconic aside, "thus it is seen why good men are disunionists under bad governments, and bad men under good ones." Still, he could hardly avoid the subjectivity he despised. He added that 1850's system was not Washington's Union. That Union had been dedicated to the rights of the weakest section or citizen.[82]

Joining in this use of the Old Union version was the rising Mississippi statesman, Jefferson Davis, who said "The North can preserve the Union, easily preserve it by . . . a due regard for the principles from which the Union arose." Equally did the concept challenge the South, for she must save it "not by submission to wrong, not by blind worship of a name, not by paeans over the corpse when the animating spirit has fled," but by firmly defending it. Should this not be done, "there might remain *an* Union but not *the* Union." Davis pledged support to the authentic Union, even if it meant leaving the transformed Union.[83]

Facing such a twist in the True Union's path, President Millard Fillmore affirmed Adams's faith in the public. Said the President: "I can not doubt that the American people, bound together by kindred blood and common traditions, still cherish a paramount regard for the Union of their fathers, and that they are ready to rebuke any attempt to violate its integrity." [84] Fillmore's successor, Franklin Pierce, was more affirmative, even to being incredulous that Union could be challenged out of "a fanatical devotion" to a few Africans. He announced that against Union "the storm of frenzy and faction" would dash in vain. True Union, built upon the Constitution, was an "unshaken rock." Thus Pierce's bravado: "I know that the Union is stronger a thousand times than all the wild and chimerical schemes of social change." [85] With a tone only slightly varied, the two Presidents, Whig and Democrat, were as one in praising the Old Union and scorning change.

Ralph Waldo Emerson led the protesters against this unyielding version of the Union of the Founding Fathers. There was to him a moral dilemma in sacrificing all for the preservation of a single value, no matter how complex that one ultimate might be. In 1851 he observed to his journal, "... *The Union;* nothing seems to me more bitterly futile than this bluster about the Union. A year ago we were all lovers and prizers of it. Before the passage of that law which Mr. Webster made his own, we indulged in all the dreams which foreign nations still cherish of American destiny." Emerson found the Fugitive Slave bill a high price for the Founders' heritage, bringing degradation and dishonor. Because of this costly Union, "we sneak about with the infamy of crime in the streets and cowardice in ourselves."

Once unleashed, Emerson's sentiment would not stop. "The Union! Oh yes, I prized that, other things being equal," he said, then asking: "but what is the Union to a man self-condemned, with all sense of self-respect and chance of fair fame cut off,—with the names of conscience and religion become bitter ironies, and liberty the ghastly nothing which Mr. Webster means by the word?" The conclusion was obvious: secession and disunion could not compare with the moral calamity now created by obedience to the Old Union. Put bluntly, said Emerson, if the price was the Fugitive Slave Law, "the Union is no longer desirable." [86]

Somehow the Emersons had to be answered. For one, Gerrit Smith tried to serve Union and virtue at the same time. Stating his opposition to slavery, he admitted such an utterance some considered hostile to the Union: "hostility to the Union is, in the eyes of American patriotism, the most odious of all offenses—the most heinous of all crimes." But Smith was not finished: "I prize the Union, because I prize the wisdom, courage, philanthropy, and piety, of which it was begotten." Out of the Founding Fathers had come a Union treasurable "for the great power it has to honor God and bless man."

Having cut a broad swath, Smith took the stand Emerson apparently could not, that any desecration of the True Union should be candidly discussed. If this was impossible, then there were indeed two Unions, that of the Fathers, and that of the present. "The Union of early times," Smith said, was "openly based on the doctrine of the equal rights of all men." Now, a concept, professing beautiful aims, seemed determined to extend slavery and commercial gain. The great question for Americans, according to Smith, was, "Which is the better Union? By their fruits ye shall know them." He was certain that the choice was simple, for the intruder was "distinctly and entirely another Union." [87]

This concept could be used in other ways, though. Especially appealing was Stephen A. Douglas's version of the Founding Fathers' labor, a Union whose essence was diversity among local institutions. Replying to the Smiths and Emersons, Douglas asked: "Why cannot this Union exist forever divided into free and slave States as our fathers made it?" The Union of old could still prevail, "if each State will carry out the principles upon which our institutions were founded, to wit: the rights of each State to do as it pleases, without meddling with its neighbors." This astonishing dream of localism was for Douglas the proper reply not only to Emerson but also to the Lincolns who spoke of divided houses being infirm. With True Union meaning a fragmented system, Douglas could plead: "Just act upon that great principle and this Union will not only live forever, but it will extend and expand until it covers the whole continent." [88]

Lincoln made no more stirring rejoinder to the Douglas version than his famous Cooper Institute speech. Sweeping aside the Old Union, Lincoln said, "Let us be diverted by none of those sophistical contrivances such as groping for some middle ground between the right and the wrong . . . such as a policy of 'don't care' on a question about which all true men do care—such as Union appeals beseeching true Union men to yield to Disunionists, reversing the divine rule, and calling not the sinners, but the righteous to repentance." [89]

The ultimate Union, scion of the noble Fathers, thus fell upon unfortunate days. Struggle as Douglas might for total surrender to this concept, new ultimates now pointed toward other True Unions, all masterpieces touched by the Founders' brush. But, by definition, only one could be authentic. Then how to test for the false? Most Southerners agreed with a Texan's manner of resolving the dilemma, "So far as this Union is concerned, the cold sweat of death is upon it. Your Union is dead." The lingering efforts to preserve it were "but the mournful ceremonies, pomps, and pageants which are seen around the mighty dead." Nothing, according to Senator Louis T. Wigfall, could refute the grim fact that for the Old Union "the spirit has departed, and it has gone back to those who gave it—the sovereign State." [90]

Others joined President Buchanan in repeatedly asserting reverence for the True Union, which he called a "sacred trust left by our Revolutionary fathers to their descendants, and never did any other people inherit so rich a legacy." Buchanan supported the Adams thesis that the people's unyielding reverence for the True Union could be affirmed, even though their spokesmen might have lost this veneration. Then, curiously, Buchanan washed his hands. In a gesture suggesting that True Union could be destroyed in spite of the public's mandate, he boasted, "I at least meant well for my country." [91] For the President, it was simple: the spirit of the Founding Fathers still lingered; only an errant few kept it from speaking through the voices of the people.

The Buchanans seemed to be saying: "We loved the Union because we have been taught to love it. It was the work of our fathers; and if it could be preserved in the spirit in which they made it, it would live fresh in eternal youth." Such words, from a Virginian, reflected the enormous physical and ideological gulf which had betrayed the Old Union: "But, sir, it exists no longer. Its spirit has fled." [92] This assertion heralded the death of a generation's fond idea of Union. For much of America, veneration for a True Union, legacy of the Fathers, was now impossible, since it could not embrace a common idealism. Inexorable change had destroyed the usefulness of the Old Union image as conveyor of America's dreams and needs. The worship of the Fathers' labor was now disturbed by such symbolical gestures as that by John Brown and by the success of the Republican party.

Out of that victory Abraham Lincoln spoke on March 4, 1861, marking the repudiation of what had been, after all, a spiritual core for the True Union concept. Asking for more than a Union built upon respect for the Founding Fathers' design, Lincoln introduced larger absolutes, for he insisted that "universal law" made Union perpetual. Fundamental truths, reflected in the Constitution, might show this to the new President; but they also returned him to the True Union, in the assurance that by executing the "express provisions" of the Constitution, "the Union will endure forever... it being impossible to destroy it except by some action not provided for in the instrument itself." [93] But this Union Absolute was hardly a mystical system emanating from memory and tradition. To solve the collapse of the Polity, Lincoln needed more than Buchanan offered for the public's edification. Now an ultimate Union established on mysticism was untenable.

Lincoln was left no alternative but another Absolute idea, one to which even Webster had resorted, wherein Union was linked to written fundamental law. It permitted him to say that, even if there was disagreement over goals and techniques of Union, still Union prevailed. For "if destruction of the Union, by one, or a part only, of the States, be lawfully possible, the Union is *less* perfect than before the Constitution, having lost the vital element of perpetuity." Lincoln's purpose differed little from that of John Quincy Adams, Andrew Jackson, William H. Seward, James Buchanan, and a host of others who yearned for Union ultimate and unchanging. For them, as for Lincoln until 1860, it seemed attainable by the nation-wide appeal of the past embodied in the Founding Fathers. It was Lincoln's lot to declare this idea obsolete, wrought though it was from awestruck dedication to the Founders' inspiration.[94]

IV

There was, however, one quality accompanying Union Absolute with which Lincoln could be sympathetic, since it was more active than the pale enshrinement in tales of the omniscient Fathers. This further aspect simply said that Union required an "elevated patriotism," and this was located in the majority's will. With this attractive idea, Union became again essentially an outlook or attitude, but one which had elements beyond simply the ideational Union, for this system assumed an Absolute Union always backed by public consensus. Additionally, it existed apart from the instrument, Constitution. Here was victory for Seward's higher law view, and thereby capitulation to the organically conceived Union.

The search for this idea began in the Continental Congress, where John Dickinson, for one, was concerned with the unifying and governing of an area "so extensive." Fretting at the possibility a "particular State may be more interested in certain points than other States," he took a hopeful perspective: "I am bound to prefer the general interest of the Confederacy to the partial Interests of Constituent Members, how manysoever they may be, and however respectable and meritorious." [95]

Dickinson's claim for wide vision as Union's essence often was repeated, and nowhere more earnestly than by George Washington. Remembering wartime divisions, the weary General dreamed of a "wisdom" among the states that led to "a great, a happy People." Only this kind of perspective would force "local politics, and unreasonable jealousies" to yield to a system "as will embrace the whole and make our Union respectable, lasting." Unless such an outlook emerged, Washington believed that "we have spent our time, spilt our blood, and wasted our treasure." [96] This semblance of perspective entered Stephen Higginson's call for "a thorough disposition in the States . . . to act honestly, to take their respective shares of the common burden, and to adhere strictly to the principles of the Confederation, or the Union will necessarily be dissolved." Only in this way would strength vital for the indispensable association be secured.[97]

The passage of months into years, however, lent no sign of the perspective's presence. Washington became exasperated. How could there ever be anything but this essential attitude or no Union? "We are either a united people," said the Mount Vernon planter, "or we are thirteen independent sovereignties, eternally counteracting each other." He added that, in such a Union, whatever the majority considered beneficial for the whole should be accepted by the minority.[98] These thoughts from the great Virginian, circulated widely, both shaped and reflected the rising determination that a Union perspective lived in the process of majority decision. Washington contended that spokesmen from the states must be free to sense and pursue the spirit of Union's councils. Opposed to binding delegates through state instruction, he insisted that each state's advantage was to rise above its own concerns—"there must be a yielding of the parts to coalesce the whole." Only through free representatives could come deliberations containing the sense or perspective essential to Union.

A year later, after the close of the Philadelphia meeting, Washington extended his remarks. Some communities who otherwise favored Union resented parts of the Constitution. These states, said Washington, "would do well to consider that it does not lye with any *one* State, or the *minority* of the States to superstruct a Constitution for the whole. The separate interests, as far as it is possible, must be consolidated." Over and over, this Virginian repeated a point fundamental for those building Union upon lofty outlook. It was that simple—"If then the Union of the whole is a desirable object, the component parts must yield a little to accomplish it." And both sides should remember, said the General, "not a single State, nor a minority of the States can force a constitution on a majority." [99]

These pleas for perspective, whether from Washington or from his cohorts, demonstrate the impact of the Confederation's lesson. Union could exist only in dynamic consensus. The consensus made the Union. If the minority might thwart the perspective's implementation, then it followed there was no Union. Being the mandate of a majority's view, Union was inherent in the dictate of a formal perspective which had to prevail for Union to prevail. Noah Webster combined the legend of the Founding Fathers with the idea of consensus; "Perfection is not the lot of humanity. . . . The mutual concessions made by the gentlemen of the convention reflect the highest honor on their candor and liberality; at the same time, they prove that their minds were deeply impressed with a conviction that such mutual sacrifices are essential to our union." [100]

There was widespread recognition both of this "conviction" and of the need to conserve Union by its maintenance. During Pennsylvania's uneasiness over the Whiskey tax, feelings were soothed by just such emphasis. Viewing the crisis, the Committee of Fayette County, Pennsylvania, declared that the Union lived or died in an attitude. The great fear here was the prospect of civil war and a "probable annihilation of the Union." To save the Union, no mere adherence to the Constitution was adequate, more vital were manifestations of good will and forbearance. When fraternal blood was spilled, this spirit would forever be gone, "whatever might be the future duration of a nominal Union, its reality would no longer exist." But to make a conviction of Union would not elude the dilemma of majority rule. The committee statement emphasized that "if any one part of the Union are suffered to oppose by force the determination of the whole, there is an end to government itself, and of course to the Union." [101]

Harmony restored, Pennsylvania then issued a general endorsement of the Fayette Declaration's philosophy. In gently reproving Kentucky for the imprudence of its action against the Alien and Sedition legislation, the Pennsylvania House of Representatives reminded that state that "Our country's dearest interest demands everywhere unanimity and harmony in our councils." How to achieve this attitude? By placing "confidence in the wise and honest labours of those in whose hands is reposed the sacred charge of preserving her peace and independence." According to the rules of the Union, "the voice of the greatest number ... shall pronounce the national will." But this would not be Union itself "unless it be followed by the unfeigned and practical acquiescence of the minor part." [102]

Similarly, John Quincy Adams later chided his restless neighbors from a vantage of favor within the Jefferson circle. Writing to Harrison Gray Otis, Adams said that every region could recognize its interest only after "a full and impartial consideration of the whole subject," from which "the whole truth ... be discerned, of questions involving the rights and interests of this extensive Union." When he was repudiated as his state's senator, Adams considered his triumph over localism a victory for Union's proper perspective, "Union at the center will send forth shoots of vigor to every part of the circumference." In true Union, "we must bear and forbear, we must conciliate and harmonize. Every man must set himself and his pretensions aside." This meant for Adams a

Union become absolute majority will. "Whatever difference of opinion there may be on the system to be adopted, when once resolved upon by the concurrence of the majority, there must be no hesitation or wavering to carry it into effect." [103]

Shifting sands of sectionalism soon brought new defenders of Union as reflected in majority will. South Carolina's gestures of defiance against tariffs distressed newly comfortable Kentucky. Kentucky's General Assembly called for the enforcement of national law, even if civil war might result. Should the law be abandoned, it meant a "virtual dissolution of the Union." No matter whether the federal system emanated from all the people or from the states, there still could be but one guide, "that the majority must govern." [104]

Such changing views explained Andrew Jackson's position to one observer. While approving the President's firmness, Justice Joseph Story noted that this transition had come only because circumstance compelled Jackson to adopt "the true principles of the Constitution," which threw him in with old foes and alienated him from his friends.[105] Writing to a new Chief Justice of his plans for a farewell message, Jackson told Roger Taney that "the events of my administration necessarily bring into review, that subject of all absorbing interest, our glorious Union." The President yearned to encourage in the public mind the proper attitudes from which alone Union would proceed. Especially was he eager "to impress the public with an adequate aversion to the sectional jealousies, the sectional parties, and sectional preferences for these would disturb and shake our happy confederacy." [106]

Meantime, the Union as outlook crept into Massachusetts' sentiment. Harrison Gray Otis told an 1835 Boston public meeting that extreme sentiments must be cast aside, and particularly must abolitionism cease if Union would endure. Without a properly moderate attitude, poison would enter the "sweet fountains of domestic safety." [107] W. E. Channing, also of Massachusetts, offered a corollary: "The bearing of measures on our Union should be the chief aspect under which they should be regarded by Congress." This required simple administration, since the mass mind in Channing's opinion was easily led into confusion, always a menace to a Union of disposition. He then proceeded to discuss positive ways of strengthening the vital "sense of the sacredness of the Union." [108]

In contrast, Calhoun suggested that only through literally a negative means could the disposition toward Union be firmly established. From his regional veto system Calhoun expected a Union Absolute to emerge, resting upon a universal feeling of security. Only thus could "the whole resources of the Union, moral and physical" be "at the disposal of the government," giving Union at last the strength "which never could be acquired by the enlargement of its power beyond the limits assigned to it." [109] As a statement of Union's essential quality as a perspective, Calhoun's observation would be difficult to surpass.

Yet President Polk did excel it, in recalling Washington's admonitions. True, he mused, "It *is* difficult to estimate the 'immense value' of our glorious Union" to which "we are so much indebted for our growth in population and wealth and for all that constitutes us a great and happy nation." He saw Union as a compelling perspective: "How unimportant are all our differences of opinion upon minor questions of public policy compared with its [Union's] preservation." For Polk this perspective revealed "how scrupulously should we avoid all agitating topics." A year later, in his final message, he seemed to side with Calhoun when he declared that the idea of Union as majority numbers was nothing less than a revolution. A Union-based attitude was one which embraced the freedom-preserving system of Constitutional balances. Polk returned the debate to the venerable ground: Union versus consolidated tyranny.[110]

The discussion seemed to be back to the point where debating issues like the Bank, Internal Improvements, and Tariffs would destroy the deferential attitude which was Union itself. Zachary Taylor, by contrast, veered toward Union's nature being what the consensus thought it was. In his Inaugural Address he said that he looked to Congress for those "measures of conciliation as may harmonize conflicting interests and tend to perpetuate that Union which should be the paramount object of our hopes and affections." Taylor pledged co-operation for "any action calculated to promote an object so near the heart of everyone who truly loves his country." [111]

During the bitter disagreements of 1850, when those who sought Union's purity clashed with those who settled simply for preserving Union extant, Daniel Webster announced that simple determination would prompt Union's endurance. It seemed as if Union would emerge from positive thought: "let us devote ourselves to those great objects that are fit for our consideration and our action; let us raise our conceptions to the magnitude and the importance of the duties that devolve upon us; let our comprehension be as broad as the country for which we act, our aspirations as high as its certain destiny; let us not be pigmies in a cause that calls for men." [112]

The divisive quality of the pre-war issues betrayed the Websters, as they made ever more awkward the effort to entrust Union to the majority. Increasingly, this concept settled for a version of Union Absolute through predisposition. The rising author, Edward Everett Hale, made one last effort in 1856 in the *North American Review* by recalling Jefferson's presidency, when many leading men contemplated disunion. Union had survived, however. The enduring lesson here was "that this Union of States—the greatest Peace Society which the sun ever looked upon—is more strongly woven together than the politicians of an hour suppose," because it now controlled men's political speculation, thus "winning their sentimental loyalty." Accepting men's inability to think without Union, Hale observed: "All this makes one hope that it may yet survive the dangers that bid timid prophets cry 'Ruin,' and that our children may write of the disaffections of 1856 as indifferently as we do of 1803." [113]

Thus could Edward Everett, politician, orator, educator, tell a group of Bostonians that he remained willing to be ridiculed for "'Union-saving.'" He urged riddance of "Buncombe" present in each section to allow a return to the unity of old, where wishing seemed the essence of Union.[114] As Everett's remarks hint, the construction of a Union upon a people's awareness of the total picture proved awkward, so that in moments before the war

Union Absolute was easier portrayed as simply indispensable and irreplaceable. It became difficult to rely on some mysterious National Character, usefully ambiguous as that concept once had been. Equally dangerous was dependence upon the soothing implication of a Union in numerical majority, now that basic decisions seemed inevitable.

Perhaps James H. Hammond, the South Carolinian, struck the truth when he observed in 1860 that for the North Union had become a "policy" rather than a "principle." [115] This seemed to be the lesson of the Republican victory: that Union Absolute need no longer tarry upon equivocal ground. Now a predominant part of America felt itself to be the Union in purpose and deed. Did not belief and majoritarianism, both ingredients of such a version, condone submission to unity? Were not those whose submission had to be compelled merely a misled or evil few for whom the Union as belief was either meaningless or something to be overcome?

Yet many were loath to surrender the conviction that all Americans shared a belief from which Absolute Union could emanate. If such a fragile device is to seem other than ludicrous, we must turn to its emotional assets in the realm of imagery and mythology. From this realm such a concept drew strength, making possible the marriage between belief and majoritarianism. The Spirit outlook was thereby bolstered, since Union Absolute was obliged to guarantee self-preserving capacities. This suggests why Seward's concept of the higher law proved more important in the history of Union sentiment than did the Constitution itself.

Of Ideal and Image

America's struggle to clarify Union's form and function required levels of meaning involving images and ideals. Consequently, Union's attributes were entwined with many of the values and concerns of the time. During this phase of Union's ideological development Americans were devising a vehicle ample enough to contain most of their dreams and desires. "The Union is part of the religion of this people," Emerson said.

5: *Mission*

Many people felt the Union incorporated a great cause. This mission variously displayed three qualities, none of which was always distinguishable from the others. These were Union as a divine instrument, as Liberty's harbinger, and as the nation's triumph. Together, they expressed America's burdensome sense of destiny.

I

When Americans spoke of the Union as a moral or supernatural instrument, they discovered that this role was more readily understood if it was associated with some cause. The Union seen simply as an ethical force was too abstract. Its enormous energy clearly sought some desirable purpose within the American dream. Nevertheless, Union sometimes appeared as a vague moral agency employed by its followers to rebuke those who preferred Union's material raiment.

A Rhode Island senator, Asher Robbins, scolded his fellows for talking of "the value of the Union as if it could be counted in dollars and cents." Speaking during the controversy over Senator Foot's resolution to diminish public land sales, he insisted that Union's value was something "which no power of numbers can express, no stretch of imagination can embrace, and which baffles every effort of the mind to comprehend." Then, ignoring his own advice, Robbins spoke of Union's mission, "this happy work," as "the offspring of something more than human wisdom." Obviously the Almighty's hand had designed Union "as the guardian angel of this country," leading it to a glory "that eye hath not seen . . . in whose blaze the master States of the world will be lost, as the stars are lost in the blaze of the noontide sun." [1]

Hezekiah Niles presented Union as embodiment of men's universal hopes for self-government, but he feared that foreign nations would be hardly dazzled, as Robbins later suggested. The editor argued that Europe simply could not comprehend the role of *"moral force"* in a land of law like America where this force became a Union whose purpose was "common effort for the common good." [2] The idea was useful for a poet. New York City closed its golden anniversary of Washington's inaugural with lines by William Cutter which made the ark the symbol representing Union. Cutter proclaimed a moral crusade:

> Priests of this holy land,
> Bear on the hallowed ark—
> Blest symbol of the God at hand,
> Our guide through deserts dark.
> There, by God's finger graven,
> Is our eternal creed,
> Drawn from the liturgy of heaven
> In freedom's hour of need. [3]

Another poet called for recognition of Union's moral force in the *Democratic Review*. Emphasizing the spirit of brotherhood in Union, the poet saw its influence as:

> A union of hearts and a union of hands,
> A Union of principles none may sever,
> A union of lakes and a union of lands,
> The American Union forever. [4]

This concept always appealed to William Ellery Channing, who wrote that Union transcended materialism to find its true form in sentiment. Here men held Union in profound reverence, and with good cause, said Channing, for it "has been called by

Providence to a twofold work,—to spread civilization over a new continent, and to give a new impulse to the cause of human rights and freedom."

The Unitarian added that America recognized this agency, "a people having such a history should be bound by sentiment to the national Union is a necessary result of the laws of human nature." Convinced that Americans had a "passion" for belonging to such a great country, Channing warned that the agency of Union could not be fulfilled until the blemish of slavery was removed. Here entered Union's purpose as a crusade for human rights. As the center of American ideals, it offered "the only unity which sums up our history . . . the grand bond of national union." For Channing, Union could accept its calling only with the elimination of chattel bondage.[5] Usually, the mission had universal implications, which was a logical result of the sense of uniqueness.

Long before, another New England man of letters had expressed his own version of the Union instrument. In the aftermath of Independence, Dr. Jonathan Mitchell Sewall of New Hampshire implored:

> May Heaven's blessings descend on our United States,
> And grant that the Union may never abate;
> May love, peace, and harmony ever be found,
> For to go hand in hand America round.[6]

Once this prayer for divine blessing seemed answered, people's conviction that Union had a calling thrived. George Washington found in a strengthened Union proof that miracles still occurred. Said he, in 1788, "We may, with a kind of grateful and pious exultation, trace the finger of Providence through those dark and mysterious events," working by true Union toward "a lasting foundation for tranquillity and happiness." [7] Both Hamilton and Madison had stressed this capacity of Union in *Federalist* contributions. Hamilton argued that Union was called to vindicate the honor of the human race, "and to teach that assuming brother, moderation." Madison put the matter more tersely, asserting that "in a word," the Union was sent to insure "the happiness of the people of America." [8]

Some such lofty calling was commonly agreed to. Yet the striking quality of this guise was its supernatural design, for Americans readily made Union the instrument for some great purpose. There was more than one purpose championed in this age of growth and uncertainty. This casual approach to overarching schemes irked Fisher Ames, who said: "Are we not, on the whole, a very incorrect people—not more than half in earnest in our best principles," with the latter usually either "visionary or pernicious." Surely, he observed in 1798, the Union "would have been years ago in its grave, and in oblivion, if the providence of man had alone watched over it." As if in echo, the United States Senate formally referred to Union as "the sacred bond," one which Providence would deliver "unimpaired to a grateful posterity." [9]

A generation later, however, the acceptance of a Supreme role carried a sense of pride. Had it not been decreed that, under God, Union would "effect for us in a political, what faith does in a religious point of view—everlasting salvation?" These words of Kentucky Congressman Richard A. Buckner were typical of a widespread belief, and many also agreed with Buckner that Union's mission should encourage an "honorable pride" which "swells with patriotic emotions the heart of an American, in whatever clime he may be, when he exclaims that he is an American citizen." [10] Assent came even from as unlikely a source as Robert J. Turnbull's *The Crisis,* which acknowledged that from Union stemmed all good and happy things—"it is by Union that we take our high rank among the nations of the earth." Properly understood, Union's mission was to bring order and joy. "In Union," Turnbull said, "is the bright, and the glorious hope of perpetuating those principles which have been and will continue to be a light to lighten mankind to their rights and to their liberties." [11]

A future president, John Tyler, added his "look into the distant future," prompted by "a reverential affection for the Union." He reported seeing the Union "walking on the waves of the mighty deep, carrying along with her tidings of great joy to distant nations. I have seen her overturning the strong places of despotism, and restoring to man his long lost rights." In the face of this noble calling, Tyler could but moan, "Wo, wo betide that man who shall sow the seeds of disunion among us! Better for him had he never been born." [12]

In treating of the 1832 crisis, Alexander H. Everett spoke of superior purpose, asserting that some powerful cause was working to make America pre-eminent in all fields. Arguing that the Union's population was held together by the stern morality of the Pilgrim Fathers, Everett found Union an extraordinary instrument in the great design where the "Genius of Civilization" lifted some people higher than others, for it only could discharge the task of nurturing a free society. "If, in an hour of wild delusion,—of mad insensibility to the cause of our present prosperity, —of criminal ingratitude to the Giver of all good,—we should burst these flowery fetters, the only possible result would be ... we would exchange them for the chains that are now clanking round the limbs of every other people on the globe." A year later, returning to this theme, Everett proclaimed "the will of Providence has decreed that these States shall be united," and that all future events would dictate the truth of this.[13]

By the 1830's there was general agreement about Union's ordination by Providence to rescue humanity. Even Alabama lawmakers, in calling for a convention of states in 1833, echoed it. Assuming sincerity in "our Northern brethren," could they not see that noxious tariffs "peril the union of these states, and make shipwreck of the last hope of mankind." [14] Encountering this sentiment in her travels, Harriet Martineau took heart because "the sectional hatred, if not an abstraction, is founded mainly on abstractions, and gives way at once when the parties are confronted." This confrontation reminded Americans that their Union carried destiny's test of human intelligence against passion, making sectional bickering trifling and unseemly. Miss Martineau concluded with a striking analogy: "It is melancholy to see how the crusading chiefs quarreled for precedence on the soil of the Holy Land: it would be more so to see the leaders of this new enterprise desecrating their higher mission by a like contention." [15]

But when American leaders did fall to quarreling over issues like anti-slave petitions, the concept of Union as a mission grew cumbersome. A New York Congressman, Charles Rogers, saw Union "as freighted with the hope of humanity—as the last mighty stake in this wide world in the experiment of self-government." From everywhere "the oppressed and down-trodden" were "stretching to us their eager arms with hope and confidence." Therefore, rather than "submit to have an atmosphere of repulsion thrown around this Capitol," he said, "I'd whistle this Union 'down the tide of time,' and give its fragments to the winds." [16]

This qualification was answered by Robert J. Walker, Polk's Secretary of the Treasury. "The American Union is a moral and physical, a political and commercial necessity, and never can, or will, be dissolved." The entire American past testified "that a higher than earthly power still guards and directs our destiny, impels us onward, and has selected our great and happy country as a model and ultimate centre of attraction for all the nations of the world." [17] Walker's response typified the Mission concept's support for those advocating America's territorial destiny. Thus, President Polk called attention to Union's incalculable value as "a model and example of free government to all the world," and as "the star of hope and haven of rest to the oppressed of every clime." He contended that, the more Union fulfilled itself through expansion, the greater would be the need for Union's sense of calm.[18]

Perhaps the most famous response to Polk's appeal was Longfellow's "The Building of the Ship," a poem first appearing in 1849 and a useful oratorical device during the agitated days of 1850. Weaving the then familiar themes of Mission and providential purpose into a majestic expression of this role the poet wrote:

> Thou, too, sail on, O Ship of State!
> Sail on, O UNION, strong and great!
> Humanity with all its fears,
> With all the hopes of future years,
> Is hanging breathless on thy fate!

The remaining lines implored Union to be unafraid, since neither rock nor gale would stay the completion of the mission. Let the Union proceed:

> Our hearts, our hopes are all with thee,
> Our hearts, our hopes, our prayers, our tears
> Our faith triumphant o'er our fears
> Are all with thee,—are all with thee! [19]

Not inappropriately, a clergyman, the Reverend H. W. Bellows, offered in the *Whig Review* a more explicit basis for accepting Union's high calling. He blessed the sentiment of New World dependence upon it, making Union a solemn reminder of "the Providence over us," whose hand moved clearly in its history. Nothing else would explain the miracle of Union's enduring the strains of rapid increase amidst fearful questions. Had the Founding Fathers foreseen these events, "it certainly would not have been credited that the Union would have continued beyond half a century!" Now, said Bellows, one beheld "the centripetal ever counteracting the centrifugal forces, and in the very nick of time asserting new energy, until we are almost forced to believe the integrity of the Union a providential decree!" [20]

In the 1850 crisis, all factions testified to Union's agency for order and perfection. The universal implications were lovingly perused, as when Seward found Union "perfectly adapted to secure domestic tranquility." The Union would then cause "a more perfect civilization" to arise in America "to bless the earth." [21] James Buchanan called "our blessed Union" a "glorious platform, on which the downtrodden nations of the earth gaze with hope and desire." In the face of this admiration, said Buchanan, "our Union is the Star in the West, whose genial and steadily increasing influence will, at last, should we remain a united people, dispel the gloom of despotism." [22]

Four of the Union's great orators stood in the afterglow of 1850's reconciliation to speak of Union's agency. Edward Everett rejoiced that more than material or geographic considerations were recognized as basic to Union. It was "as if it were the design

of Providence that we should be bound together," bound, that
is, "by the cords of love." From this, "the genius of the Union,
with the law of the land in the right hand, and the law of love in
the left," came national order. In eulogizing Clay, Abraham Lincoln praised any man who would accept "as the truth" the belief
"that the world's best hope depended on the continued Union."
Clay and all good men clung to Union, said Lincoln, recognizing
that slavery could not "be at *once* eradicated, without producing
a greater evil, even to the cause of human liberty." Jefferson Davis,
touring the northeast with President Pierce, called Union a
"brotherhood . . . binding and perpetual." Though there were
many states, "we have but one history, one pride, one destiny."
Under "one destiny," which Davis quietly associated with local
rights, "this Union may go on expanding wider and wider until
its great temple reaches not only from sea to sea, but from pole to
pole." Even now, said the Mississippian, rays from the Union's
"constellation" were "world-wide," so that "wherever man raises
his hand in the cause of freedom, its light illumines his path,
cheering and directing him on to the goal of constitutional
liberty." [23] As Davis spoke, a fourth orator, Rufus Choate, ad-
dressed Dartmouth College in memory of the departed Webster.
Choate labored to place his hero's moral Union above such smaller
considerations as the Fugitive Slave Act. The Union made easy
the choice "between the greater good and the less." After all, said
Choate, those who shared Webster's grasp of Union's lofty purpose knew that for "the highest degree, and widest diffusion of
human happiness, a Union of States such as ours, some free, some
not so, was necessary." He concluded by pronouncing Union indispensable for advancing "the dearest interests of man, through
generations countless." [24]

James Buchanan, in his Inaugural Address, deplored the fact
that people now calculated "the mere material value of the
Union." If only men did not fret over the values and purpose of
Union! Surely, said the President, "the kind Providence which
inspired our fathers with wisdom to frame the most perfect form
of government and union ever devised by man will not suffer it
to perish until it shall have been peacefully instrumental by its

example in the extension of civil and religious liberty throughout the world." [25]

As the crisis deepened, Union's international mission invited larger emphasis, as it distracted attention from the divisive matters. Delight with this theme permitted Representative William Reilly to justify the proposed Kansas constitution prepared at Lecompton, which allowed slavery in the area. Supporting the admittedly dubious document in the shadow of Union's larger purpose, he anticipated the day "when all nations shall acknowledge our superiority, and when, through the benign influences of our free institutions, the kingdoms of the earth shall be regenerated, and the whole human race disenthralled." This, Union's purpose, must be cherished, so Reilly urged: "Let us environ our Union with an impenetrable wall of strong arms and stout hearts. That Union! Who does not love it?" It was the grandest edifice "ever erected by men of other-worldly wisdom." Its mission would be safer if guarded "with half the vigilance exercised by those who spent their energies and lives to secure its perpetuity." [26]

Reilly's position is instructive, representing as it does a merger of the organic with human design. Since this was possible only if the Founding Fathers were portrayed as inspired or other-worldly, it was a curious effort to add a supernatural quality to John Locke's rational process. Certainly this concept of Union had to endorse man's ability to design and maintain his own polity.

Attacking those who accepted less than Union's broad mission, the *Democratic Review* announced as the goal, "developing, elevating, and refining mankind." Men should, "rather than seek to derogate from our national character, and our national position, endeavor to elevate, to consolidate, and to perpetuate that Union which has already accomplished so much for mankind in solving the problem of man's capacity for self-government." [27] The Democrats' outstanding leader at the time, Stephen A. Douglas, used this argument in debating with Lincoln. Calling Union "the hope of the friends of freedom throughout the world," Douglas emphasized the universal need for its preservation. Surely mere Kansas matters withered in the presence of the true objects of Union, "the down-trodden and oppressed people who are suffering under European despotism." These looked "with hope and anxiety to the American Union as the only resting place and permanent home of freedom and self-government." [28]

In the Senate, Seward took comfort in knowing that the "coolness, calmness, and resolution" of the people's character would rescue the Union. Why? Because "this Union has not yet accomplished what good for mankind was manifestly designed by Him who appoints the seasons and prescribes the duties of States and empires." Seward said any impediment would be momentary, and Union "would rise again and reappear in all its majestic proportions tomorrow." [29] This Christ-like quality often assigned Union befitted the mission of universal regeneration which so many attributed to Providence. Among the clergy accepting this design was James Craik, who found that Union, next to Christianity, was the most precious gift of God to any people. Through a combination of the Almighty's power and the fact that Americans came from superior Teutonic stock, Craik said the American Union in its complexity stood forth to preserve freedom everywhere.[30]

These appeals to mysticism seemed again the way to avoid the occasional awkwardness of pursuing Union's lofty purpose. None was more noteworthy than 1856 lectures by Professor Henry Reed of the University of Pennsylvania. He spoke in hope that reviewing "the Providential processes which created the Union may not be without interest and use at a time when adverse sectional excitements endanger it." Reed's prescription demanded unquestioning reverence for the fact of Union and condemnation for those who looked "at the Union as the mere creation of human agencies." For himself, Reed "humbly and intelligently looked upon the Union as the blessed work of God," and as such he "loved and revered it." While the Constitution and the Declaration were due to human endeavor, "for the UNION, our thanksgiving must be laid at the foot of the throne of God; and, therefore, treason to the Union cannot be conceived of but as a crime which heaps upon the traitor an accumulated guilt of thankless impiety." [31]

The idea of Union's purpose allowed two positions, as Reed's appeal shows. It was possible to see both the Declaration and the Constitution as representing the rational contractualism which remained at men's disposal, but the broader element, the community itself, rested on a supernatural decree, hence giving the organic idea considerable security. This necessitated bypassing Webster's strategy of associating Union and Constitution, as well it might, since the Union's mission, effectively conceived, had to be supra-human. There was a rich background for this idea of purpose, involving especially Calvinist concepts. For American thought these promised more appeal than did contrivances like the Constitution. But Polity and Mission could not be kept safely apart for long.

Indeed, the concept of Union as an agent engendered an explosive question. So long as Union's Messianic quality remained majestic but obscure, local defects might be tolerated. More often, however, it became useful to explore the Mission concept, disclosing Union to some eyes as Liberty's harbinger. This was a transition easily made within the concept of Mission, for a Divine Instrument had to face the question, "for what?" The answer almost had to be the role of prophet for Liberty, both within America and throughout the world.

II

While Providence and Liberty seemed cause and effect, the latter became increasingly controversial within America's socio-economic contrasts. The Union religion which Emerson had seen needed more theology than a vague sense of mission for order and happiness. Consequently, Americans often reviewed the advantages of their system, which came down to argument in a circle: the notion that Union alone could perpetuate the freedom vital to America, and that freedom was possible only through the integrity of Union. Expert at drawing this design was Daniel Webster, champion of Union's libertarian mission. He rose to the occasion at the 1843 celebration on the completion of the Bunker Hill monument. "Woe betide the man," said Webster, "who brings to this day's worship feeling less than wholly American." Again the appeal, in unconscious irony, warning men lest they depart from approved thought in a system dedicated to freedom.

This ubiquitous theme demonstrated a continuing uneasiness over Union's success. Only evil, deranged, or pitiable people would dwell beyond Union's true quality. As for the strife-torn story of localism, Webster invoked the great antidote to such "festering and rankling," which was "Union, established in justice, in patriotism, and the most plain and obvious common interest." Here, above all, "Union, founded in the same love of liberty," conceived in the "common cause" of freedom, was easily "the source of all our glory and greatness thus far and is the ground for all our highest hopes." Pointing to the monument which symbolized America's quest for Freedom, Webster announced: "This column stands on Union." When Union fell, the monument and all for which it stood would collapse.[32]

Even in the era commemorated at Bunker Hill's ceremonies, Webster's version of Union had been present. James Iredell sought early to portray the mission as a "great truth," calling its importance such as to make it "the watch-word of American liberty and safety." Union sustained would allow America to become "as it seems destined to be, an asylum for all the oppressed upon the globe." Thus the Constitution proposed in 1787 was a delight to Iredell because of its "many provisions calculated to make us as much one people as possible." [33] When some of his neighbors failed to see this "useful and important truth," Iredell pleaded throughout the North Carolina ratification convention for staying with Union and avoiding the "great danger of a separation forever . . . so awful an event." Why "awful"? Because, said Iredell, "our freedom," source of all things dear, "has been derived from that Union we are now going rashly to dissolve." [34]

Far to the North, on Christmas Day, 1787, the Union was similarly cast. In the *Massachusetts Gazette,* James Sullivan insisted the people themselves wanted a more perfect Union as the only way they could "support and transmit, inviolate, to the latest posterity, all the blessings of civil and religious liberty." [35] In the West, Pennsylvania frontiersmen gathered at the Harrisburg Conference in 1788 to consider young Albert Gallatin's draft of a report. Only through Union, this document contended, could liberty and happiness be assured. Thus, given "the present situation of the Union," there was no doubt that all men motivated by prudence and conciliation should support any changes needed "to prevent a dissolution of the Union." [36]

Throughout a period of experiment, the Union's role as messenger for liberty continued useful. On the eve of the War of 1812, ex-President Adams affirmed his faith in Union as "the rock of our salvation," and his belief that the people generally shared this, for "prophecies of division have been familiar in my ears for six-and-thirty years." Such incessant sentiment had "no other effect than to increase the attachment of the people to the Union." In fact, Union as preserver of liberty had extraordinary significance for Adams who felt it was one of those "fundamental questions" which politicians tended to ignore. He observed to Josiah Quincy, "However lightly we may think of the voice of the people sometimes, they not infrequently see farther than you or I . . . and you may depend upon it, they see in a partition of the Union, more danger to American liberty . . . and a total loss of independence for both fragments, or all fragments of the Union." [37]

America's liberty-oriented system of republicanism, more and more self-conscious of its uniqueness, took its cue from the elder Adams. Governor Gabriel Slaughter told the Kentucky legislature, "Let us remember that ours is the only republic on the globe, and that a union among ourselves is necessary to insure success to our system." While there might be honest differences of opinion, woe betide the day when the Union should "be divided by the mere magic of unmeaning names and terms." Like Adams, Slaughter wanted Union's role as guarantor of the American paradise uppermost.[38]

At this point, it was often prudent to add another aspect of Union, the legend of the everlasting fathers which is discussed in the ensuing chapter. The "patriots of other days," as Kentucky

Congressman Richard Buckner called them, had a regard for Union's liberty-bearing mission which waxed with the passing years. Buckner's tie of past to present was much used in the bitter campaign of 1828, during which Jackson endorsed this mission of Union, saying, "there is nothing that I shudder at more than the idea of a separation of the Union." Should it occur, "which I fervently pray God to avert," said he, "from that date, I view our liberty gone." The durability of Union alone "must prolong our liberty." [39]

As a chief executive confronted by many crises, Jackson announced happiness and liberty would persist, since Union could not be dissolved. Falling back on old John Adams's useful dictum, the President insisted that the "national voice" decreed Union with unanimity, recognizing it as "the sheet anchor of our liberty and prosperity." The rough draft of Jackson's second inaugural message discloses his growing preoccupation with this idea. If Union, bearing liberty off with it, were lost, then he beheld "our sons made soldiers to deluge with blood the fields they now till in peace . . . and military leaders, at the head of their victorious legions, becoming our lawgivers and judges." In brief, "dissolution of the Union" meant the "loss of liberty." And it was more than America's freedom that Union impelled, since the world watched for the outcome of Union's effort. Before this combined charge, Jackson was confident that anyone who might "lift his parricidal hand against this blessed Union, which, like Heaven's Canopy, spreads over us all," would be met by the "curse of millions." [40] On this point there was a remarkable affinity of sentiment between the old Federalist, Adams, and the popular Democrat.

Jackson's image of a liberty-charged Union was endorsed by Governor Henry Johnson of Louisiana. "The character of our liberty is too sacred thus to be sported with. Separate the Union and our free institutions may be forever destroyed." The faith of John Adams was reflected in Johnson's words: "The character of the American people, the devotion they have displayed to the principles of true liberty," all this was "a sufficient pledge for its [Union's] preservation." [41]

But South Carolina, the source of so much alarm, also claimed reverence for Union's mission. The legislative statement of 1831, prepared by Calhoun, agreed that Americans had "the deepest interest in the preservation of the Union, as the only certain guarantee of their peace and security." It was necessary to eliminate the alien "spirit of interfering," and Americans should recognize that wisdom meant "a wise and masterful inactivity." Once this vision had been cleared, "an invaluable blessing will be conferred; our liberty will be saved, and our Union preserved." [42]

A crucial disparity appeared in the use of this idea of Union. South Carolina led the way from the Adams-Jackson mystical Union of mass sentiment toward the antithesis, a concept literally devoid of power. The nature of Union's mission was challenged, for Calhoun considered liberty both technique and condition. To this, the aging James Madison objected. An 1829 outline of his ideas on federalism insisted that Union was "without a model, and to be explained by itself, not by similitudes or analogies." One thing was clear, "The happy Union of these States is a wonder; their Const.ⁿ a miracle; their example the hope of Liberty throughout the world." Obviously moved by the idea of mission, Madison suggested forgetting the curiosities of federalism in the face of Union's enthralling purpose.

"Woe to the ambition," he cried, "that would meditate the destruction" of the happy calling.[43] Here Madison abandoned his long concern with techniques of politics to investigate the organic aspect. He now supported its emphasis on eternal principle and purpose, which made Union's role as harbinger of freedom surpass the trivia of origin and procedure. Since Union as Liberty's agent seemed indispensable and absolute, it doomed the idea of reasoned contract.

Webster was indebted to this trend for letting him shout that nullifiers would become "the great blasters of human hopes," while he reiterated that the cause of universal liberty depended upon preserving Union. Webster, unlike Adams and Madison, feared to shelve the Constitution, but he enjoyed stressing the unique nature of Union. In it was "the peculiar and cherished idea of United American Liberty.... The noble idea of United American Liberty, of *our* liberty." Little would survive if Union crumbled. "Fragments and shattered columns of the edifice may be found remaining; and melancholy and mournful ruins will they be. The august temple itself will be prostrate in the dust." [44]

In this way, perpetuating the American order became a truism as Union's mission increasingly preoccupied American attention. President Zachary Taylor called Union's dissolution "the greatest of calamities" because all happiness depended upon Union for "countless generations to come." [45] On the eve of Taylor's election, the *North American Review* took Europe's tumult to be the moment when Union's libertarian mission could be fulfilled. Thus, "It becomes us, by fidelity to our own republic, to keep the model to which they all turn, and by which they must all work, fair and bright before their eyes." In London, Francis Grund's *The Americans* used this theme to say that America's freedom, honor, power, even "her existence are explicitly pledged in the Union. If this palladium of her liberty should once be lost or destroyed," there would vanish what Grund admired, the lofty patriotism which gave the American mind its broad sweep.[46]

Once again, the sense of duty to the world was used to surmount internal feuds. Senator Thomas Metcalfe of Kentucky said a distraught world saw Union "as the bright resplendent polar star of human liberty." He added, "the different nations of Europe are endeavoring to shape their governments so as to imitate our own." Thus, "Let our motto ever be, Union now, and Union forever." Said an Indiana spokesman: "This Union which is the germ that is leavening the world with the spirit of freedom! This Union which is the nucleus of the liberties of mankind." [47] To Massachusetts' freshman senator, Charles Summer, Union was especially blessed "as model and beginning of that all-embracing Federation of States by which unity, peace, and concord will finally be organized among the Nations." [48] Secretary of State Webster told of sleeplessly worrying about Union's preservation for its republican mission, "that throws a shade, and sometimes a deep and black shade, over the monarchies and aristocracies, and despotisms of Europe." [49] Webster hoped men would keep

Union for its world influence if its national mission were not enough to rally public support.

Others, like George Ticknor Curtis, who claimed Webster's dying blessing, thought it wise to rest content with Union's domestic mission. In the preface of his *History,* Curtis pictured Union as purveying the twin blessings of liberty and order. Here was the tone of Lincoln's reply to the first toast, "The UNION," at an 1856 Republican banquet. In it, he reiterated that Republicans believed liberty could be obtained best through the agency of Union.[50] Many like Lincoln were stressing Union's guise as bearer of freedom while they recognized that not all Americans responded to it. Instead of seeking escape in the global ramifications of Union's agency, the Republicans accepted an ominous fact which worshipers of Union had avoided for a generation. A Connecticut Lincoln paper went directly to the point: "It is clear that we can even now have Union, but it is not so clear that we can have Union *and Liberty.* The object of the Union was to rescue the blessings of liberty." But now the danger was "that the Union might be preserved by measures which would render it wholly false to its original object." [51]

An additional feature of Union's mission for liberty was the appearance of Union as a veritable temple or shrine for freedom. This idea had a more commanding quality than was usually present in Union's guarantor role. The powerful Democrat, Silas Wright, talked of such a Citadel shortly before his death. Speaking on July Fourth, the New York leader pleaded in 1839 that men revere the Founding Fathers' assumptions. "What American citizen will now rise, and claim to be purer than Washington . . . purer and more patriotic than the sages who supported him in the great work." There being no takers, Wright could safely proceed to the climax, asking who "will cast the first stone at that temple of human liberty which they erected?" Speaking as strongly as American legend permitted, Wright wished the fate of Benedict Arnold upon him who would dismember Union, "Our proud Temple of Freedom." [52]

Wright's emphasis suggests the subtle implications in this variation of mission. Union seen as an agent for liberty could not escape a tentative note, while the idea of a Citadel for Freedom was incontrovertible. It therefore justified Wright's charge of betrayer upon the person failing to worship. Futhermore, the question of organic or compact derivation remained happily confused. Although the Founding Fathers built the Temple, their design was clearly an inspired one.

While Union's latter days, filled with anguish, especially encouraged the Citadel or Temple version of mission, this symbol had appeared earlier. Addressing the South Carolina ratification convention, Charles Pinckney asserted: "To the Union we will look up, as to the temple of our freedom—a temple founded in the affections and supported by the virtue, of the people." [53] The citizen body as worshippers in a cathedral-Union was a frequent image. Philip Freneau used it in an editorial of 1792: "The people of *fifteen united parishes,* in a certain part of America, have agreed on one common religion, and erected to themselves a temple. . . . They have entrusted this temple to the care of a set of priests chosen and paid for the express purpose of performing service in it, keeping it in repair, and writing catechisms and books of useful instruction to promote 'the general welfare' of the fifteen united parishes." [54]

Later, when slavery, tariffs, and internal improvement agitation troubled the Shrine, a Pennsylvania congressman spoke of a Western congregation which performed "an annual pilgrimage over yonder rough and rugged mountains, to worship here with 'a more than Eastern idolatry,' at this temple of liberty, this altar of our Union." Should this shrine be destroyed, "you extinguish the last lamp of liberty, you prostrate the last citadel of freedom." With the mission frustrated, freedom was "left without a friend, and liberty without a sanctuary." [55]

A failure to appreciate this spiritual calling was ascribed to the South by Webster, as the tariff tested some men's faith in Union's mission. Robert Y. Hayne was obliged to deny any Southern materialism, saying that, when Union called, "the sons of Carolina were all seen crowding together to the temple, bringing their gifts to the altar of their common country." Hayne could not resist wondering where New England had worshipped during

the Hartford apostasy. Where, he asked, was Webster then? [56]
Such an exchange prompted a faithful Temple servant to reprove
the congregation. John Bell, then a Tennessee congressman,
pleaded for moderation without which the world would behold
"sooner or later, the Union broken up, and this last and noblest
sanctuary of freedom polluted and destroyed." Undismayed, in
1835 South Carolina's legislature demanded that the North halt
its agitation, for "they not only owe it to us, but they owe it
to themselves, to that union, at whose shrine they have so often
offered up the highest pledges by which man can plight his tem-
poral faith." [57]

Northerners replied in kind. One New Yorker said of disunion,
"you might just as well talk, in this nineteenth century, of overturning the Christian religion." In fact, said Representative
Samuel Gordon, "Next to the Christian religion, the people of
these United States, from north to south, from east to west, all
cherish and adore this holy and sacred Union of ours." To the
lover of freedom, "the cry of dissolution of the Union is second
only in insanity and blasphemy to the cry in France that there is
no God." It was, he added, "an impossibility," the Union would
never, could never be dissolved.[58] Blasphemy had now joined
insanity and treason as impulses for those wretched challengers of
Union. Certainly no hint of human origin is discernible in the
Shrine image. Instead, an ever more passive role was assigned to
the citizen-worshipper. More and more the issue of who had
erected the temple was lost.

Threats to the Citadel called forth no more valiant defender than
James Buchanan. The Temple idea served admirably for one who
sought a view without an irksome mixture of light and shadow.
It permitted Buchanan to assert: "God forbid that fanaticism
should ever apply a torch to this, the grandest and most glorious
temple which has ever been erected to political freedom on the
face of the earth." This language became stock-in-trade for those
like Buchanan who met each divisive issue with warnings that
it might "destroy this the grandest temple which has ever been
dedicated to human freedom since the world began." Should
the temple fall, liberty's friends would everywhere be crushed,

"and a long night of leaden despotism would enshroud the nations." [59]

Some of the congregation decided to be explicit. Senator John J. McRae of Mississippi insisted, "in the American Pantheon . . . in which American freemen make their worship to the divinity of their country, there is no separate statue of the Union." Rather, McRae found around "its great altar" were "the several statues of the several, sovereign, independent States, as they came one by one, to build up the great compact of the Union." And in the midst of these McRae saw an image of the Constitution.[60] Others, of course, were taken aback at finding a controversial polity within. Less disturbed was Owen Lovejoy, the Illinois congressman, who believed like John Adams that the mass of men would save freedom's shrine. In Lovejoy's view, it was "the sturdy yeoman class" which would "protect from violence or dismemberment the temple of freedom where in the holiest of holies, the Constitution and the Union repose." It was this class which would drive out the "traitorous hordes of disunionists, as the Son of God drove their prototypes, the fallen angels, over the battlements of heaven." [61]

Such assured dedication made a voice from New York tell the South, "You may shatter the Union; but the holiest associations for ages to come will gather round and garnish its ruins." The Union's role as Liberty's Citadel would go on in spite of Southern apostasy. "The travel-stained pilgrim in liberty's cause will, through all time, weep its overthrow. . . . You may destroy our temple, but, like the sacred olive on the Acropolis, the burnt stump will immediately put forth 'a fresh shoot.' " [62] A New Jersey senator disagreed only by asserting that "This Union cannot be destroyed." Men might attempt it, but God would not permit it. Such prospects invited a long poetic passage which conveyed admirably the tenets of Union's mission for liberty:

> Who would sever Freedom's Shrine?
> Who would draw the invidious line?
> Though by birth, one spot be mine,
>   Dear is all the rest.

Dear to me the South's fair land,
Dear the central mountain band,
Dear New England's rocky strand,
    Dear the prairied West.
By our altars, pure and free,
By our law's deep-rooted tree,
By the past's dread memory,
    By our Washington,
By our common parent tongue,
By our hopes, bright, brilliant, young—
By the ties of country, strong
    We will still be one.
Fathers, have ye bled in vain?
Ages! must ye droop again?
Maker! shall we rashly stain
    blessings sent from thee?
No! receive our solemn vow,
While before thy throne we bow,
Ever to maintain, as now,
    Union—Liberty.[63]

Such lofty sentiment did not entirely dominate the idea of Union's agency. Granting that Freedom and Union were intertwined, some held that as liberty clearly needed material achievement, Union became the only source of mundane advance. Rarely, however, was Union and Freedom's marriage in material triumph discussed after Jackson's era. For instance, Henry Clay's apotheosis of Union became much different after the economic crises of the Jackson Administration. Before then he was renowned as much for popularizing the material mission of Union as for his compromise artistry.

During the House's 1816 effort to create several military academies, Speaker Clay met contention that the distribution of these institutions would further sectional consciousness by saying that "the moral effect" of the proposal "would be to increase the affection of the people for the Union." Inquiring: "If the bond of Union was to be strengthened by the measures of the government, what ought to be the character of them?" he replied that government must always try "to afford to every man in the Union" some palpable evidence of the Union's benefits. Once this occurred, sectional feeling would vanish, since, said Clay, "the bosom turns with thankfulness to the source of benefits received, as unerringly as the needle to the pole." [64]

Sensing the agony which befell Clay's dreams in the years following 1816, Tocqueville relied upon the Union's role as mystical spirit to observe, "the government of the Union watches over the general interests of the country; but the general interests of the people have but a questionable influence upon individual happiness, while state interests produce an immediate effect upon the welfare of the inhabitants." In Tocqueville's view, Union was limited to securing "the independence and the greatness of the nation, which do not immediately affect private citizens." Unaware that he was speaking about a dying age, Tocqueville lauded decentralization with its negative materialism. [65]

Clearly, Tocqueville, like the time in which he wrote, was charmed alternately by localism and centralism. Through its federal arrangement the Union seemed the way to make harmonious these often anachronistic elements. But when the material Union's effect grew, it seemed to omit or endanger a significant portion of those localities which Clay once strove to rally. If the neglected South appeared unlikely to benefit from the material Union's success, as many Southerners believed, it made rather useless the idea of material agency, and it left Union's more mystical versions of mission in control.

Earlier, in an age of uncertainty and novelty, the material feature of Union's mission could be stressed heavily. Hamilton often expressed belief in "the necessity of the Union" for the "safety and prosperity" of the people at large. In speaking on these matters to Jefferson, George Washington claimed Union effective if it brought commercial order and national respectability. Union, Washington said, would make America "the asylum of pacific and industrial characters from all parts of Europe." Wealthy men would come to America, since Union would be "giving security to property and liberty to its holders." [66] Washington's Farewell Orders to the army in 1783 made his soldiers Union's ambassadors of good will, seeking "to remove the prejudices which may have taken possession of the minds of any of the People of the States." An unprejudiced mind, Washington thought, would try "to confirm and perpetuate that happy Union of the States and its citizens which under Providence has so visibly been the means of our deliverance." [67]

Union's material mission was therefore built around a simple idea—that the good society with freedom properly implanted would thrive in America only with economic assurance. The latter, according to many, demanded Union. Thomas Smith Grimke of Charleston emphasized this in an 1809 Fourth of July address. Union, he announced, was "the vital principle of our permanence and happiness," because it meant prosperity and "renovation," thus providing the proper channel for "the influences of the social principle." [68]

In a few years the nation's path seemed clearer, but most Charlestonians did not like its direction. Union's physical advantages no longer could be easily pictured as encompassing men of Massachusetts and Georgia. Even President Jackson found it prudent to be more vague in his attempt to synthesize Union's material and spiritual designs. His Second Inaugural Address, devoted as it was to glorifying Union and the "sacred duty" of all to support it in its "incalculable importance," said simply that "loss of liberty, of all good government, of peace, plenty, and happiness, must inevitably follow a dissolution of the Union." Given such a Union, "in supporting it, therefore we support all that is dear to the freeman and the philanthropist." [69]

The very crisis which obliged the President to stress Union's worldly mission was forcing the idea of Union to loftier ground so that materialism's shortcomings might be abandoned. Little remained but such safe generalizations as Edward Everett used in his benediction on the career of Webster: "The key to his whole political course is the belief that, when the Union is dissolved, the internal peace, the vigorous growth, and the prosperity of the States and the welfare of their inhabitants, are blighted forever, and that, while the Union endures, all else of trial and calamity which can befall a nation may be remedied or borne." [70]

III

Everett's summary suggests another version of mission, the Union cast as America's triumphant deliverer. Here the lures of prosperity and liberty could be reconciled in a broader design emphasizing national ascendancy and glory. Union's mission became that of evoking an American character. Thus, talk of Providential Agency or Liberty's harbinger often concluded by disclosing national triumph to be the reward for continued Union, an achievement comprised of two attributes: status in the eyes of the world, and the establishment of the long-coveted national character among Americans. So great was the eagerness to produce an "American people" that Union was pictured not only as entailed by the character of Americans, but also as having a mission to produce just such a character.

Edward Everett's 1824 Phi Beta Kappa oration at Harvard was an excellent early formulation of this idea, seeing a mission intending not merely one government, one language, but ultimately, "one character over so vast a space as the United States of America." Then, "should our happy Union continue," here would dwell "the mightiest kindred people known in history." In fact, the prospect of this mission's triumph was staggering. Everett drew back, "the vision is too magnificent to be fully borne." But looking anyway, he found a national mentality under Union, with two or three million citizens guided into one great consensus, there swayed by the master spirits of the time.[71]

Many had shared Everett's hopes for a Union character, including George Washington. "We are a young Nation," said Washington, "and have a character to establish. It behooves us therefore to set out right for first impressions will be lasting, indeed are all in all." For the General, only Union brought true character and with it that badge of triumph, "a place among the Nations of the Earth." Without it, America would be "contemptible." Yet the draft of a 1792 Farewell Message for Washington could speak of Union's perpetuity through brotherly affection among the people. "We may all be considered the children of one common country. We have all been embarked in one common cause." To assist in this mission was an "affectionate and permanent Union." [72] By 1797 Justice William Paterson could see in the fact that President Adams and Vice President Jefferson shared lodging something emblematic of the united national character that was needed. Paterson was encouraged to "hope that, in a short time, we shall have no interests or views but what is purely American. In this wish will all wise heads and honest hearts unite." [73]

What Paterson called the "purely American," Hezekiah Niles termed "a NATIONAL CHARACTER," whose establishment was his dream. The Baltimore editor conceived Union as called to establish "the whole American family—divested of local partialities and sectional prejudices." Foreseeing a successful mission, he said in 1820, "Certainly men are more and more esteemed according to their merits." The Union's victory Niles beheld was the triumph once seen by old John Adams, for citizens were beginning "to see that their interests are more clearly united together than demagogues . . . would have suffered them to believe was the case." Niles found Union progressing in its effort to command America's mind. "A general desire for the welfare of the Union, the pride of the age and the hope of posterity," said Niles, "is superseding the petit clamors that formerly prevailed." [74]

Failure to succumb to this appeal some considered to have been South Carolina's sin in 1832. "The animated and persevering expressions in favour of the Union from every division of the country," quickly revealed to Carolinians, said one analyst, "that they had mistaken the voice of a few partisans for the voice of the people." This writer for the *American Quarterly Review* awarded Union a full measure of achievement by arguing that its destruction now meant violence to the character and habits of the American people. To this idea, George Bancroft added that history confirmed Union's agency, and more especially the public as carriers of the cause. Another historian, William H. Prescott, said it was certain "we shall be true to our *mission*—the most momentous ever entrusted to a nation." [75]

This American character which many accepted as Union's great goal was a commonplace by the 1840's. An able expositor of it was Levi Woodbury. Speaking to the New Hampshire Historical Society in 1845, the year he joined the federal Supreme Court, Woodbury said that "Peculiar Traits of American Character" was a topic meriting attention so that "all, living within the glorious brotherhood of our Union, will come to prize each other higher, because they will know each other better." There was an American character, Woodbury stoutly maintained, coming out of diverse backgrounds and in a varied country, yet one "as uniformly and strongly marked as any of the nations from which we sprang." Seeing the political anguish around him, Woodbury insisted that only unity in character had made it possible to "preserve a political Union, indissolubly and gloriously, amidst all the trying scenes of more than half a century." Thus Union's essence once more was seen as Spirit, surpassing mere form.[76]

Desires for national character and for world respectability were obviously related. The latter was another facet of Union's mission to bring America greatness. John Quincy Adams, a cosmopolitan in a nation becoming increasingly introverted, sought especially to enhance this role. Appropriately, it was the first President who launched Adams as a world citizen by making him Minister to the Netherlands. For over a quarter of a century, Adams was obliged professionally to see his Union from the world's eye. Writing from The Hague in 1796, he asserted, "All my hopes of national felicity and glory have invariably been founded upon the continuance of the Union." Here was the fundamental ingredient in his concept of the public welfare. Therefore, "much as I must disapprove of the general tenor of southern politics," Adams said, "I would rather even yield to their unreasonable pretensions and suffer much for their wrongs, than break the chain that binds us together." He added, "there is no one article of my political creed more clearly demonstrated to my mind than this, that we shall proceed with gigantic strides to honor and consideration, and national greatness, if the Union is preserved." [77]

Fifteen years later, writing to his mother from Russia, Adams's views were even more strongly internationalist. He urged that disunionist sentiment be put down, or else, "Instead of a nation, coextensive with the North American continent, destined by God and nature to be the most populous and most powerful people ever combined under one social compact, we shall have an endless multitude of little insignificant clans and tribes at eternal war with one another for a rock, or a fishpond, the sport and fable of European masters and oppressors." [78]

Fifteen years later, as Chief Executive, Adams marveled at the failure of all to share the majestic view of Union's mission. His inaugural remarks admitted that, while divisions within the Union were "inseparable from the enjoyment of freedom," these had "more than once appeared to threaten the dissolution of the Union, and with it the overthrow of all the enjoyments of our present lot and all our earthly hopes of the future." But Adams felt that a new day brought courage, because most Americans now accepted as "articles of faith," the belief that "the policy of our country is peace and the ark of our salvation, Union." [79]

Adams was quickly disillusioned about Union's triumphant mission. A decade after his tenure ended, he complained that Union's true mission was thwarted by "the Sable Genius of the South." As a consequence, "the American Union as a moral Person in the family of Nations, is to live from hand to mouth, to cast away, instead of using for the improvement of its own condition, the bounties of Providence." [80]

For a time, Adams's preoccupation had been widely shared. But that was during the uncertain early years when Madison could say hopefully, "America united, with a handful of troops, or without a single soldier, exhibits a more forbidding posture to foreign ambition than America disunited, with a hundred thousand veterans." Thus the moral: "Let it never for a moment be forgotten that they are indebted for this advantage to the Union alone. The moment of its dissolution will be the date of a new order of things." [81] Thomas Jefferson, Madison's companion in nurturing Union, assented, saying to Elbridge Gerry, "Whatever follies we may be led into as to foreign nations, we shall never give up our Union, the last anchor of our hope, & that alone which is to prevent this heavenly country from becoming an arena of gladiators." The pacifist Jefferson confessed a willingness to join with "my brethren" in battling Europe as preferable to separating from any of his brothers.[82]

Here Adams's idea of Mission rested for two decades while America faced an international menace. Certainly in the hour of New England's discontent, most of the nation took heart from the sense of Union's international ramifications. By the time of Monroe's presidency, however, this world visage dwindled as domestic issues became paramount. It lingered in only an occasional reference. After 1830, despite the inner turmoil, Union's mission of national ascendancy kept to a domestic setting, as when Abbott Lawrence tried to persuade Virginia's statesman, William C. Rives, that the "destiny of our beloved country" was in "upholding and maintaining the Union." Just so would a tariff program bring strength and security to all the Union, Lawrence insisted.[83] The newly launched Whig journal, *The American Review,* announced in 1845 that no "true-hearted" American would disrupt the Union, for he always appreciated the great mission. Those who did not should look to Europe, where men still fought for crumbs amid indolence and want. Unity had brought to America power, prosperity, and law. The man who shared this vision, said these editors, "will nerve himself for every contest in which he can do service for the CONSTITUTION and the UNION." [84]

Elias Peissner's little volume of 1861 made this even more clear. "The American question has gradually become one of nationality." This author ridiculed such efforts to thwart the march of Union as drawing the Missouri line.[85] Here were sentiments which could have introduced James Russell Lowell's great statement of Union's mission, the 1861 essay, *"E Pluribus Unum,"* one revealing a profound tie between this mid-century man of letters and the man of affairs, George Washington. While their concepts were much the same, the elapse of seven decades had transformed Washington's wistful glimpse of mission into Lowell's triumphant affirmation. "The United States are not a German Confederation," he observed, "but a unitary and indivisible nation, with a national life to protect, a national power to maintain, and national rights to defend against any and every assailant, at all hazards." The Union's existence, Lowell said, "is all that gives value to American citizenship." In denying this, the South merely toyed with words. "The United States are a nation, and not a mass meeting," Lowell affirmed, adding: "We want neither Central Republics nor Northern Republics, but our own Republic and that of our fathers, destined one day to gather the whole continent under a flag that shall be the most august in the world." [86]

In the thirty tense years preceding Lowell's statement, Union's mission had assumed an inviolable quality that contributed to the increasingly organic nature of its design. Instead of hoping that men might choose to join in Union's effort, many people could now insist that no choice existed. A few days before Lincoln was inaugurated, a Kentucky Congressman, John Y. Brown, said that a citizen had to see his "first, highest, holiest ambition" as contributing "to the perpetuity, prosperity, and renown of this Union." Here the "grand mission has been one of civilization, of advancing the cause of civil liberty, of nurturing and developing the arts and sciences, and of expanding our power on land and sea." Yet the Kentuckian foresaw the mission's failure, "some of the pillars of the Union are fallen, others crumbling, and the magnificent fabric reels. . . ." Then, dramatizing the fatal equivocation in Union's purpose, he acknowledged that, if Lincoln drew the sword, his own sense of Union would force him to aid the South.[87]

Union's evocative mission for national character proved a failure in its own terms. Once, at a time fraught with international insecurity, when technology had yet to shape national design, Washington placed Union's mission in its safest terms when he demanded that Americans live in a global context. Such a course would surely discourage any foolish inner strife. But when a later generation took to isolation of a kind Washington could not have foreseen, the American character split. In asking Union to work its purpose within national dimensions, two national selves claimed to embody this purpose. A clash was certain.

Ultimately the advocates of national character were vindicated, but at a price few desired to pay. Lincoln fought a war for both versions of mission, American character and national glory. Yet the fact of disruption was essentially a repudiation of these ideas as they had been traditionally understood. Out of this comes another aspect of Union ideology. In portraying Union with brushings of moral instrumentality, libertarian agency, and great-ness' design, such efforts point to the lore and legend in which so many of Union's concepts finally were interred. To these versions of Union we now turn.

6: *Legend*

Few people demurred when an 1850 Mississippi pamphleteer declared: "I love the Union . . . for its proud and glorious associations with all that is dear to an American heart." [1] Yet these legends proved unwieldy for the Union consensus sought by the followers of Clay and Webster. Eagerly, such believers pursued versions of Union that might combat what Dr. Benjamin Rush of Philadelphia once had called a mind so "bedollared." Rush wondered what could be offered the American people to inspire unity. The Constitution would never do, Rush was convinced. It was so controvertible that he never did "meet with a man who loves it." In 1808, Rush could see only the presidential office as a "center of Union" which "we rally round." But this required a popular chief, and after the death of Washington Rush found none capable of assuming the symbolical function. [2] While Rush lived too soon to see the Union become self-contained, many others labored in the hope that the lore of Union itself might bring the indispensable spirit of Union. These devotees failed to see that Union was becoming an indisputable physical fact, and thus an Absolute in American thought. Consequently, the legends of Union would become superfluous.

For the time, however, a hunger for national identity fed upon Union as the supreme legend. The generations after 1776 found America's domestic and foreign travail too overwhelming for any

human to succeed as a demigod figure, and so the legends to which
America consistently responded were largely the supra-individ-
ualistic ones inspired by the Union. For those who considered
Union a vast and comforting organic process, as well as those who
were convinced that the American nation could exist only through
mystical association, the Union was supported by three legends.
Of these the most familiar entailed Providence's care. With as-
surances of predestined success, it conveyed an appealing story of
Union's divine appointment. The second legend cultivated the
Everlasting Fathers, emphasizing not so much their omniscience
as attributing their Timeless Insights to Inspired Soundness. This
idea's strength was Union's apparent changelessness. The difficulty
was agreeing what that Union was. Finally, Union lore invoked
the concept of Nature's Decree. Here were such qualities as the
call of natural outlines; the belief that unity flourished the more
because of diversity; and the Union's essence as a family. Closely
allied to these ideas was that will-o'-the-wisp, National Character.

Together, these legends combined to endorse a Union so absolute yet so ambiguous that, quite understandably, brother was
led to destroy brother. It was through this lore that most Americans came to understand Union.

I

So much has been said in these pages about the association of
Providence with Union that here we need only acknowledge the
legend of Providential Care. Its early appeal can be sensed in
John Jay's *Federalist* comment: "This country and this people
seem to have been made for each other, and it appears as if it was
the design of Providence, that an inheritance so proper and convenient for a land of brethren, united to each other by the strongest ties, should never be split into a number of unsocial, jealous,
and alien sovereignties." [3] In another contribution, James Madison recalled the hazards of agreeing upon a new plan for Union.
The result was so splendid that Madison insisted: "It is impossible for the men of pious reflection not to perceive in it a finger

of that Almighty hand which has been so frequently and signally extended to our relief in the critical stages of the revolution." [4] Contemplating the same marvel, George Washington told La-fayette that the adoption of a new instrument of Union was "little short of a miracle." Aware of the need to be fastidious about reason, Washington added, "I think we may rationally indulge the pleasing hope that the Union will now be established upon a durable basis, and that Providence seems still disposed to favour the members of it, with unequalled opportunities for political happiness." [5]

The legend of a Providential design soon became commonplace. The simple idea was widely used in a fashion typified by George McDuffie's assertion: "All of us must agree that our hope of reaching the high and happy destinies for which Providence seems to have formed this country and this Government, absolutely depend upon the preservation of the Union." Others, like Vir-ginia's Ballard Smith, wanted legislation to create the crucial "sympathy of feeling," the "harmonious connexion," the "reci-procity of interests," needed if Union should bring America "to that high destiny to which the God of nature hath allotted it." All this pleased Henry Clay, who often called upon the legend of Providence, joining it with the storied Founders' devotion to "UNION." [6]

During the Manifest Destiny agitation, when Union's fated geographical growth was disputed, a Providence legend became even more useful. The Reverend H. W. Bellows' essay was rep-resentative in its assertion that Providence had deliberately withheld the American continent until men's ideas were ready to use it. Elaborately tracing divine guidance in America's unifica-tion, Bellows made much of the purpose behind recent develop-ments. "May we not feel that steam in its application as a motive power was discovered with express reference to our enormous rivers and lakes?" he asked. Where steam had simply aided other nations, "it has recreated ours. Was not the railroad expressly in-vented to hold together in its vast iron cleats our broad and otherwise unbound country, threatening to fall to pieces by its own weight. Its ponderous trains flying like great shuttles across our land, weave into one seamless web the many-colored interests and varied sentiments and affections of our scattered country-men."

Bellows thereupon concluded that the technological triumphs of the steamboat, the locomotive, and the telegraph all had come from Heaven "to reconcile in our favor physical incompatibilities —the benefits of vast area with none of its evils—its varied climates, products and spaciousness, without its separation, conflicts of interests, or jealous diversity of sentiments." [7] Not to be outdone, the *Democratic Review* drew hope from the legend. "Providence has been so watchful over us, that jealousies have been quieted, the fires of animosity have been quenched at the altar of patriotism." All had receded before "a deeper sense of the value of the Union, and the importance of unflinching fidelity to its true intent." [8]

Thus grew the myth, contributing especially to a deterministic setting. At the Bunker Hill monument, Edward Everett proclaimed that "the necessity of a Union was established by the same law of our nature, or rather of the Author of our Nature, which sets the solitary in families, and has melted families into clans, and clans into States, which binds the particles of matter together; which suspends a planet in the sky, or hangs a dew-drop upon a rose-leaf." Joining Everett in popularizing the legend was George Bancroft's history, in which he claimed its goal was to explain that America's achievements were due to "a favoring Providence, calling our institutions into being." [9]

These excerpts, all typical of their genre, convey how easily the Providence legend merged with demands for an evolving organic quality, thereby strengthening the Union Absolute. Men simply needed to recognize their part in carrying out the dictates of a supernatural plan. From this vantage dissent could more easily be castigated than if the rational contract scheme with its individual-state power had persisted. Also the legend blended with national awe for the Founding Fathers' work. The Reverend James Craik offered his audiences the obvious bridge between Providence and the Fathers. He emphasized the latters' unique wisdom which allowed them to know that God had ordained two facts for America: "That the American people have always been ONE NATION under one common allegiance; and have always been divided into separate, and to some extent, independent sovereignties."

Struggling to reconcile these, Craik contended that Union displayed how God could design order out of conflicting elements, to bring harmony out of "mutual antagonism of opposing forces, rightly ordered." In fact, the legend helped Craik insist just before the Civil War that in Union harmony depended upon antagonism. Only God could have brought "the separate sovereignty of the States, and the Union of the States under one government into one nation." [10]

Craik was only one of many to advocate accepting Union's contradiction as the plan of Providence. Henry Reed made a more elaborate presentation in 1856 when he contended that simply recalling Union's past did much "to inspire a thoughtful loyalty . . . and a deep sense of responsibility for each generation coming to live within that Union and to transmit it unimpaired to posterity." The fact that Union orginated from the "Providential government of the world" meant for Reed the comforts of an organic character. "In truth, the Union was not made; *it grew.* . . . The Union grew as the forest grows, and the seed was not sown by man's hands."

Reed used Providence's organic design to introduce another legendary detail. With America's exposure to German universities and the ideas of Herder and Hegel, there was increased enthusiasm for the mystical Saxon or Teutonic origin of American institutions. For the Romantic mind, the woodland of Europe, rather than the English origin, was a happier place for suprahuman design to originate. After eulogizing Providence's European labors, Reed turned to the Saxon respect for local government. Thus, "the first element of Union is separation,—distinctiveness of existence and of character. The history of Union begins not with unity, but with the creation of such separate existences as in the future may . . . become united but not consolidated." [11]

From this point, Reed could talk of the Union's emergence as "a slow, a laborious, and a reluctant process," happily under the inspired hand of leaders. These leaders, in carrying out Providence's plan, became an important part of Union's legend. In fact, many who fashioned Union ideology seemed to use Providence most effectively to introduce the mythical Everlasting Fathers.

II

As time passed, these Founders had their place strengthened in America's memory. This brought a useful dividend for most defenders of Union, since it meant that to attack Union was to impugn the Fathers, a doubly irreverent act. Those who relied on the fable of the Founding Fathers first emphasized the memory of them and their wisdom. Consequently, so much effort was given to demands that the American mind unite in revering these early leaders that this reverence became itself a basis for Union. An even sterner regard, however, grew from insistence upon Union's original principles as timeless. Partaking of an inspired soundness, it was argued that these precepts must remain unaltered. Once more the trend ran toward organic design and Absolute character for Union.

The Fathers' myth was deliberately conservative in impact, since, like the legend of Providence, it was employed to hurry Union beyond awkward demands made by relentless change. An invocation of the spirit of the Fathers normally accompanied genuflection before the portrait of Union's establishment. The Union's majestic triumph over diversity was due to the sublime, even mysterious wisdom of the Fathers. Theirs was so awesome an accomplishment that succeeding generations ought to pray that eternal vigil before such achievement might cause the elders' wisdom to linger in Union's hour of crisis. While the decade of the 1850's brought the Fathers' value to its peak, the legend had proved useful much earlier.

For instance, shortly after Burgoyne's defeat in 1777, an anonymous poem called "A New Song" became popular. Its most successful stanza was an idolization of Union's leaders:

Charge your glasses lip high, to brave Washington sing,
To the Union so glorious the whole world shall ring;
May their councils in wisdom and valor unite
And the men ne'er be wrong who yet so far are right.[12]

Of similar tenor was James Wilson's plea that the Pennsylvania
ratification convention recognize how ponderous was the burden
on the Philadelphia meeting a few months earlier. All praise to
the triumph of what Wilson called "a spirit of mutual forebearance and conciliation" among the founders. Having been one
himself, Wilson should have known.[13] A newspaper appeal to the
people of Massachusetts late in 1787 urged: "Consider that those
immortal characters, who first planned the event of the revolution . . . have now devised a plan for supporting your freedom,
and increasing your strength, your power and happiness." The
opposition were "emissaries of hell," men who wished "to ascend
the chariot of anarchy" to ride triumphant over Union's ruins.
There was no alternative to heeding the tried and true Founders.[14]

Addressing his neighbors in New York, John Jay cited the
legendary creation of Union. After describing the dangers surrounding its colonial birth, he recalled: "Union was then considered as the most essential of human means, and we almost
worshipped it with as much fervor as pagans in distress implored
the protection of the tutelar deities. That Union was the child of
wisdom. Heaven blessed it and wrought out our political salvation." Now, in the midst of rising security and peace, the wisdom
of the establishment days was, in Jay's view, fading. This failure
to keep faith with the founders, he argued, "loosened the bonds of
Union." [15] James Madison called this straying from the early work
a "state of imbecility." He urged Congress to make as its first
act an effort "to revive those principles of honor and honesty that
have too long lain dormant." [16]

Launched by many who were themselves soon to be canonized,
the legend of the Everlasting Fathers quickly thrived. Its usefulness was especially apparent in discussions of Union's future.
Typical was the pained response of Virginia's Congressman

Thomas Gholson, who insisted that past events "are connected with too many precious, too many proud recollections, to permit a man easily to think of realizing a dismemberment of the Union so achieved and so established." [17] With an unpopular war just begun, an 1812 Independence Day orator pleaded that the nation would be spared disunion and civil war only if the Fathers' wisdom tarried with the sons. Only such insight would assure that the "great pillar of our salvation, *UNION*" would not "be swept away and the remembrance of it only preserved, to embitter the sorrows of our posterity." [18] Edward Everett's Phi Beta Kappa oration reflected the happier mood of a decade later. He noted with satisfaction that population's spread westward kept sturdy ties between regions old and new. Of these links of Union, Everett emphasized history, where the Fathers' deeds shone as a patrimony the children would always keep.[19]

Unfortunately, the labor of the Founders became a storm center as the nature of the Union grew more equivocal. President Jackson used his Bank veto message to invoke the spirit of the "fathers of our Union." Only this would soften the sectional antagonisms, thus recementing Union's foundation. Others called the Fathers' time "the purer days of this Republic." It was absurd to think that these men could "entertain the idea that faction and fanaticism would one day shake this Union to its centre.... In those days men trusted each other." [20] For some, the legend had come to mean not so much what the Fathers had done, but the spirit in which they had operated. President John Tyler expressed it simply at a dinner following the 1843 Bunker Hill celebration. He saluted: "*The Union*: Union of purpose—Union of feeling—the Union established by our fathers." [21]

Of course the spirit which had moved the Founders became increasingly more elusive. Struggling against what one person called the disenchantment with Union, many urged new hosannas. Said a Pennsylvanian: "I love our Union as I love my Country. It was obtained by the blood of heroes and the wisdom of sages," and it "makes us one great commonwealth of nations." Union was irreplaceable, since such an achievement was within reach only of those "schooled in the revolution, and in whose memory the recollections of its scenes and sufferings were fresh." [22] To those of a new generation tempted to become a Union-destroying majority, memories of the Fathers might rekindle the saving spirit. This was the hope of Tennessee's Senator Ephraim H. Foster, who spoke of loving Union "for the veneration I bear to the statesmen and patriots who constructed its parts, and sanctified them with their prayers and benedictions." [23]

Young Congressman Jefferson Davis described his region's sympathy with the faith Foster had expressed. "From sire to son" had descended a "creed" of Union. Thus, "if envy, and jealousy, and sectional strife, are eating like rust in the bonds our fathers expected to bind us, they come from causes which our southern atmosphere has never furnished." Davis urged that all men "retrace the fountain of our years and stand beside its source; to contemplate the scene where Massachusetts and Virginia, as stronger brothers of the family, stood foremost to defend our common rights; and remembrance of the petty jarrings of today are buried in the noble friendship of an earlier time." [24]

To those for whom the Territorial issue seemed so important, Senator Sam Houston read lines about Union's sublime character. The poem, sent to Houston from Wheeling, Virginia, rebuked men who dared favor disunion:

> Can such prove worthless of their great bequest,
> And smile upon *Disunion's* Gorgon crest?
> Who will surrender up his joint estate
> In the rich memory of our country's great?
> And who his blood-bought share consent to yield
> In Saratoga's or in Yorktown's field?

Houston felt the past's meaning was so real to the masses of Americans that they would emerge from lethargy to save the Union of the Founding Fathers.[25]

The Texas hero's contribution came early in the crisis of 1850, a year in which the legendary Fathers were tirelessly invoked. Senator James Cooper of Pennsylvania used the lore to justify his state's belief that disunion was unmentionable. Recalling that Union was achieved only "by the outpouring of the blood of the citizens of all the States," Cooper now coveted the spirit of these Founders. By it Union would remain intact, even when granite and marble had crumbled. This spirit had, through the Revolutionary experience, been purified from all the dross of selfishness. No less than this venerable outlook could extinguish the terrible fire within Union in 1850.[26]

But here Jefferson Davis had to dissent. "I cannot agree . . . that the liberty we inherit from the heroes and patriots of our revolution is one and inseparable from the Union." For himself, Davis preferred to think that "Union was the result of the liberty and independence of the States, not the converse." This position exposed a weakness in the fable of the Fathers. Union was formed by the liberty-loving states, said the Mississippian, "and, if the sons be worthy of their sires, [liberty] might be maintained though the Union should perish." Davis had made it possible to revere the Founders while discarding Union.[27] Normally, this gloomy twist to the legend remained in hiding, for most people joined with Webster in recalling that the Fathers had been filled with a glorious love of Union. Thus, said he, did the illustrious dead cry out from the ground, beseeching from the grave that all men hold firm to the Union.[28]

William H. Seward made a similar appeal in his 1854 Phi Beta Kappa address at Yale. Was "ever higher genius, or greater talent, displayed, in conducting the affairs of men," than when Union was formed? Seward described the forging of all parts "into one great machine with such wonderful skill, that at the very first touch propelling popular spring, it went at once into full and perfect operation." Seward must have challenged the credulity of his listeners at Yale when he added that Union so launched by the extraordinary Founders had continued in perfection "not only without interruption or irregularity, but even without a jar." [29]

For many, the threatening Republican movement encouraged more parading of the Founders, a group often enlarged to include Daniel Webster. Maine Congressman John Perry's contribution was typical: "We talk of disunion; and yet how can we do it without waking up the memories of the past? Comes there not a voice from the sequestered shade of Mount Vernon, rolling over the waters of the Potomac in trumpet tones, exclaiming: 'Stay the rude hand, already uplifted to disturb the peaceful repose of the mighty dead and desecrate the quiet home of the sleeping hero?' " Refusing to believe that any man "who owes allegiance to American soil" would hazard the Union, Perry was so confident of the will and work of the Fathers that he actually challenged Union's foes to "dress up your hideous, ghastly goddess of disunion with habiliments stained with human gore, drawn from the veins of our own brethren," and call upon Americans "to fall down and worship the image." If ever disunion's flag appeared, men "of brave hearts" from all quarters of America would rally to defend the "UNION," responding to the "old battle-cry of our fathers, ONE DESTINY, ONE COUNTRY!" [30]

Beyond the walls of Congress, this legend flourished in such editorial expression as that of the Bell paper in Cincinnati which asked shortly before the 1860 election, "Why should we quarrel? Are we not the bondslaves of reason?" The rational path led to the Fathers' lesson. "We are all of one family—we are all of one nation. The wisdom of our fathers, inspired from Heaven, gave us a government unequalled in the annals of the world for the exquisiteness of its machinery." [31] A Union College professor, Elias Peissner, published *The American Question in its National Aspect* early in 1861. Here Peissner contended that all Americans were duty-bound "to wander religiously to the graves of our noble forefathers who have made us one and united, and to seek at their shrine light and knowledge from our fear-beset ways." [32]

This variation of Union's legend spread confusion by combining rational and mystical elements. Were the Fathers moved by reason—or by the hand of God—or by some great political process? Now the sons were challenged to use the same reason or to submit before Plan and Process. A clear answer was impossible, since the lore skillfully employed all features, seeking to satisfy everyone. Among the unmoved was Georgia's Robert Toombs, who opposed the Fathers' legend as unhistorical. He argued that no Union existed until the Constitution was devised as a way for government to pick the public's pockets. Goaded by this absurdity,

Toombs told the Senate, "The country is deluded with the nonsense that this bond of union was cemented by the blood of brave men in the Revolution. Sir, it is false. It never cost a drop of blood. A large portion of the best men of the Revolution voted against it." He added, "This talk about the blood of patriots is intended to humbug the country, to scare the old women. Why, sir, it never cost a drop of blood. It was carried on in some of the States by treachery, by men betraying their constituents. That is the history of the times." Even more vital in causing Toombs' dismay was the critical inference from the Founders' appeal—the timelessness of their guiding principles. Although Toombs reduced his objection to the simple assertion that Union under the Constitution was "not a good bond," he was not really oversimplifying.[33] Many worshippers of the Fathers had strengthened the legend by insisting that Union was achieved under inspired precepts which must be kept unaltered.

One of the most influential carriers of this version was Joseph Story's *Commentaries,* whose goal was to bring new generations "a profound reverence" for the Union. He described the Union as a "structure [that] has been erected by architects of consummate skill and fidelity; its foundations are solid; its compartments are beautiful as well as useful; its arrangements are full of wisdom and order; and its defenses are impregnable from without." Then the concluding salute: "It has been reared for immortality, if the work of men may justly aspire to such a title." This was not unreasonable, thought the conservative Story, if original principles and acknowledgement of wise leadership prevailed.[34] Francis Grund, ardent Democrat, was more casually confident, holding that those ideals which produced Union "are still operating with a tenfold greater force." Such were the factors which once brought Americans to be so "intimately connected with each other, that they voluntarily established that union which has since become the means of their greatness." [35]

Rebuking those who failed to recognize this Union, John Wise of Virginia wondered how one as old as John Quincy Adams, "who had himself looked upon Washington and heard his living voice," could now trifle "with things too sacred to be trifled with?" Wise's attack disclosed how contrived was the Fathers' legend, for Adams sprang from a Founder and received political appointment from the most Jovian figure of all. Yet desperation for the comfort of immutable precept gave Adams's generation an astonishing sense of time and allowed Wise to demand of Adams himself: "Was not this Union a thing too valuable, not to us alone, but to all the nations of mankind—to every subsequent age of the world?" He pictured Adams so bent upon attacking slaveholders that he lost sight "of the greatest blessing of Heaven." When the House debated a resolution to censure the former President for presenting an abolitionist petition calling for disunion, it accused him of failing to recognize the changeless quality of the Fathers' legacy. The man perhaps closest to the legend failed.[36] The lore of the Founders here worked nearly to exhaustion.

More troubling was the thought, often expressed in the days of Tyler and Polk, that the original premises had somehow been stolen and replaced with dangerous substitutes. A Union so transformed would be defiled. This, the Calhoun argument, allowed Carolinians and others to escape the charge of hostility to the Union. "There is not a member of our Union more devoted to it than she [South Carolina] is," said the Secretary of State in 1844, but he added hurriedly, "I mean the Federal Union, as it came from the hands of its framers." The great menace to this original Union was, of course, consolidation, which Calhoun said threatened the Founders' plan more dangerously than did simple despotism.[37] Another Carolinian contended in 1848 that in the days of the Fathers even party rivalry had been different and superior, for it was "a manly and generous rivalship between the North and the South." All Founders had accepted "the diversity of the human mind," as "one of the most powerful elements in the progress of human society."

To this principle, Representative Daniel Wallace told his colleagues, "we are indebted for much of the intellectual power of American statesmen." Unfortunately, the South had been unable to keep the Union upon these "fundamental principles of the true Republican faith." Now he beheld "gentlemen recklessly descending from the high position of an elevated statesmanship, and forgetting the imperious calls of patriotic duty." This inevitably would bring "a state of things which would tear asunder every tie which binds this Union together...." So drastic seemed the estrangement from the fabled ideals that this South Carolinian issued what became a familiar declaration. His region "had yielded the last inch," and if inscrutable Providence willed "that the temple of human liberty, reared by our patriot fathers in a purer and better age of the Republic, shall fall—upon your heads, not ours, will rest the guilt of the mighty consequences." [38] As the Mississippi legislature declared, in calling for a convention at Nashville: "We continue to entertain a devoted and cherished attachment to the Union, but we desire to have it as it was formed, and not as an engine of oppression." [39]

Northern moderates sensed how awkward it was to dispute the Founders' motivating ideals and sought ways for men of good will to escape by invoking simple respect for the memory of the Fathers. Although a sturdy organicist, Edward Everett helped in the rescue by taking Union back before the controvertible Constitution. The critical moment in Union's career, he argued, was after 1776, when the path "branched off in a twofold direction, leading on the one hand to union, growth, prosperity, and power, and on the other to discord, civil war, and despotism." It was at this point that a Union of spirit, existing since 1764, asserted its primacy, said Everett. Here the fundamental fact was that the real Union was "unconsciously formed. It sprang from the historical conditions of the past." [40]

Such vague principles grew in value during the 1854 Kansas-Nebraska crisis. Ohio Congressman Edward Ball was typically preoccupied with the folly even of talking about breaking the Union. The Union had "for nearly seventy years, stood as a *towering monument* of the wisdom and patriotism of our fathers." Under its "blessed influence" the nation had flourished. The original spirit would persist, predicted Ball, long after politicians of the nineteenth century were dead and forgotten. The public mind treasured the Fathers' wisdom. In neither North nor South did the people want disunion, and they would never "submit to it, under any circumstance." [41] Abraham Lincoln used this im-

plication of the Founders' story in the autumn of 1854. He praised
the Missouri Compromise as originating "in the hearts of all patriotic men, who desired to preserve and perpetuate the blessings
of our glorious Union—an origin akin that of the Constitution of
the United States, conceived in the same spirit of fraternal affection, and calculated to remove forever, the only danger, which
seemed to threaten, at some distant day, to sever the social bond
of Union." [42]

Now tied to abstract process, the legend of timeless principles
had to settle for good intentions and fraternal spirit as its paternal
legacy. These were essentially all that a generation of disputants
could hope to agree on. So meager a harvest out of the Founders'
legend can be seen at the heart of a partisan poem honoring
Buchanan in 1857:

> O, ye souls of the mighty! Who flamed in the past
>   And the banner of the Union above us unfurled,
> When its stars shall be swept by the factionist's blast,
>   That would hurl into wreck the last hope of a world—
> O, ye glorious shades of our ancestors! Pray
>   That we always may see such a chief on the sod
> As the one who thus scourges the black Lie away
>   From a land where Truth's patent was given by God.[43]

To the last, the legendary omniscience of the Fathers and the
unwavering persistence of their doctrines remained appealing,
even as the myth became obscure through efforts to retain some
common ground. This produced at least one memorable moment
involving the old Unionist, Sam Houston. He told the Senate, "I
am a Union man. The great champion of the Union was Andrew
Jackson. To him descended from the fathers of the Republic, in a
direct line, the principles upon which he stood; and his declaration, 'The Union; it must and shall be preserved,' will never be
forgotten. Sir, that will tingle in the ears of patriots for ages to
come." Asserting that he had never seen a Jackson Democrat who
was "a man to make hypothetical cases, and to say that in such
and such events in case such and such things would be done, the
Union would be dissolved," Houston joined others in dismissing

all the Founders' lore save that of faith in Union itself. While not expecting disunion, Houston admitted being uneasy when some leaders of the 1850's claimed more wisdom than Union's own founders. To Houston it was sacrilege "when a man profanely derides the memory of our glorious ancestors who established this Union and consecrated it by their wisdom." [44]

The myth of the Fathers failed for the same reasons that Union itself failed. Utilizing the Founders' legend in the turbulent nineteenth century, men found themselves simply imploring fidelity to an historical occurrence. Apparently such lore must offer more. Ernest Cassirer defines myth as "a unitary energy of the human spirit: as a self-contained form of interpretation which asserts itself amidst all the diversity of the objective material it presents." [45] The story of the omniscient Fathers, with their immutable guiding precepts, was betrayed by intervening revolutionary changes. While Sam Houston's version was charming, it would not help an increasing number of Americans sublimate the challenges raised by industry, slavery, and centralized democracy.

The myth's sterility often disturbed thoughtful men. Dr. Thomas Cooper noted, in 1836, "I disapprove of the eternal panegyrics on our union, which as construed, is worse than good for nothing, and is at its best, worth little but for imaginative declamation; that is, to the South." However, for the North Cooper said Union was "the widow's cruse of oil, a fountain of living waters, an inexhaustible pretense for solemn cheating under the forms of Law; and protected by grave exclamations about the inestimable value of our national compact, which the rogues well know is made only to be broken for their benefit." [46]

Speaking for the opposite view, Vermont's Congressman William Slade emphasized that Union made everyone brothers and was concerned with every man's problems, including slavery. Yet Union had become simply a device which the South employed. "The Union is . . . thrown around slavery as a shield of defense against the power of truth." Ironically, before the Union existed, the North might have spoken for freedom and truth. "But the Union has been formed, and we must be silent!" Slade added, "This whole land is to be shrouded in the darkness of Egypt and

hushed in the silence of death on the great subject which has
moved Christendom, because we have formed the Union!" Slade
was exposing the myth's weakness twenty years before Lincoln's
election.[47]

The intrepid "Josh" Giddings, anti-slavery spokesman from
Ohio, relished emphasizing this weakness. President Fillmore's
reference to the Union of the Founding Fathers impelled Giddings to say, "There is something pleasing and solemn in the
recollection of that Union. . . . But it is now nearly half a century
since that Union ceased to exist." Nevertheless, Americans still
sought "to sanctify every enormity in legislation by referring to
the *'Union of our fathers.'* " Now the President was victimized by
this legend, said Giddings; he added that calling upon loyalty to
the British crown was no more irrelevant than appealing to the
original Union. Giddings insisted that some men would discard
the Union when they felt it oppressive, just as England had been
shunted aside. This returned him to his thesis that Union-saving
cant was a device by which outrages were perpetrated upon the
North.[48]

While agreeing in principle with Giddings, Charles Sumner
put his objections to the Founders' lore more subtly. Now, for
many Northerners, the Higher Law meant the same as the True
and Original Union did for the South, allowing Sumner to remain with the Old Union while converting its basis to mystical
verities. Writing to the Massachusetts legislature, Sumner said,
"If I decline to recognize as my guide the leading men of today,
I shall feel safe while I follow the master principles which the
Union was established to secure, leaning for support upon the
great Triumvirate of American Freedom,—Washington, Franklin,
and Jefferson." What Sumner meant here was that the Founders
had stood for principle; but the Websterians, fearing the divisive
effect of unveiling these precepts in the mid-century crisis, hid
them in order to worship only the fact of Union. Insisting that
true politics "are simply morals applied to public affairs," Sumner
declared himself able to soar beyond the currently popular ambiguities, aided by "those ever-lasting rules of right and wrong
which are a law alike to individuals and communities." [49]

Similarly struck, Wendell Phillips eagerly attacked the perversions to which the legend of the Fathers had been put, especially those Websterian efforts to overcloud the slavery question through appeals "to the superstitious and idolatrous veneration for the ... Union." Later, as the Civil War began, Phillips endorsed a view like Robert Toombs's, "We are one in blood, trade, thought, religion, history; nothing can long divide us.... The only thing that divides us now, is the artificial attempt, in 1787, to force us into an unripe union." It was as if one placed an acorn in a vase, and then saw the vase shatter. Said Phillips, the Websters, Clays, and Everetts "have been anxiously clasping the vase, but the roots have burst abroad at last, and the porcelain is in pieces." For this famous agitator, it clarified everything to know that, in spite of elaborate mythology, the "Union of 1787 was one of fear; we were driven into it by poverty and the commercial hostility of England." The result was a Union useful only to the South.[50]

The Southern repudiation of the legend was conveyed in the Richmond *Enquirer*'s assertion that deprivation of just rights would make any honorable person a disunionist. A penny tax on tea caused a vast revolution by 1776. This disunion from England "had not more enemies nor less friends, because of the insignificant penny abstraction cause; nor will disunionists in 1861 be deterred by the tory cry of Union when a majority of the States have authoritatively pronounced for 'the irrepressible conflict' against the rights, interests, property, and lives of the minority." [51] Perhaps Emerson made the sternest assault upon the Fathers' myth, however, when he wrote the senior Oliver Wendell Holmes in 1856: "The cant of Union like the cant of extending the area of liberty by annexing Texas & Mexico is too transparent for its most imprudent repeater to hope to deceive you." Scorning the Websterian myth, Emerson asserted: "The 'Union' they talk of, is dead and rotten, the real union, that is, the will to keep and renew union is like the will to keep and renew life, and this alone gives any tension to the dead letter and if when we have broken several inches of the old wooden hoop [it] will still hold us staunch." [52]

III

Emerson's rejection of the Old Union legend suggests a third ingredient of the lore, an invocation of Nature. Obviously, in an age so deeply conscious of the natural, it was inevitable that Unionist ideology should seize opportunities implicit in Nature. Since the latter, like Union, was a varied idea, its use blended well with most versions. Essentially, this blending entailed two considerations. First, when were Union and Nature in accord? And, second, when did Union become unnatural? Our knowledge of American nationalist sentiment recognizes the marriage of Nature and Union. Both Merle Curti and Henry Nash Smith have noted how American geography was described in the period as insisting upon Union.[53] Neither scholar, however, was concerned primarily with Union's function as an idea. This ideology contained a complicated relationship between Nature and the legends of Union.

Both localists and centralists used Nature and geography to sanctify their concept of Union. Friends of expansion as well as containment confirmed their expectations by citing a natural decree. Idolators of Union proclaimed it the embodiment of Nature's grandest design, human brotherhood, thus permitting Nature's own triumph to be allied with Union.

A leading advocate of this geopolitical legend was William Gilpin, whose 1860 volume presented Union as the child of Nature, a contribution important most of all for its rich organicism. He argued that Union's inevitability would occur to all men with the triumph of scientific understanding. That each citizen should sense the unity imposed by Nature, Gilpin considered as crucial as knowledge of the federal polity. Since the North American continent "opens toward heaven in an expanded bowl to receive and fuse harmoniously whatever enters its rim. . . . The American Republic is then *predestined* to expand and fit itself to the continent." Out of Nature's inducement would come Union's citizenry with identical manners, interests, and even impulses.

Attacking those who blocked the people's fusion with Nature's

Union, Gilpin said: "Counterfeit geography, promulgated with official dogmatism will cease to be fashionable, or to defeat the divine instinct of the people." Truth and science, aided by patriotism, would comprehend Nature's mandate, which was "huge in dimensions, sublime in order and symmetry, a unity in plan." Obviously, "Our political and social empire, expanded by the same dimensions, harmonized to the same chequered variety, will assume a similar order, a like symmetry, and crown hope with a similar solid and enduring perpetuity." Thus, Union's continental destiny would be completed "with intense celerity," and "according to a system understood and self-disciplined ... uniting in one homogeneous order, with the same energies, a single aim, and rushing to consummate a common destiny." [54]

Repeatedly Gilpin insisted upon the inevitability of Nature's decree; men must accept the omnipotence of a plan which guaranteed "the perpetuity and destiny of our sacred Union." Consequently, "the political storms that periodically rage," Gilpin found "but the clouds and sunshine that give variety to the atmosphere." In a Kansas City speech of 1858, however, Gilpin was despondent. Perturbed by the critical events at hand, he blamed the crisis on an old foe, eastern fanatics who fought Nature's Union with "every form of meretricious and deceptive political agitation," as well as with false geography. Because of these faithless assailants, Union "has seemed to approach the twilight of its existence." Gilpin could only stress the legend's vital quality, the public's awareness of Nature's plan, much as John Adams so memorably had done. Soon the popular mind would reclaim Union, and through a period "of stern virtue, of holy zeal, of regenerating patriotism," the "devoted citizens" would dutifully accept the lofty decree of Nature's unity. [55]

Actually, William Gilpin belatedly served as myth-maker. Before him, a generation equally alert to Nature had testified to its alliance with Union. Writing from Paris in 1786, Thomas Jefferson looked placidly upon the growth of political Union. "Our present federal limits are not too large for good government, nor will the increase of votes in congress produce any ill-effect. On the contrary, it will drown out the bitter divisions at present existing there." Jefferson then added an optimistic note: "Our confederacy must be viewed as the nest from which all America, North and South, is to be peopled." [56] His statement contained two prime elements of the legend: one emphasized the geographical abundance in which Union had been set; the other said that, as Union experienced its natural growth, this fulfillment would repulse any political conflicts.

For over a generation these implications of Union's alliance with Nature comprised an important segment of Unionism. James Monroe, a devotee of this legendary quality, was converted to the vision late in life. Earlier, he had regretted that Kentucky broke from Virginia, and had felt that this separation would diminish Virginia's prowess in a Union he considered to be simply "the states upon the Atlantic." These states must realize that the Ohio Valley would "necessarily be but little interested in whatever respects us." In fact, the West might soon outweigh the Old Union in Congress, said Monroe, "unless we confine their number as much as possible." [57]

Upon becoming President, however, Monroe could hardly ignore the aid given the Republican cause by this region whose inherent tastes he once dismissed. Perhaps this encouraged him to support the great myth of Union as Nature's child. His First Inaugural Address declared that more than political reasons "admonish us to cherish our Union and to cling to the government that supports it." Indeed, said Monroe, there were physical reasons. The bounty of a natural fusion was such "that there is not a part of our Union that is not particularly interested in preserving it." He then recounted the extraordinary interdependence wrought by Nature.[58]

Monroe's second annual message acclaimed the admission of Illinois for Jeffersonian reasons, saying that the bigger the Union the less chance for central despotism. Nature's invitation for Union's growth was an opportunity to create the good society. As Union extended itself to accept Nature's offer, Monroe pointed out that the "impracticability of one consolidated government for this great and growing nation will be more apparent and will be universally admitted. Incapable of exercising local authority except for general purposes, the General Government will no longer be dreaded." Even so, Monroe was dimly aware of technology's knitting effect, for he spoke of commercial developments as meaning that "those parts of the United States which are most remote from each other will be further bound together by the strongest tie which mutual interest can create." [59]

Monroe retold again and again the myth of Nature's invitation for the achievement of a truly good Union. In the midst of fiery debates over slavery, tariffs, internal improvements, and banking, Monroe drowsed in his ideological refuge, foreseeing "the Union blessed with plenty and rapidly rising to greatness under a National Government which operates with complete effect in every part without being felt in any except by the ample protection which it affords." With Nature and Union allied, Monroe considered that the Missouri controversy demonstrated "the connection and dependence which the various parts of our happy Union have on each other, thereby augmenting daily our social incorporation and adding by its strong ties new strength and vigor to the political." [60]

For his last address Monroe reserved the greatest ecstasy over Union's growth: "We have daily gained strength by a native population in every quarter—a population devoted to our happy system of government and cherishing the bond of union with fraternal affection." Diversity within Union, Monroe reiterated, led to interdependence. Thus, out of Nature's contrast, "causes which might otherwise lead to dismemberment operate powerfully to draw us closer together." [61]

As Monroe reiterated Nature's myth, there came a jarring note. He vetoed an internal improvements bill, as did Madison before him, because of belated proddings by a Republican conscience. Although the President yearned for these technological advances, since the effect they "would have on the bond of union itself affords an inducement for them more powerful than any which have been urged or than all of them united," he began doubting the myth. "The only danger," said Monroe, to which the Union was exposed, "arises from its expansion over a vast territory. Our Union is not held together by standing armies or by any ties other than the positive interests and powerful attractions of its parts toward each other." From this point, Monroe's labors with Nature's lore became significantly confused.

Foreseeing how ambitious men might appeal to unreal sectional considerations, Monroe said, "I have little fear of this danger, knowing well how strong the bond which holds us together is." But he urged reliance upon technological improvements "and the intercourse which would grow out of them," so that Union "would soon become so compacted and bound together that nothing could break it." Growth could be an asset. It was "only when the expansion shall be carried beyond the faculties of the General Government so as to enfeeble its operation to the injury of the whole that any of the parts can be injured. The tendency in that stage will be to dismemberment and not to consolidation." [62]

With such assertions Monroe sought an artificial unity from technology. This ambivalence was to characterize later American thought which looked both to Nature and the Machine. Yet neither the fundamental commitment nor the possible antithesis was usually confronted. One person who did so, Vice President Calhoun, had the bad grace to tell the aging Monroe in 1828 that Nature's vastness might entail inequity, thus abusing some segments in the Union. Calhoun was certain "that the system is getting wrong and if a speedy and effective remedy be not applied a shock at no long interval may be expected." The continuing rifts in Union which could be expected under the circumstances did "render doubtful," the South Carolinian told Monroe, "the beautiful idea, which you cherished so fondly, that our system might under its natural action sustain itself without exciting party feeling." [63]

An early encouragement for the "beautiful idea" had come from Fisher Ames: "Nature has so arranged our circumstances, that the people of the several States pursue various employments which support each other." Consequently, "so far from being rivals," the regions of the Union, according to Ames, were "in both a natural and political sense ... necessary and beneficial to each other's interests." Thanks to the great scheme of things, individual interests were compatible with Union's intent. The public knew this, said Ames, since one found everywhere expressions of attachment to the Union. On this fact of nature, Ames contended, "our existence as a nation depends." [64] Although Ames and Monroe were for once on the same side, the legend of Nature's Union was much controverted by 1820.

In that year, Hezekiah Niles rejected the Jeffersonian lore to predict that "political power will soon rest where the effective population is located." Except for Florida, Niles expected the Union would be enlarged no further. "Our territory is already *large enough*," he said, "and the dispersion of our population must be measurably restrained, that the physical power of the nation may be preserved." Jeremiah Mason deplored President Monroe's flimsy generalizations about supplanting partisanship with a "Union of talents for national objects, and consequently an union of strength, which would enable the country to do whatever was desirable both at home and abroad." He was hardly surprised that Monroe could only hope that this natural Union would be achieved.[65]

More sensational conflict over Nature's Union entered an 1823 congressional exchange. Francis Baylies of Massachusetts based his argument on the legend when he recommended that the United States occupy the Columbia River's mouth. To the widespread fear that western expansion would endanger Union, Baylies replied: "In my opinion, the unity of this nation depends in some measure upon its extension." Then followed the Jeffersonian argument that disunion's potential declined as Union's membership increased and the familiar proof: Nature's variety neutralized distinctions. As for the gloomy prophecies about new regions, Baylies said, "the region west of the Mississippi is as much attached to the Union as that on the Atlantic." Why, therefore, should men see the Rocky Mountains as the natural limit for Union? Beyond this range Nature had reserved a space of greater advantage than all of the area between the Rockies and the Mississippi, "Sir, our natural boundary is the Pacific Ocean," said Baylies, and the tide of population "must and will" roll on to it. Fusing Nature and the Almighty, Baylies dwelt on the greatness ahead for a Union willing to accept such a future.[66]

In reply, John J. Breckinridge drew a frightening picture of Oregon clamoring to participate in the Union. The Kentuckian bluntly rejected the myth: "There can be no community of interest or feeling between governments so situated," since "the wholesome blood which flowed from the heart of this confederacy cannot reach the confines of Oregon. There can be no bond of Union between them; and the limb, thus separated from the body, must perish." [67] Most persons were finding it easier to agree with James Fenimore Cooper, who said, "It strikes me that as the confederation of the United States is the most natural government known, that it is consequently the only empire on whose stability the fullest confidence can be placed." [68]

This hope was joined by a movement to merge technology's aid with Union's natural fulfillment. Those who espoused the American System, especially men surrounding Henry Clay, were not consciously impatient with the myth of Nature's Union. Rather, they believed that it offered a broader meaning to the concept of Nature, just as some Americans would affirm that the machine was merely servant to Nature. John Quincy Adams vigorously praised technical improvements; Andrew Jackson, Nature's own child, added his endorsement. In his third annual message, Old Hickory predicted synthesis with the Union's far distant parts. For, "in the construction of railroads and the application of steam power, we have a reasonable prospect that the extreme parts of our country will be so much approximated . . . as to remove an apprehension sometimes entertained that the great extent of the Union would endanger its permanent existence." Abbott Lawrence similarly bolstered his faith in Nature's Union. The industrialist told Henry Clay that through the American System "Union would be bound by ties stronger than all the constitutions that human wisdom can devise." [69]

Lawrence and Jackson accepted the myth which Jefferson had gladly embraced, but for a different purpose. Where Jefferson saw Nature's bequest as the freedom-assuring dispersion, Jackson and Lawrence now beheld Nature, aided by the machine, as an integrative force. Lawrence's cry to Clay, "It is intercourse we want, and that I desire," reflected assurance that a railroad between

New England and Georgia would do more for real Union than any Constitutional amendment could. Ultimately, Nature's legend betrayed the Old Union, forcing it through an agonizing metamorphosis so that the mechanized nineteenth century could embrace a congenial idea. It became unrealistic to say simply, as did William Ellery Channing in the year of his death, "It is by the fusion of various attributes that rich and noble characters are formed." Contrasts were a part of Union's nature, being the result of "climate, that mysterious agent on the spirit." Channing followed the Jeffersonian view: "The Diversities . . . are inducements, rather than objections, to Union." [70]

Nevertheless, the comforting myth grew more useful as the nation found that opportunities for growth would bring broadened sectional provocation. For instance, Robert J. Walker said of the area dominated by the Mississippi that the Creator had "planed down the whole valley, including Texas, and united every atom of the soil and every drop of the waters of the mighty whole." Nature having preserved the great inner continent for one people, Walker insisted that "it is impious in man to attempt to dissolve this great and glorious Union." [71]

President James Polk was struck by this legend. He saluted Texas joining the Union by asserting that annexation served everyone's interest. Speaking lovingly of "the whole Union," Polk observed, "In the earlier stages of our national existence the opinion prevailed with some that our system . . . could not operate successfully over an extended territory." How groundless this had proven, for "as our population has expanded," one found "the Union has been cemented and strengthened." Explaining further, Polk insisted that the growing population needed to expand or there would be trouble. In an early version of the "safety-valve" idea, he said that sparsely distributed population meant security for the Union, and he concluded by saying that for a Texas-blest generation the message of Nature was not lost. It could now be "confidently believed that our system may be safely extended to the utmost bounds of our territorial limits, and that as it shall be extended the bonds of Union, so far from being weakened, will become stronger." [72]

While keeping the pace, John C. Calhoun savored the legend's Jeffersonian flavor. His *Discourse* observed, "it may be laid down as a principle, that the power and action of the Union, instead of being increased, ought to be diminished, with the increase of its extent and population." Here was a version of Nature's bequest very close both to Polk and Jefferson. Nature offered constantly greater diversification of interest for Union, which promised happy news of "the less *closeness of Union,* (so to speak) ." [73] Many other Democrats, pondering the relationship between Union government and local authority, were able to put the Jeffersonian version in a modern setting.

The result was "popular sovereignty," a proposal redolent with Union's mythical relationship to Nature. For instance, when Daniel S. Dickinson of New York pleaded for unrestricted annexation, he argued that just as the Founders' glimpse of Union domain had been far exceeded, so now the new glory which Nature along with technology offered the Union was only dimly perceived. Soon each of Union's parts "may be made more accessible to every other than were the original States to each other at the time they formed the Confederacy." With America yielding "to the influences of laws more potent than those which prescribed artificial boundaries," Dickinson foresaw a political Union worthy of the natural Union. Within a continental domain in which the spirit of freedom was the unifying element, Dickinson declared that local determinism embodied this idea of freedom; in fact, it offered a stronger bond of Union than any congressional enactment.

Beyond this, of course, Dickinson could hardly go, for here were combustible elements. Little wonder he used abstraction to avoid a dilemma provoked by the marriage of Union, Nature, and Technology. The legend demanded following Nature while preserving the Union's curious political qualities, despite the advantages which technical achievement offered the economy. Here was, of course, a mature version of the issue which once parted Jefferson from Hamilton. An age generally desiring Nature's bounty, Steam's bequest, and the traditions of Union forced Dickinson to a mystical conclusion: "The rich heritage we enjoy," he said, "was won by the common blood and treasure of the North and South, the East and the West." In several wars, "the brave sons of every section of the Union have fought and fallen side by side; the parched sands of Mexico have drunk together the best blood of New York and South Carolina." Such general contribution to achievement across the continent should, Dickinson insisted, compel true Union men "to spurn all attempts at provoking sectional jealousies and irritations, calculated to disturb the harmony and shake the stability of the Union." [74]

In fighting to keep the legend of Natural Union from becoming a catalyst, Dickinson was aided by the venerable Whig, Daniel Webster. At the New York Pilgrim Festival he noted the great natural growth of Union. "I confess I have had my doubts," he said, "whether the republican system under which we live could be so vastly extended without danger of dissolution." Whereupon the orator hastened into the legend, insisting, no matter where there was extension, "it seems to create a strong attachment to the Union and the Constitution that protects it." The Massachusetts statesman also employed the familiar references: "nature, the seas, the gulfs, the lakes, and the rivers, bound us together by ties nearly impossible to be broken." Finding suitable poetry for the lore, Webster sent these anonymous lines to a Georgia farmer:

> The States are united, confederated,
> Not, chaos-like, together crushed and bruised,
> But, like the world, harmoniously confused;
> Where order in variety we see,
> And where, though all things differ, all agree.[75]

In the words "harmoniously confused," Webster wrung the essence from Nature's myth on which he elaborated in a Maryland speech, "I may express myself too strongly, perhaps, but there are impossibilities in the natural as well as in the physical world, and I hold the idea of a separation of these States . . . as such an impossibility." Webster insisted, "there are natural causes that would keep and tie us together, and these are social and domestic relations which we could not break if we would." He also used a favorite theme of the Nature argument, the Mississippi's grandeur, a symbol for many of Union's natural design. Webster was so struck by Nature's message for Union that a violation of this edict gave him "an utter disgust." [76]

Local determinism seemed the feasible antidote to the troubles between Nature, Technology, and Union. Stephen A. Douglas could thus oppose Lincoln's concept of national uniformity by insisting that the Fathers understood Nature's decree that North and South must differ. Using the Founders' legend, Douglas reproved Lincoln for establishing himself as wiser than the Fathers. In a reply which defended uniformity in only a vague way, Lincoln surrendered. Excepting the issue of free labor, he made his own peace with Nature. Said Lincoln: "The great variety of the local institutions in the States, springing from differences in the soil, differences in the face of the country, and in the climate, are bonds of Union. They do not make 'a house divided against itself;' but they make a house united." Hailing the American System's ghost, he praised the natural function of sections as that of specialized production for the whole, so that Nature's differences became "not matters of discord but bonds of Union, true bonds of Union."

Although accepting Nature's lore, Lincoln added a qualification which somewhat tempered his obeisances. Slavery, he insisted, was not among the variety imposed by the natural order. Lincoln emphasized how the Fathers had fought the further spread of bondage.[77] In another way, Jefferson Davis blended Nature with the Founders. He told a gathering of Mississippi Democrats that "Our fathers wisely saw harmony in diversity, and mutuality in the opposite character of the climate, population and pursuits of the people in the different States." Thinking perhaps of Lincoln's dissent, Davis added, "But to them the proposition was far less apparent than it is to us." [78]

For Davis's age, the problem was to keep the national mind content with magnitude and diversity, when in fact magnitude was now inviting unification. Just as the industrial revolution modified communication, attacking the once sacred community insularity; so it began altering the status and views of farm and factory workers. The latter agreed when Lincoln denied that chattel bondage was within the ken of Nature-ordained mutual diversity. Consequently, Nature's legend seemed circular reasoning for many people in the new generation. Facing this debacle, some Unionists resorted to a last device, the concept of Union as an American family created by Nature.

Here was the legend's final appeal, for, if Nature decreed such a vast physical community, any spiritual rupture was unconscionable. Just as a family struggled together, surmounting differences for the sake of Nature's basic social unit, so the Union seen as brotherhood or family would achieve similar accord. Nature demanded tolerance, if not acceptance, of social as well as material variations. A younger orator, Thomas Starr King, announced in 1851 that an ordinary dedication from the citizen body was not enough, "it is the striking glory of our land that the patriotism it asks for is of the highest stamp." Uninhibited affection was required by Union's circumstances. "To a mind of ordinary capacity," said King, "the extent of our territory and the various needs of our population, furnish as fine a temptation, certainly, as can well be offered for the exercise of the sentiment of *universal brotherhood*." [79] Or, as Samuel Dexter had put it earlier: "The eastern and southern Atlantic states are made for each other. A man and a woman might as reasonably quarrel on account of the differences in their formation." [80]

The family quality implanted by Nature in the American character especially encouraged Union's legends, since it made possible appeals beyond the physical inducements usually cited. These further strengthened the organic interpretation, and thus Union Absolute. This was illustrated by Hezekiah Niles, whose fury with the recalcitrant New Englanders after 1812 made him say that they "have lost sight of the *American* character." Certain that appeals made "to the *reason* of the people will not be in vain," Niles announced that in True Union, "the majority must and ought to govern." Therefore Niles must have been greatly pleased to print a speech in which Louisiana's Governor William C. C. Claiborne said that "concord—harmony and mutual confidence sweeten the private and domestic circle; they tend no less to give tranquility, and force, and safety to the political communities." Just so had Louisiana "been received into the bosom of the American union, and with equal privileges. Let then no improper jealousies be fostered, no injurious distinctions be made—we are members of one family, and with the same common interest." [81]

Monroe, of course, lost no chance to emphasize this ideal. His New England tour made every public utterance a plea that men from all sections should "embrace each other as brethren of the same family." The trip's chronicler, S. Putnam Waldo, spoke hopefully of achieving this mood with its consequence of "National feeling." This must be, for "the division of the Union will be the destruction of the Republic. The bundled reeds can withstand the arm of the giant; separately they may be broken by the child." [82] In 1823, a Kentucky newspaper editorial, in strong agreement, asserted: "The spectacle now presented for the admiration of all good men, by the Union, is that of a family of States, each regarding the other with fraternal affection; and the citizens of each, feeling as a band of brothers, jealous only of themselves, resolved to preserve the compact of association or perish with its dissolution. He who would disturb the harmony of this happy family, is an enemy of the human race." [83]

Francis Lieber pointed out the danger of this attitude. Asserting that tribes and states followed the same fundamental law which regulated the intercourse of private individuals, he added: "The more sympathy or natural relations urge for Union, the more bitter will be the conflict if this inner urgency is counteracted by external separation." Hence the relevance of Tocqueville's warning that "Slavery, then, does not attack the American Union directly in its interests, but indirectly in its manners." [84]

Both Tocqueville and Lieber said that Union existed fundamentally and naturally as a family. Only an unnatural intruder could create the violence and dissent which might destroy the familial tie. This reading of Nature's legend had more internal consistency than the other implications of Nature and Union's marriage. Most portraits of Union as family, furthermore, were quite simple. Typical of these was Abbott Lawrence's comment in 1846: "We are, I hold, one great family, and indissolubly linked together, and the chain cannot be touched, without vibration being felt at either extremity." Lawrence used his own response as an example: "I entertain and cherish a strong American feeling; although born and bred in Massachusetts, I have a feeling of pride in the honor and character of every State in our Union." Whether he found himself in Maine or in Georgia, "I am an American citizen." [85]

William H. Seward saw clearly the usefulness of the legend of a natural family. Touring the West for the Republican ticket in 1860, he admitted in St. Paul that men now were genuinely conscious "of the high necessity" to be as one. More than ever, men felt "that fervent heat of love and attachment" which compelled all citizens "to be members of one great political family." Seward insisted that Minnesota especially revealed "the unity . . . that constitutes and compels us to constitute, not many nations, not many peoples, but one nation and one people only." In St. Joseph, Missouri, a few days later, the New York Senator rejoiced at the presence of so diverse a group. "This is exactly what will always occur," he predicted, "whenever you attempt to divide this people. . . . The moment you have brought the people to the point where there is the least degree of danger to the national existence felt, then those whom party ambition have arrayed against each other as enemies, will embrace each other as friends and brethren." Rejecting the Tocqueville hypothesis, Seward announced that "there is no difference whatever in the nature, constitution or character of the people of the several states of this Union. They are all of one nature. . . . The very effect of their being American citizens is to make them all alike." [86]

In Seward's organicism lingered hope born from Nature's lore that in the process of things all Americans were bound by an innate character. The myths of Providential plan and Everlasting Fathers brought much inspiration, as did the version of Nature's decree. Only the last, by insisting that each participant in Union shared a brotherhood where similarities transcended differences, placed Union in men's souls. While most versions exalted Union as an externalized system before which puny man rejoiced, the family ideal put responsibility upon every citizen rather than on history or Providence. But the more popular legends were those in which Union was awarded to the citizens, a development which became general especially after the era of experimentation. This would seem fitting, as troubled times encouraged an organic view of the American community. The march toward a Union of absolute proportions would be painful if Union's nature was often placed within each citizen's soul. It was much easier to talk of a Union bestowed upon a fortunate people by Providence, Inspired Founders, and Nature.

An examination of Union's symbols will help in illuminating this tendency.

7: *Symbol*

Illinois' anti-slavery congressman, Owen Lovejoy, observed early in 1861: "Every nation has some nucleas thought, some central idea, which they enshrine, and around which they cluster and fashion." Rome had its Pantheon; France embraced Napoleon; England claimed the constitutional monarch; and Lovejoy found America no different. "The American people have this one central idea or thought ... to which they adhere with a spirit of superstitious idolatry." The Union, joined by the Constitution and the flag, were "a sort of trinity, to which the American people pay political homage and worship." Lovejoy, a former clergyman, contended that it was unwise "to tamper with that holy instrument around which all American hearts cluster, and to which they cling with the tenacity of a semi-religious attachment." [1]

Lovejoy made his analysis without the literature on images and symbols which now helps the student. There is, for instance, the provocative conclusion of Herbert Read's 1953 Norton Lectures at Harvard University: "The general tendency throughout the history of mankind has been to suppress all traces of a self—*not* to betray the self, but to remain faithful to what is superior to the self, namely the group." He adds: "In other words, social consciousness has in general been far stronger and far more imperative than self-consciousness." [2] Certainly as ante-bellum Americans thought about their national career, the individual hero filled a symbolic role with difficulty. Rather, it was the group concept, redolent with historical and preternatural implication and personified in the Union, which triumphed as the more evocative American concept.

In the recent analysis of important American images and symbols, only passing reference has been made to the concept of Union. Yet this concept must be placed among such figures as the Garden, Jackson, the American Adam, and Washington.[3] Union's symbolical devices offer further insight into the significance of its ideology. If, as Merrill Peterson has suggested, symbols as objective vehicles for a myth are most successful when they are fully charged with the emotional background inherent to that myth,[4] we can see in Union's imagery certain strengths and weaknesses. For just as Union became increasingly important, so did its symbols from necessity develop the impression of transcendence or intransigence. These images help in understanding why Union Absolute cost a terrible struggle, a civil conflict which Unionist sentiment ironically had been calculated to avoid.

Union's symbols invariably conveyed a sense of comfort and reassurance. The figures used were familiar, often in fact inherently unexciting, and usually mechanical. But each suggested a quality of synthesis indispensable to the idea itself. The images chiefly encountered are chains, ships, constellations, and other markedly tangible representations such as vases and architectural patterns. The figure of Washington also acquired interesting symbolical attributes. All convey an impression of the indisputable and the indispensable through a necessarily irrefrangible career, one that exceeded the human sphere.

The chain image was Union's most popular figure. Certainly it carried an unequivocal visage, being either united or ceasing to exist usefully. It also boasted a superhuman quality. Actually, the early attempt at union was scoffingly portrayed as a variant of this image, a rope of sand. This offered interesting and disturbing possibilities, as the dynamic Georgian, William Jackson, observed in 1790. "The Union had been frequently compared to a rope of sand; it was well to beware, lest the argument be carried too far the other way; lest this ligature, this cord, by its too great extension, may snap, and be rendered more difficult to bring together than the rope of sand divided in a dozen places." [5]

Such early misgivings soon receded before figures showing Union's increasing appeal. We have already noted how an enfeeblement of Union's Experiment design characterized the Jeffersonian era. During a non-importation bill debate, Speaker Nathaniel Macon stepped down to scold his colleagues. "The dissolution of this Union ought not," he said, "to be mentioned in this House on any pretence whatever." Emphasizing that every part of the nation was attached to the Union, Macon said, "Indeed, the Union may be compared to a chain, the value of which depends upon its being whole, but may be destroyed by taking any one of its links away." Acknowledging the chain's fragile nature, Macon warned that "whoever breaks the chain by which the States are linked together, will render the whole people miserable." [6]

The chain image was often used during the Nullification crisis. In urging caution, ex-President Madison spoke of the universal tragedy accompanying "a break in the chain which unites their interests and binds them together as neighbors & fellow citizens." Severing the chain, said the old statesman, would be "fatal to the Union, and fatal to the hopes of liberty and humanity." [7] Daniel Webster similarly warned: "Let us not, sir, deceive ourselves by the imagination that the Union may subsist though one State secede from it." If the elements of Union could not all be kept linked, it would be fatal to the whole. From the moment rupture occurred, our "whole Union is virtually dissolved. Whatever link may be struck from the golden chain, breaks the whole." Webster, who grew fond of this symbol, underscored his point by saying that the chain broken meant farewell "forever not only to the glorious *idea,* but to the glorious *reality,* of the United States of America." [8]

Yet there was a significant effort to make a chain not a chain in the frequently repeated stanzas from William Cullen Bryant's ode sung as New York City celebrated the fiftieth anniversary of Washington's first inauguration. The poem, preceding John Quincy Adams's oration, was set in the Everlasting Fathers' legend; it concluded:

That noble race is gone; the suns
Of fifty years have risen and set;
The holy links those mighty ones
Had forged and knit, are brighter yet.

But a Democrat might hope that the chain would have resiliency:

Wide—as our own free race increase—
Wide shall it stretch the elastic chain,
And bind, in everlasting peace,
State after state, a mighty train.[9]

A more impatient poet-citizen, John Greenleaf Whittier, chose the chain symbol, but not without difficulty. In his oft-revised "Texas," Whittier urged the North to say to the South:

'Make our Union-bond a chain,
Weak as tow in Freedom's strain
Link by link shall snap in twain.

Vainly shall your sand-wrought rope
Bind the starry cluster up
Scattered over heaven's blue cope!'

And then a challenge to the South:

'Boldly, or with treacherous act,
Strike the blood-wrought chain apart;
Break the Union's mighty heart;

Work the ruin, if ye will;
Pluck upon your heads an ill
Which shall grow and deepen still.'

Originally the first stanza had been written as:

'Make our Union-band a chain,
We shall snap its links in twain
We shall stand erect again!'

The second revision put the thought:

> 'If with added weight ye strain
> On th' already breaking chain
> Who will bind its links again?' [10]

The Quaker poet's doubts about the chain were, in spite of their eloquence, hardly typical of the general sentiment, which preferred the Websterian invocation. Typical of the latter was Rufus Choate's prediction that the Taylor Administration "will be memorable for having strengthened and brightened the golden chain of the American Union." A more tangible moment occurred when Webster received a golden chain as a gift. An accompanying tribute called the resplendent links "a fitting symbol of that glorious Union, of which you stand preeminently the ablest defender." [11] But while most sentiment rejoiced with Webster over this symbolism, Whittier grew more vexed. His poem, "In the Evil Days," included the lines:

> For pity now is crime; the chain
>   Which binds our States
> Is melted at her hearth in twain,
> Is rusted by her tears' soft rain.
>
> Our Union, like a glacier stirred
>   By a voice below
> Or bell of kine, or wing of bird,
> A beggar's crust, a kindly word
>   May overthrow.[12]

Webster, of course, continued to support the chain-Union's enduring quality. In a fascinating 1851 speech, he used the great-chain-of-being concept, lingering fondly over its connotation of a mutual dependency within the frame of things. "There seems to be some analogy between this great system of the universe and our association here.... What the poet says of the great chain that holds all together in the moral, intellectual, and physical world, is applicable to the bond which unites the States." After this richly organicist observation, Webster could not resist a line:

> 'Whatever link you strike
> Tenth . . . ten thousandth, breaks the chain alike.' [13]

Such a figure became a familiar reference on most occasions when political moderation prevailed, as in the refrain sung at Washington's tomb during 1851 Masonic ceremonies:

> Let the Union he founded forever remain!
> Strike powerless the arm which would sever its chain! [14]

The South made similar references. North Carolina Congressman Thomas Ruffin's pleasure in the symbol was typical. After reciting Northern measures against the Union, Ruffin deplored John C. Frémont's nomination as Republican Presidential candidate in 1856, and pleaded that Union's cords be restored,

> 'Unbroken as the sacred chain of nature
> That links the jarring elements in peace.' [15]

In this fashion the symbol persisted, building its obvious appeal upon units necessarily linked, as in anonymous lines quoted in the House of Representatives early in 1861:

> Dissolve the Union! Who would part
> The Chain that binds us heart to heart?
> Each link was forged by sainted sires,
> Amid the Revolution fires:
> And cool'd—oh! where so rich a flood?—
> In Warren's and in Sumter's blood.[16]

As these instances suggest, Union's symbolism was frequently joined by some legendary aspect, usually appeals to Nature or to the Everlasting Fathers.

While the chain apparently suited the era more than any other figure did, the ship symbol offered similarly useful superhuman or trans-individual qualities. As the ship's purpose was a joint enterprise, its success obviously required the crew's accord. Jefferson told the venerable John Dickinson of the grave "storm" just passed in 1801. Now one could say "the tough sides of our Argosie have been thoroughly tried. Her strength has stood the waves into which she was steered, with a view to sink her. We shall put her on her republican tack, & she will now show by the beauty of her motion the skill of her builders." [17]

The continued turbulence of American politics encouraged frequent use of Jefferson's analogy. For instance, during the Missouri debate William Pinkney warned that such agitation promised to "push from its moorings the sacred ark of the common safety, and to drive this gallant vessel, freighted with every thing dear to an American bosom, upon the rocks, or lay it a sheer hulk upon the ocean." [18] In quiet corners, the symbol also had appeal. An obscure Massachusetts citizen, William Lee, told his daughter in Berlin that slavery was a savage menace to Union. It was, he said, "the leading bone of contention among these states, and the great rock on which the Ship of State is to be wrecked." [19] But the figure gradually became more ornate, as Union's versions grew more complex. One commentator beheld a voyage under Providential auspices, and asserted that the latter would "smile upon labors of a disinterested wisdom." And with the "most bountiful benignity" did Providence bless the builders of Union. Using a design far superior to the pompous but disintegrating lines of the older world's plan, the Founders launched the ship. "The little craft was just put into perfect trim, her complete suit of new gear had been strongly set up . . . and the world's best pilot had grasped the wheel." Into the storm it went, and, though the ship "staggered and reeled," said the narrator, "she minded her helm like a beauty." [20]

It was this image which prompted Longfellow to exult in the most famous expression of Union symbolism, "The Building of the Ship":

> Thou, too, sail on, O Ship of State!
> Sail on, O Union, strong and great!

These widely repeated lines, using the popular ideas of Mission and Inspired Founders, proceeded with deliberate majesty:

> Humanity with all its fears,
> With all the hopes of future years,
> Is hanging, breathless on thy fate!
> We know what Master laid thy keel
> What workmen wrought thy ribs of steel...[21]

Longfellow's confidence in the vessel's triumph, that neither rock nor gale would stay the completion of the noble mission, diminished in later uses of the simile. The familiar storm setting became a hurricane by 1850, giving pleas for the "Good Ship Union" a note of desperation. Mississippi's Congressman William McWillie, after crediting God with marine construction, peered into the fury: "The Ship of State approaches the dreadful maelstrom of disunion. She already feels and answers to its circling currents." With every hand upon the deck and every sail set, McWillie called: "Cast out the anchor, the anchor of the Constitution; even yet it may take hold upon the minds and the hearts of the people, and save the ship; which that God may grant, should be the prayer of every heart." [22]

Heeding such calls, ex-President John Tyler sought to save the craft, asserting: "My attachment to the Union may have carried me far into error. If it be so, the reason is one I am proud to avow." Yet only the future knew if the Union would continue as a "majestic ship," fraught with hopes and bearing glad tidings to distant lands. Seeing a lifting sky in 1850, Tyler added: "Let justice preside at the helm, and all will be well. But if she be stricken down, and a dark and gloomy and remorseless fanaticism usurp her place, then is this argosy, so richly freighted, inevitably wrecked." [23]

As Tyler's remarks suggest, the ship image entailed a question of guidance, for destination was not readily within the ship's discretion. Here the figure was usually strengthened by adding the inspired helmsman. Deaths of leaders like Calhoun, Clay, and Webster made such portraiture possible. Of Clay, for example, it was said that, "when the waters of the great political deep were up-heaved by the tempest of discord, and the ark of the Union, freighted with the hopes and destinies of freedom, tossing about on the raging billows, and drifting every moment nearer the vor-tex which threatened to swallow it up," it was his "clarion call . . . that admonished the crew of impending peril, and counselled the way to safety." [24] Even Seward enjoyed the comparison, recalling that during Clay's early career, the Union, like a "bark" had "gone to sea, thus unfurnished and untried." Stressing the ex-perimental quality of the early Union, Seward could escape the question of the vessel's inspired design and construction. The ship of Union, at the beginning of its voyage, "seemed quite cer-tain to founder by reason of its own inherent frailty." [25]

A deepening crisis suggested the vessel might yet fail, thus permitting further moralization about the dismal fate of frag-mented or individual struggles. Edward Everett Hale wrote of the absurdity of disunion: "It would be like breaking up a noble ship, which whatever its imperfections, still bears those on board safely across the seas, in order that the dismembered and scattered crew might find greater safety and independence on the loose rafts constructed out of the fragments." [26] Such use of the symbol reveals how the ship figure eased the anxiety of a people adrift in seas of alarming uncertainty. That a raft might provide as-surances and safety was impossible. Mindful of this, President-elect Abraham Lincoln issued his own plea to the citizens while travel-ing to Washington: "If all do not join now to save the good old Ship of the Union on this voyage, nobody will have a chance to pilot her on another voyage." In responding to New York's Mayor Fernando Wood, Lincoln enlarged the image, emphasizing that a ship was made to preserve and carry cargo—it should never be left while it might be saved. "This Union," said he, "should likewise never be abandoned unless it fails and the probability of its preservation should cease to exist without throwing the pas-sengers and cargo overboard." [27] No analogy shows more clearly the dilemma of those who sought to embrace both principle and Union.

Yet, as the dream of a prosperous journey faded early in 1861, one essayist used the raft figure to escape the absolute quality of a ship while preserving the image. Granting that the crisis came upon most of Union's citizens "like a thunderbolt out of the clear sky," still it was an emergency which the all-knowing Founding Fathers had anticipated. Consequently, they allotted the Union a short life. "The permanent union of even the thirteen States, with their wide dissiliency of character, industry, and interest, seemed to them beyond hope." Thus, they "constructed a raft which should bend and yield, take the very shape of the waves, let the water in and out freely through its seams and junctures, and by its loose couplings and elastic movement divide and dissipate the force of any sudden shock." Here was an amazing attempt to make the ship image pleasing, much as Bryant had ventured to speak of an elastic chain. The analogy announced that the crisis had stemmed from "the attempt to consolidate it [the raft], to bind its lashings more closely, and to leave a less free scope and sway to its separate members." [28]

Another popular image for Union with extraordinary qualities of endurance and invariableness was a heavenly solar system. Man's puny notions of time and energy should quail in such a presence. Brooding over the events of 1798, Jefferson observed that it was not "for the interest of the general government itself, & still less of the Union at large" for the states to be so little respected. After suggesting this interesting distinction between Union and polity, Jefferson argued that the Union was comparable to "the planets revolving around their common sun," and the result should be "that beautiful equilibrium" which would exhibit to the world "a degree of perfection unexampled but in the planetary system itself." [29]

Soon thereafter, some of Jefferson's disenchanted Virginia brethren began to disagree. One of these "Quids," John Clopton, explained how he disliked the image now made of Union—"a grand, primary planet, and its surrounding satellites." Stressing the obvious objection to this symbol, Clopton noted: "These states do not, like those satellites, shine with borrowed, reflected light, emanating from a great central planet." Rather, he said, "they display a radiance solely their own. Their splendors issue from their own bodies. They are so many original sources of light and heat." In this system, Clopton argued, Union simply brought "the members of this constellation together in harmonious intercourse, and produces to the system the benefits of their collective energies." So long as this was its real nature, Clopton believed such a "grand and beautiful system" would exist "co-extensively with the duration of time itself." [30]

Despite his uneasiness with the solar system symbol, Clopton succumbed to its charm. What imagery could be more timeless, unvarying, and awe-inspiring, than one constructed of heavenly elements? While the simile was impressive in its power and simplicity, it had another quality that enhanced its popularity, as shown in John Rowan's fervent insistence, during the Nullification period, that while "I am, with my whole heart, and in all its feelings, in favor of the Union," most desirable was a "Union of the States, and not an indiscriminate union of the people." This Kentucky Senator urged that each star "brighten with its benign and unclouded light the whole sphere of State sovereignty. I would have them all to shine with confluent lustre throughout the legitimate sphere of the Union." Speaking during the Foot Resolution debate, Rowan made clearer use of the stellar symbol than did Daniel Webster. In first replying to Hayne, Webster urged Union's indispensability by pleading: "Far, indeed, in my wishes, very far distant be the day . . . when that happy constellation under which we have risen to so much renown shall be broken up, and sink, star after star into obscurity and night!" [31]

Later, Webster was more concise with this symbol. Speaking in New York City during an election year, 1852, he offered a surprisingly simple and appealing version of the Union as solar system. "Here we are," he said, "thirty-two sisters revolving around a common centre, like the planets, all enjoying the same light as illumination, all enjoying its protection, and keeping steady in their places, by its even, equal, and tranquil gravitation." [32] John Quincy Adams liked this imagery, using it on one occasion with such flourish as to make Webster's effort seem feeble: "If, in the institutions of the Grecian mythology, the lyre of Orpheus was transferred to the heavens for its attractive virtues in civilizing and harmonizing the solitary savage of the desert into the social denizen of a community, may its fascination still bind in Union, never to be dissolved, the stars of our confederate hemisphere, till the harmonious movement of the globe shall be involved in the orb of its revolution!" With poetry Adams described Union's ultimate exultation:

> Now of the starry orbs it leads the course,
> Extends its virtues to the welkin's bound,
> And, rolling, whirls the universe around.[33]

These symbols—chain, ship, and solar system—dominated the imagery in Union's ideology, emphasizing as they did an irrefrangible essence. Intactness was the most prominent quality of other symbols of Union, the vase and the inspired architectural design. The vase's requirement for wholeness and delicacy is obvious. Matthew Carey called it a "great and solemn truth," that "as well might we expect to reunite, without a flaw, the fragments of an elegant porcelain vase, shattered to pieces, as to restore the Union, if dissolved but for one hour." Benjamin Franklin had been optimistic on this score for Union, for he told a friend in England to pay no attention to rumors that "the cement of the confederation may be annihilated . . ." In the wise Doctor's opinion, "There is sense enough in America to take care of their own china vase." [34]

Architecture invited more variation of the theme. Possibly the most famous effort to represent Union as a structure was Francis Hopkinson's happy allegory, "The New Roof," published in Philadelphia at the beginning of the ratification struggle. Hopkinson portrayed the confederation as a mansion, the roof of which proved in poor condition, despite being used for merely a dozen years. The owners consulted skillful architects who reported that the fabric of the building was generally weak because the thirteen key rafters were unconnected by the kinds of braces or ties necessary for effective union. Some of the rafters were enlarged and warped from too much weight, while others, smaller, had shrunk from no weight at all. The shingling Hopkinson described as fastened by wooden pegs rather than iron nails, so that bits of roof flew off. The cornice was so ill-proportioned and badly put up as to be neither ornamental nor useful. Clearly a new roof was necessary, and Hopkinson concluded his allegory with the family debating changes in design.[35]

A few months later, the Grand Federal Procession which celebrated Pennsylvania's consent to ratification, prompted Hopkinson to write his poem, "The New Roof: A Song for Federal Mechanics." It included a stirring invocation:

> Come muster, my lads, your mechanical tools,
> Your saws and your axes, your hammers and rules;
> Bring your mallets and planes, your level and line,
> And plenty of pins of American pine:
> *For our roof we will raise, and our song still shall be,*
> *Our government firm, and our citizens free.*

After describing the labors, the poem concluded:

> Huzza! my brave boys, our work is complete;
> The world shall admire Columbia's fair seat;
> Its strength against tempest and time shall be proof,
> And thousands shall come to dwell under our roof;
> *Whilst we drain the deep bowl, our toast still shall be*
> *Our government firm, and our citizens free.*[36]

This symbolism became very successful, because it readily supported the hope for intactness. Union Absolute was clearly present in the popular analogy of the Federal Temple where the loss of one pillar would cause disaster. Friends of retiring Secretary of State Henry Clay, dining in his honor, found such symbolism pleasant. The occasion's outstanding toast used the arch motif: "Our Union—the keystone of the mighty arch of the western empire—the bond of twenty-four states." [37] In the meantime, a worried Madison, brooding over Southern feeling, feared that "local prejudices and ambitious leaders may be but too successful in finding or creating occasions, for the nullifying experiment of breaking a more beautiful China vase than the British Empire ever was, into parts which a miracle only would unite." [38] A curious juxtaposition, perhaps, but Madison placed together the ambitious individual as symbol of disunion and the fragile vase as the idea of Union.

The design became more elaborate, but the implication remained similar during the later use of the construct figure. For instance, an Indiana congressman, William W. Wick, denounced sinister schemes at work "undermining the foundation of the symmetrical structure composing the Union of the States. That structure," said Wick, "is of the composite order, combining the majesty of the Gothic, the sturdy strength of the Doric, the chaste neatness of the Ionic, and the ornate beauty of the Corinthian orders. It can never be overthrown by open attack, but it may be subverted by undermining and removing the foundation." [39] So extravagant became the symbolism that it paled even such curious references as the elderly Josiah Quincy's mournful assertion at the close of the Mexican War: "Even now I feel the upheaving of the advancing tempest. I see the broken columns of our Union, and realizing the grinding of their massive materials as they dash against each other—*not without blood.*" [40]

Out of this symbolism emerged a heightened impression of tangible Union, as if to challenge the defiler. Rufus Choate's attempt represents such efforts on the eve of Civil War. He called Union "a castle; a capitol; suppose the capitol at Washington. It is a fortress at once, and a temple.... Titan hands might have built it.... But one imperfection there is, a seam in the marble; a flaw in the iron; a break scarcely visible ... yet a real vertical fissure, parting by an imperceptible opening from top to foundation the whole in two." Commitment to other preachments of Union ideology obliged Choate to say of the flaw, "The builder saw it, and guarded against it as well as he might; those who followed ... tried by underpinning, by lateral support, by buttress and buttress alternatively, to hold the disjointed sides in contact." Gradually, said Choate, the crevice representing slavery grew less troublesome, "the moss began to conceal it, even." At this point appeared Union's private devil, a violent individual unimpressed with

Union, a workman who proposed to "knock out the well-planned lateral supports, loosen the underpinnings of the ends, dig a yawning excavation under both of them, and then set on each the mountain weight of a frowning and defiant dome of its own." Whereupon, predicted Choate, "Down the huge pile topples in an hour. Small compensation is it that the architect of ruin finds his grave too, beneath it!" [41]

Inveighing against the rude hand threatening the shell of Union, William Seward said: "Our fathers undertook a great work for themselves, for us, and for our successors—to erect a free and Federal empire, whose arches shall span the North American continent, and reflect the rays of the sun throughout his whole passage from the one to the other side of the great oceans. They erected thirteen of its columns all at once. These are standing now, the admiration of mankind." Work continued, however, asserted the New York Senator, with many more pillars added and planned: "Some among us prefer for these columns a composite material; others the purer white marble. Our fathers and our predecessors differed in the same way, and on the same point." Looking directly at the Territorial question, the New Yorker made his final point. Surely all dwellers in Union would wrathfully oppose the wayward soul who from "disgust at being overruled in his choice of materials for any new column, should have laid violent hands on the imperfect structure and brought it down to the earth, there to remain a wreck, instead of a citadel of a world's best hope!" A year later, with the edifice toppling, Seward switched his allusions to the vase's chaste simplicity. Confessing his loss at knowing the value of a Union "saved by the use of the sword," Seward could not consent to separation. After all, he said, "the strength of the vase in which the hopes of the nation are held consists chiefly in its remaining unbroken." [42]

The contention that human default would cause Union's failure invited a mystical sense encountered in a final symbol, George Washington. Given the precariousness of Union, its experimental version, the controversy over its nature and purpose amidst quaking fear of foreign and internal disorder, it was not surprising that Washington became a national symbol. More extraordinary are the levels of achievement his symbolical role encountered. Even before the writing of the new Constitution, John Adams's avowal of faith involved a fascinating use of Washington. Adams said that "Instead of adoring a Washington, mankind should applaud the nation which educated him." Just as he later deposited Union in the public heart, safe from aspiring politicians, so then Adams confessed: "I glory in the character of a Washington, because I know him to be only an exemplification of the American character. I know that the general character of the natives of the United States is the same with his, and that the prevalence of such sentiments and principles produced his character and preserved it, and I know that there are thousands of others who have in them all the essential qualities, moral and intellectual, which compose it." Then Adams added revealingly of Washington's symbolical role: "If his character stood alone, I should value it very little." [43]

Adams's insight is useful. Union had called Washington forth; it had designated him. Thus he became an oracle, a prophet, but with little independent capacity. Adams was on solid footing when he insisted that, wrested out of context, Washington's character was insignificant. Here one glimpses why America disliked the Carlyle-Emerson version of great men's contributions. It was not difficult to present Washington as agent for Union, as called to kneel didactically while Union glistened in the reverence of this true son. Washington the symbol received much the same treatment as the Everlasting Fathers.

Providence, in devising Union, was expected to single out groups, but the exaltation of any individual approached the detested concepts of the early Stuarts. Whether from the democratic or the republican vantage, Union's situation brought commendation to the group, out of which occasionally a few or even one individual might be assigned special duty. Even Parson Weems's portrait had this quality. He had Union's "Divine Founder" speak through Washington to urge mutual love: "Hear his voice from the lips of his servant Washington, 'Above all things hold dear your national Union!'" [44] Others, of course, ascribed to Washington an even more active role. On the second day of the new century, Robert Treat Paine eulogized the fallen statesman by noting that, in the desperate need for Union, "the heart-uniting Washington appeared, the political magnet in the center of discord." It was he who "reconciled and consolidated the clashing particles of the system in an indissoluble union of government." [45]

Early nineteenth century literature contains abundant allusion to Washington's role, most of which describes the first President as exemplar of the spirit or motive which should pervade all hearts. It was not Washington the powerful, the dynamic, but Washington the agent, who was most often celebrated and invoked. Nothing was more revealing than the protests against any other role. For instance, the defenders of the Louisiana Purchase delighted in citing in their behalf Washington's urgent desire for perpetuating Union. One reply, by William H. Wells of Delaware, suggested that Washington be left to sleep in peace. He had simply seen, like any other person, "the difficulty of uniting in one compact so different and distant interests." He, too, had no choice but to plead for Union, since it alone was the "rock of national political salvation." Wells argued that Washington's era permitted its utter dependence upon Union to discourage talk of disunion. Accordingly, Washington represented a guide pointing to public safety while stressing that "disunion was the great rock facing the ship of republicanism." [46]

By the time America warred again with England, while facing continued internal conflict, the shade of Mount Vernon was habitually on call. Hezekiah Niles's constant prayer for Union insisted that collapse could be averted if the Founders' insights remained uppermost. This being so, Niles predicted that "the spirit of Washington will descend, and cement the hearts of the people." Niles also assisted in elevating the Farewell Address to inspired station which men should accept "as the rule and guide of their political faith," and whose most solemn precept was for "us always to speak of the *union of the states* with *reverence.*" Impatient with the behavior of Massachusetts, the Maryland editor did however attribute special power to the first President personally in his challenge to the Bay Staters: "the best of you" would never have "dared" to have "spoken of the dissolution of the union, in the presence of Washington." [47]

The end of the War of 1812 did not diminish the invocation of Washington's memory, since the symbol was handsomely equivocal. Still the loudest were those who called the Mount Vernon farmer a citizen-agent appointed to advance the design of a Lofty Power. But others undertook to present Washington as Union. Edward Livingston in an 1824 eulogy extolled the name of Washington as "synonymous with every paraphrase that can express the union of virtues and qualities never found but in him." His name must never be profaned, since "the Union, formed under his auspices, cannot be dissolved without an outrage to his memory." Livingston advised against "even the unguarded expression" that disunion might someday become desirable, for this, too, diminished the lustre brought by his reputation.[48] In either case, however, the intent of the symbolization was the same. The image of Washington invited all men to present themselves, loyal and selfless, at the feet of Union.

Washington's role as symbol was to guide men into a more intimate rapport with the all-sufficing Union. During Congress's lengthy debate over moving the hero's remains to the capital named for him, Virginia's William F. Gordon simply repeated what many before him had said when he pleaded: "Let the virtues of Washington be set before us as a model. If we practice these, then will our Union be immortal." [49] While Gordon considered it unnecessary to disturb the sleeping Father, other Virginians enjoyed parading the dismal prospect of a shattered Union, with Washington entombed beyond his homeland.

Dispute over the new resting place continued, for the uneasy times made other Southerners agree with Virginia's fears. Should disunion come, then "behold! the remains of Washington on a shore foreign to his native soil." In scolding this line of thought, most voices insisted that "the sacred name of Washington should never in debate or in thought be connected with the idea of a dissolution of this happy Union." Yet there was one expression of Virginia nationalism which must have seemed impossible to surpass: "Mount Vernon and Mount Calvary will descend to posterity with coextensive remembrance." [50] On the whole, in spite of these Southern alarums, the debate left a different impression, stressing that Washington's body lying in the capital city would be a fitting tribute to the Union, for the latter's most devoted son would be safely home.

This theme dominated Daniel Webster's great oration on the centennial of Washington's birth, in which Webster insisted that Washington's thoughts never strayed from the Union as he served it selflessly. By now, of course, Webster sought Union as an ultimate, and the symbolical use of Washington fitted admirably. As Union's exemplary servant, the man from Mount Vernon had regarded it "less as one of our blessings," said Webster, "than as the great treasure house which contained them all." This, of course, produced a plea to emulate the symbol, for had not Washington judged Union "the great magazine of all our means of prosperity; here, as he thought, and as every true American still thinks, are deposited all our animating prospects, all our solid hopes for future greatness." According to Webster, Washington, the example, "has taught us to maintain this union, not by seeking to enlarge the powers of the government on the one hand, nor by surrendering them, on the other." Union has been ordained, its process simply should be carried out in a "firm and moderate" spirit with "justice and equity." Like Washington, true Americans would behold and obey the changeless attributes of Union, which advice Webster doubtless meant to be soothing in the midst of the tariff wars.[51]

Yet on the same day Webster spoke, ex-President Adams confided gloomily to his diary that the fact that Washington's remains were not yet interred in the Capitol was emblematic of a tragic shift in Union's fortunes. "I now disbelieve its duration for twenty years," he wrote, "and doubt its continuance for five. It is falling into the sere and yellow leaf." [52]

In most public commentary, however, the Washington symbol continued to invoke reverence for eternal Union by acting both as example and exhorter. Reviewing Jared Sparks's biography of Washington, Edward Everett said that his "influence, unauthorized by any office, not expressed in orders, not enforced by troops, insensibly emanating, rather than visibly going forth from Mount Vernon, breathing Union amidst the elements of discord, inspiring hope when all hope seemed to have turned to sadness and despair, saved the country." [53] From that day forward, argued many laborers for Union's success, Washington's role had taught obedience to Union and its officials. Levi Woodbury of the federal Supreme Court was obviously moved by this implication of Washington's image. In stoutly condemning New England for opposing the Fugitive Slave law, the Justice pleaded that the "hallowed Union" be saved from those resisting its laws and servants. Such opposition, he said, was "in direct hostility to the injunctions of Washington," whose emphasis on fealty to Union made such license "hostile and derogatory to every sound principle for sustaining public order." [54]

So grew the symbolical meaning of Washington's memory, tied to the evolution of Union's Absolute role. Inevitably, a new generation demanded more content in the image of Union's Washington. While saluting Washington's exhortations, Charles Sumner noted the redoubled relevance of this legacy when Southerners contemplated civil war for the slavery Washington himself had condemned. Here, contrasted, were two generations of Union idolatry. The Websterian was charmed by the sheer fact of Union, symbolized by the comfort of ships and chains. But new men began using the imagery against detested companions in Union, insisting that "his great name should now be employed for the suppression of the Slave Power which is the fruitful mother of so much wretchedness." Sumner supplied a profound revision when he asserted of the Washington-symbol: "It will not be enough to quote his paternal words for Union: his example must be arrayed against the gigantic wrong which now disturbs this Union to its centre, and the very madness of its tyranny, destroys the very objects of Union." [55]

The Sumnerians' view, echoing widely, found typical support in Andrew Johnson, who warned that "if this Union is to be broken up, it shall be done by those who are stealthily and insidiously making encroachments upon its foundations." The future President also gave Washington's memory new life when he pointed out that the Father's symbol would be so powerful at the moment of disunion "that the patriot soldier who sleeps in his honored grave, will rise, shake off the habiliments of the tomb, and forbid the act." Similarly, Lincoln pleaded in his Cooper Institute speech for an end to the "invocations to Washington, imploring men to unsay what Washington said, and undo what Washington did." [56] Like Sumner, Lincoln wanted Washington to represent a Union for principle, not merely a Union cherished for safety's sake.

Here the symbolical role of Washington came to grief, as Union ideology abandoned the ambiguous Clay-Webster tradition in seeking to command a new generation's thought. Reassuring symbolism, including ships, chains, and the preachments of Washington, no longer permitted America to ignore the changing times. By 1861 Seward knew this, for he warned that disunion would "provincialize Mount Vernon and give this Capitol over to desolation." Seward dramatically pointed to the aged Secretary of the Senate who wept at every irreverent word uttered against the Union, and then to the youthful page who was obviously pleased by the tense excitement and the new considerations.[57] This young man, oblivious of Websterian appeals to Union as sufficient in itself, represented impatience with the tradition that Union soared above the divisive issues impelled by widespread change.

Terrible though the Civil War was, its coming seems to have been inevitable, given the overwhelming demands of a new age upon minds heavily encumbered by the evasions so long implicit in Union imagery. Long afterward, Alfred North Whitehead might have been speaking directly of the generation represented by Webster and Buchanan when he asserted: "The art of free society consists first in the maintenance of the symbolic code; and secondly in fearlessness of revision, to secure that the code serves those purposes which satisfy an enlightened reason. Those societies which cannot combine reverence to their symbols with freedom of revision, must ultimately decay either from anarchy or from the slow atrophy of a life stifled by useless shadows." [58] In a sense, the great conflict was an act of revision. Although symbolized by reassuring figures, the ideal Union failed to provoke an allegiance capable of diverting America from an impatient restlessness. It sought desperately to retain universality in spite of the diverse socio-economic interests adhering to it. The ideology's mortal flaw was its conservatism, born in an age of unease, which lingered to negate a new society out of fidelity to an image which demanded total surrender to intactness.

To the misgivings implicit in the Union as fact and thought we must now turn. For in them appear the fatal and frightening concepts of Union.

Misgiving

American unity provoked two apprehensions. One considered Union a yoke, resting uncomfortably upon some or even all American shoulders. The other brooded over the meaning of disunion. In these pages, Union's yoke-like design becomes more than the traditional vantage for understanding the ante-bellum South. It serves rather as a preface to the ideology of disunion itself. Certainly these misgivings mirror in a final way the concepts of Union already noted, ranging from Experiment to Absolute.

8: *Uneasy Yoke*

To those seeing Union as a burden, one that might readily be dislodged, the Union never lost its tentative quality. This version had a positive flavor, however, since it contended that Union's modification or elimination would hasten America toward the good society. While the South's fondness for this point became famous, less familiar is the dogged refusal by some to recognize a Union so indispensable as to leave no alternative but disaster. This resistance to Union's versions—save that of Experiment—came essentially from two inspirations. One was New England's well-known discomfiture during the Jeffersonian age. The other, more general, was the belief that Union corroded genuine liberty in America. From these stemmed an uneasiness which encouraged the sentiment that disunion could be universally advantageous. Such misgiving seemed confirmed by knowledge that for numerous Americans Union was not an uneasy yoke but was immutable and irreproachable.

I

Among the unenchanted, the vitriolic Wendell Phillips perhaps most eloquently spoke against the Union Yoke. He singled out Seward as the high priest of Absolute Union, and thus representative of all Americans so imprisoned by veneration for Union that they denied their own identity. "This trembling dread of

losing the Union, which so frightens the people," Phillips considered so powerful that "Mr. Seward, as a practical man, dares
not now tell, as he says, what he really thinks and wishes." Yet
this imprisonment in Union's toils was, the Massachusetts
agitator said, "the child of his [Seward's] and Webster's insincere
idolatry of the Union." Phillips ignored the irony in the fact that
these leaders themselves had warned against monstrous individuals who knew not the true Union but only personal avarice.
Apparently Phillips was content to say that the Websters, serving party and personal ambition, "made a god of the Union; and
today their invention returns to plague the inventors. They made
the people slaves to a falsehood; and that same deluded people
have turned their fetters into gags for Mr. Seward's lips." [1]

Few outside the South rejected Union as emphatically as Phillips; yet his emphasis on Union as a yoke represented a cause
which spanned Union's whole career. This idea was first popular
when New England seemed persecuted by the administrations of
Jefferson and Madison. Consequently, for the Northeast unity
with other sections appeared burdensome, so that its responses
established thought patterns for later struggles to elude the
Union-yoke. In fact, well before the Philadelphia convention,
the "Eastern delegates" to Congress were accused of plotting to
diminish the Union's strength. A North Carolinian argued that
the four New England states wanted "to weaken the power of the
union" and "sacrifice our national strength and dignity," because
they saw their status improved if they were conspicuously disunited and apart from the larger group. This analyst, Richard
Dobbs Spaight, acknowledged that, while New England probably
did not wish "a dissolution," still "they press so extremely hard on
the chain that unites us, that I imagine it will break before they
are well aware of it." Spaight could hardly believe that a region
would not see Union as its salvation.[2]

This Southern analysis of 1784 would thrive in a Northern
climate once Union's balance had been affected by nineteenth
century trends. Then New England would brood about others'
misunderstanding of Union's implication. For the moment, however, Spaight forecast Union's immediate dissolution. He con-

sidered it unlikely that New England would suddenly surrender to "the general good of the whole." In this early moment for Unionist ideology, the symbol was already a chain, each segment lost without commitment to cohesion and everyone left subordinate to the principle which Spaight put simply as the good of the whole.

Although men like Spaight underestimated the appeal for New England of sharing in national well-being, it proved true that Jefferson's election to the Presidency convinced many New Englanders that Union was an intolerable burden. The gloomy days of 1803-04 brought a succession of distressed voices. Timothy Pickering, for instance, wondered if there remained enough virtue and spirit to resist the ill-driven Union, even though intelligent persons in his region anticipated a new association, including New York and the Canadian provinces.[3] But not even Pickering proposed no union at all; only a union recast without the South and its slave-bolstered voice. It was never union in principle to which the New England dissidents objected; it was an unsafe Union which alarmed them.

Even so, most persons found the dangers described and the solutions proposed by the disunionists to be simply an interesting hypothesis. As Stephen Higginson told Pickering, disunion was a question "very delicate and important," but few saw it beyond "the abstract." Higginson was convinced that proposals for departing the Union "would indeed be very unpopular"; especially since John Adams would lead the opposition against anyone who talked beyond the theoretical. Higginson himself relied upon time, "I am for remaining at our posts, ready to seize every favorable event and to keep the robin alive as long as we can." [4]

Experimental though Higginson's Union was, already it was difficult to plan alternatives to it. While disunionism in the 1804 crisis absorbed the thoughts of more than a few men, the tormented New England region as a whole remained unpersuaded about the advantages of abandoning the Union. In town meetings which discussed Union's discomforts, New England communities gradually succumbed to the sense of inevitability about its continuance, for no plausible substitute presented itself.[5] Actually, the mere fact of whether the disunionists succeeded or failed was not significant. The nature of their appeal is what is important, for it reveals much about the early strength of Union's Absolute design. While Union might yet become a positive good, it was not often considered the worthless device portrayed by Pickering and his followers.

New England dissidents were left with such slight consolation as Fisher Ames's posthumous message, called "The Dangers of American Liberty." In describing the experimental status of federalistic Union, Ames never spoke of abandoning the effort but warned of the greed exhibited by its larger participants. Such ambitious giants like Virginia could manage the smaller members cleverly, thus leaving Union in an unwholesome arrangement.[6] In this spirit Josiah Quincy found the bill to admit Louisiana disturbing. The Union was built by sages using lofty principles, and Quincy yielded to no man in loving the Founding Fathers' effort. But, he inquired in behalf of New England, what was one to do when Union was dominated by heretical principles? Facing the latter, the true qualities of Union "are no more than flax before the fire, or stubble before the whirlwind."

Quincy's position is instructive, revealing how one might oppose while remaining loyal. Union had become a yoke only through aberrant leadership. This faith in a Union immutably grounded, threatened only by the unredeemed, captivated the Hartford Convention. The amendments there proposed were a means of purification, whereby Union—no longer a burden—was restored to the Founding Fathers' intention. But other threats to valid Union appeared, as when Quincy said of the Louisiana issue: "If this bill passes, the bonds of this Union are virtually dissolved; that the States which compose it are free from their moral obligations, and that, as it will be the right of all, so it will be the duty of some, to prepare definitely for a separation; amicably if they can, violently if they must." [7]

With a dissidence already sounding like expressions for true Union, New England moved toward an immutable but fragile ideal whose guardians resided largely in the Northeast. There the concept of Union held by men like Charles W. Hare prevailed.

Hare proposed to act, but according to a plan wherein "there is no danger of civil war or disunion." He was certain that the Federalists' way offered "the road to the restoration of peace abroad & its preservation at home & to strengthen & maintain the authority of the Union." Hare expected Pennsylvania would soon join the Northeast, so that "the national base is enlarged & the Union freed from danger." [8]

All danger had not vanished nor was an acceptable base wholly formed when some of the same New Englanders who had been distressed by events in 1804 and 1812 found new anguish in the possibility in 1820 that the Union might tolerate slavery west of the Mississippi. Whatever the anger, the lesson of earlier battles had not been lost. The advice Harrison Gray Otis offered his associates was widely endorsed: "Express always the desire of Union," he said, "which we all feel, but say boldly, that if it can't be had, but by a further subversion of the political balance, you are sorry but will not consent to that." [9] Others feared the loss of spirit in New England would hinder this response. William Tudor reported that even those of his neighbors who had encouraged disunion during the war were no longer interested, although Tudor felt the Missouri issue suggested disunion "naturally." Brushing aside those who swallowed their distress in hopes that Union piety offered political advantages, Tudor contended that, if slavery crossed into Missouri, "I believe the separation of the Union inevitable. For however the southern politicians may calculate on our supineness . . . they cannot suppose us so wholly insensible, as to be patient under the state of things that will arise when their blessed 'diffusion' of slavery has taken place." [10]

Vermont's William Plumer venerated Union in another way. He insisted that, wherever slavery went, it was accompanied by economic blight. Slavery would make the Garden of Eden a desert, he said, then adding an appeal in behalf of his region: "Is it nothing to us that, in more than half the Union, a state of things exists unfavorable to commerce, to manufacturers, to agricultural improvements?" Refusing to take seriously the South's warnings of disunion if she were not granted diffusion, Plumer delighted in the blessing wrought by the Missouri issue. It had, he said, truly united lovers of freedom; no longer was there a petty distinction between Federalists and Republicans.[11]

Plumer's satisfaction in his area's new unity was broadly shared. Timothy Fuller of Massachusetts, for instance, felt he could boast that the power of New England, the Middle region, and the West was now as one, especially should the South challenge Union further. In Boston, a proud Federal journal, the *Columbian Centinel*, following a similar line, accepted the free community's unity as "a duty which they owe to their God." On Christmas Day, 1819, the *Centinel* was hardly less candid in rejoicing that New England's dissension was healed. After admitting the importance of power and weight in the political Union, the paper stressed the loftier demands of religion and humanity which clearly called men to Union in a more imperious tone.[12]

Yet when a compromise was the solution, New England accepted Union in hope of directing its policies. Union was still a yoke when its burden could not be adjusted to suit one's self. Many New Englanders felt the Virginia-dominated Southern machine would never tolerate a Union not of its shaping. On the whole, however, there was little of the extreme despair some had displayed merely six years before. The *Columbian Centinel*, calling compromise a tragic blow to the "friends of freedom," spoke enviously of the South's unity and sorrowfully of Southern blandishments of disunion and civil war. But the Boston journal acknowledged these tactics had succeeded, leaving the hope that such Southern aggressiveness might have the "still more favorable tendency of uniting and binding the *non-Slaveholding States in a free bond* for the support of their mutual rights and liberties." Congressman Jonathan Mason simply assured his Massachusetts constituents he had voted for compromise out of fear that, unless calmed, the agitated public mind might take the Union's separation seriously.[13]

New England was caught within an economic revolution, and her doubts about Union's advantages to her epitomized the growing dilemma which faced the entire nation. Deploring these materialist-inspired defections from the true Union, Edward

Dowse of Massachusetts hoped: "If sound policy, if reason, if religion, if virtue, can ever successfully combat against the love of money—the sole root of all this evil—then we shall come off victorious." [14] Others, like Rufus King and Harrison Gray Otis called the North to repentance by pleading for a Union built upon principle. On the other side, and for the moment safely beyond the precincts of Congress, Daniel Webster cautiously agreed with the militant protectionist, Henry Baldwin, who feared that Missouri's clamor jeopardized the enactment of important economic legislation. Webster did not go quite as far so early; he simply "presumed the people of the North, among other considerations, regarded this question as one which affected their right *to an equal weight in the political power of the Government.*" [15]

Many New Englanders sensed the potential power of a fusion among all free states. No longer was Union declared a yoke because of the Republicans' strength in agricultural regions; it became, instead, submission to a more vulnerable oppressor, the slavocracy. This new design for the yoke idea not only invited Northern coalition along lines of congenial principle but also encouraged economic rapport from the Northeast through the Middle States to the Lakes region. In this sense, New England's portrait of Union as a burden remained popular through 1861, although the yoke's character changed.

Wendell Phillips's response to the later Union pietists renewed the sentiments of two Massachusetts statesmen in 1820, Jeremiah Nelson and Secretary of State John Quincy Adams, who had agreed that Union built upon the compromise was itself an evil association. As Nelson put it, "There is henceforth no remedy for it but a new organization of the Union to effect which a concert of all the white states is indispensable." Adams was personally somewhat at a loss to explain the departure of so many Northern men into slavery's camp, in spite of the wishes of their constituents. This forced him to appraise each side's commitment: "The cause of this closer union on the slavish side is, that the question affected the individual interest of every slaveholding member and of almost every one of his constituents." Such individual interest was not felt by Northerners in this dispute, said

Adams. The North battled for republican principles and the
rights of human nature. It was apparent to Adams that until
the North had strength and zeal enough to overtake and subdue
the South's concept of Union, New England would still find her-
self wearing a yoke.[16]

The question for many was how much time the free region
would require to awaken, seize its strength, and right the wronged
Union. There was a rueful, even an envious quality in a resolution
adopted in 1820 by the New Hampshire legislature, which admitted, "That slavery creates habits and interests peculiar to the
states tolerating it, and that it constitutes between them a strong
bond of union." These lawmakers foresaw how the resulting unanimity, if unopposed, would control the Union at large. Men
like Christopher Gore and Daniel Webster sent grateful messages
to friends in New Hampshire.[17] A year later, Missouri proscribed
the presence of free Negroes, and New England took heart at
what Plumer, for one, felt to be the first increase in Northern
solidarity. Rufus King shared this gratification; and John Randolph, who bragged the year before of the ease with which the
South could seduce Northerners, now in 1821 condemned these
same men as blind sheep following their leaders.[18]

Between episodes of the Missouri question, many New Englanders found another issue which clarified the difference between
Union as a burden and as a blessing. This emanated from the
appeal of tariff protection. In 1816, the House Committee on
Commerce and Manufactures had adopted a view which in time
pleased New England. The Committee predicted that "different
sections of the nation will . . . strike into that line of industry
which is best adapted to their interests and the good of the
whole. An active and free intercourse, prompted and facili-
tated by roads and canals will ensue; prejudices which are gen-
erated by distance, and the want of inducements to approach
each other and reciprocate benefits will be removed, information
will be extended; the Union will acquire strength and solidarity." [19] Thus, Union promised to be more a blessing than a
yoke.

Even those still dedicated to commerce began to concede that a domestic manufacturing program would not endanger foreign trade. During April of 1820, the Baldwin tariff bill, frankly protective, was discussed in Congress. The final vote found more New Englanders in the House for it than opposed. Had not the *American Monthly Magazine* in 1818 urged New England to favor tariff increases as the sole way of achieving a commanding position in the Union? By 1820, the *Columbian Centinel* and the Boston *Intelligencer* were in public agreement. By 1824, Webster's advocacy for the life of the soil in preference to machine toil had disappeared, and he dutifully, though belatedly, joined his region in embracing industry.[20]

A shifting economy offered New England a new basis for participating in Union, as well as guaranteeing new and powerful allies in the middle region and even in the once scorned West. Consequently, Union designed as burden went south. The tide turned with the election of John Quincy Adams as President, backed by Clay and the protectionists. Although Adams the candidate sensed that tensions within Union encouraged silence as the better part of electoral valor, his supporters often proclaimed that a true son of New England deserved the Presidency. Other New England voices actually scolded Adams's few Southern supporters for suggesting an "Atlantic" party which could crush the licentious West.

Some pro-Adams journals preferred to breathe Union piety. Unless Adams could make a true and broad appeal, the Boston *Patriot* insisted, "Our Union is a rope of sand, our National Government a farce, and we shall soon separate into bitter and unextinguishable hostilities." Meantime, the Boston *Statesman* made its case more quietly, claiming simply that there should be a "sectional rotation in office." On the eve of the election, the *Patriot* joined in, elaborately reminding the South of her three successive Presidents who had received the "cordial support" of New England. "We now offer in our turn a distinguished statesman from the North," a man of "the whole Union," who ill-deserved the attacks being launched out of Southern bitterness.[21]

Here ended New England's travail. Her son could be proudly toasted as a man of all the Union. Even many of the Northeast's citizens who disliked Adams's early departure from Federalism found it wiser to hold their tongues. Recalling Adams's election, Missouri's Senator David Barton refused in 1830 to believe there ever would be confirmation of Washington's warning that demagogues would appear "to cultivate and cherish the young devils of discord to tear out the vitals of the Union and scatter them to the dogs of civil war and horrid anarchy." Barton remembered that in 1824-5 the Americans thus warned by Washington "believed they saw symptoms of the coming evil. They beheld the people of the United States, like an agitated ocean, threatened with the storms of sectional ambition, and no revolutionary worthies at hand to seize the helm and guide the vessel of state through the tempest with the firmness of Washington." After this glimpse of an overpowering Union, Barton cheerfully explained how the people had turned to Adams in hope of calming and preserving the Union when it had been New England's turn for leadership.[22]

In his second speech on Foot's Resolution, Daniel Webster spoke frankly about New England's stigma and bluntly denied that the Hartford Convention had met to break up the Union or even *"to calculate the value of the Union."* Admitting that to have done so would have been disloyal, Webster's position revealed clearly how fifteen years had brought New England fresh assurances about Union. He insisted that, no matter what the inducement, contemplation of disunion was unpardonable. Once, in 1807, "a great majority of the people of New England" believed as sincerely that the embargo was unconstitutional as did South Carolinians now feel about the tariff. Although the embargo brought ruin and anguish, Webster said his neighbors never once considered interposing their arm against the Union. Though arguing and petitioning, New England remained true to the procedures established by Union.[23] Those Yankees whom John Quincy Adams accused of once planning dismemberment hastily denied ever entertaining a "design to produce separation of the Union." This famous tempest had little significance except to show New England's rising enthusiasm toward Union. Now all factions in the region sought to outdo each other in proclaiming a record of unwavering adherence to Union.[24]

The aftermath of New England's torment centered on John Quincy Adams and such disciples as Wendell Phillips. Arguing from libertarian principles that chattel bondage threatened Union's health, this group produced a story graphically recorded by that perceptive New York citizen, Philip Hone. In 1841, he spoke disgustedly of Adams's tactics: "Among other insane movements of the ex-President, he has presented a petition praying for *a repeal of the Union,* because the petitioners are deprived of the privilege of agitating the terrible question of slavery." Hone called this proposal "monstrous" and Adams's tactics characterized by "indomitable obstinacy." [25]

Joining Adams in this effort were certain New Englanders who considered the Union still a yoke, so long as the South, far from a majority, ruled it, For Adams and his associates, a useful example of Union's burden was the threat to free speech implicit in the detested gag rule. Some citizens, including John Greenleaf Whittier, used protests like the 1842 "Haverhill Petition" which Adams put before the House. Whittier and his fellows prayed that Congress "will immediately adopt measures peaceably to dissolve the union of these States: first, because no union can be agreeable or permanent which does not present prospects of reciprocal benefit; second, because a vast proportion of the resources of one section of the Union is annually drained to sustain the views and course of another section without any adequate return." The final plea for dismemberment was "because (judging from the history of past nations) this union, if persisted in, in the present course of things will eventually overwhelm the whole nation in utter destruction." [26]

Generally, however, Union was too valuable and too serious to a rising generation of New Englanders for it to be endangered by the ancient problem of minority rights. Sentiment more representative of the Northeast than the Haverhill statement colored the memoirs of an old Federalist, S. G. Goodrich. In 1856, he observed that, anguished as New Englanders were during the War of 1812, they "did not ... array the States in arms, and cry out for a dissolution of the Union!" Furthermore, "They did not—as is now the fashion with certain democrats in full communion with the party—claim that the Union shall be torn asunder, whenever the administration of the government does not altogether please them." Consequently, remarked Goodrich, there was singular justice in the fact that New England should have supplied the acknowledged champion of the Union, Webster. Equally appropriate, he said, was that "Southern Democracy" should be breeders of disunion and should furnish the "Arch Nullifier" himself. And yet that area continued "to point its finger at New England, and cry *'Treason, treason to the Union!' "* As Goodrich saw it, this untruth allowed a Democrat to steal a horse, while a descendant of New England "may not look over a hedge!" [27]

In his second volume, Goodrich put the Hartford conferees among the exalted Founding Fathers. The latters' legend had amazing uses, but none more extraordinary than Goodrich's picture of the participants in the Hartford meeting being like Washington, gray with service to the Union. "Look at these men," he invited, "and then tell me if there was treason, conspiracy, dismemberment of the Union, either in their hearts or in the hearts of the people who elevated them?" Indeed not, for they were great and noble men, whom time would honor, for "one truth will stand—they were of those who reared the glorious fabric of the Union, and under all circumstances taught the people to regard it as sacred." [28] Thus Goodrich testified to Union's rehabilitation in the Northeast. So deeply had Union become intrenched in the region's mind that even those who had earlier squirmed beneath the yoke version, now were in the pantheon of the Founding Fathers. Only Union conceived as an Absolute might have wrought such a change.

II

New England's experience did encourage some Americans to accept Union as a liberty-consuming Hydra. For example, Patrick Henry warned the Virginia ratification convention that surrendering tax power to the Union meant serious curtailment of local freedom, although he proclaimed that "I am a lover of the American Union." This was easily clarified by his declaring: "The first thing I have at heart is American liberty: the second thing is American Union." Echoed a New Yorker: "A Union with our sister states I as ardently desire as any man, and that upon the most generous principles; but a union under such a system as this, I think is not a desirable thing." Why? Because "the design of a union is safety, but the union upon the proposed plan is certain destruction to liberty." This was "a dreadful kind of safety." In resolutions approved by Kentucky's legislature, Vice President Jefferson wrote that "the several States composing the United States of America, are not united on the principle of unlimited submission to their general government." [29]

Passage of a quarter-century strengthened Jefferson's patience. Pleading in 1825 for tolerance, he observed that, if every suspected misdeed were to entail dissolution, Union would not last a year. Dismemberment should come, said Jefferson, only "when the sole alternatives left are the dissolution of our Union ... or submission to a government without limitation of power. Between these two evils, when we must make a choice, there can be no hesitation." [30] Similarly, Senator William Hendricks of Indiana deplored the "habit" which "has grown up amongst us, of talking of this General Government as a great political hydra, destined finally to ingulph and destroy our liberties." But he added that if he felt some misgivings were justified, he, too, "would raise my voice for the dissolution of the Union." [31]

Here, of course, was a prominent feature of American political thought. Those who feared a powerful Union compared it to George III. The only practical escape was to use the legendary original Union, as did many Southerners who found libertarian appeals the best means of reaching True Union's refuge. Not everyone was so bold as Dr. Thomas Cooper, who insisted to Van Buren in 1829 that Union no longer had any value for intelligent men in South Carolina, Alabama, and Georgia.[32] He accurately foresaw that to "intelligent" Southerners Union's visage would become the grim features of oppression.

Hendrick's Hydra of Tyranny did not vanish, no matter how

the South might grip Democratic party councils. Pointing to the visage, one speaker at a Georgia anti-tariff rally shouted in 1832: "No more of the sickly cant about *brotherly love,* and the *sacredness* of the Union." For "they who shook off the tyrannical oppression of their mother country, will not hesitate to resist that of their *sister* states—and if need be even unto death." As if in proof, Robert Barnwell Rhett boasted in 1841 that, a few years before, he and a few House associates had been alarmed enough to draft disunion resolutions. Reading from these, Rhett charged that for enemies of the South, "the bonds of the Union constitute the cords by which they propose to bind the victim to the altar." [33]

It remained for John C. Calhoun to give heroic proportion to the portrait of Union devouring liberty. In his *Discourse,* he sought to justify Southern alarm. "All this has brought about a state of things hostile to the continuance of the Union," he concluded. "Alienation is succeeding to attachment, and hostile feelings to alienation; and these; in turn, will be followed by revolution or a disruption of the Union." The latter might still be saved, admitted Calhoun, although it would take more to salvage Southern freedom than restoring the old federal character. Calhoun had been too near the grim Hydra: "What has been done cannot be undone." [34] In his last utterance during the 1850 Compromise debate, Calhoun warned that Union's appointments were increasingly those of a tyrant. Might Union be spared this fate? "It cannot be saved by eulogies on the Union, however splendid or numerous. The cry of 'Union, Union, the glorious Union!' can no more prevent disunion than the cry of 'Health, health, glorious health!' on the part of the physician can save a patient." Thus Calhoun dismissed the Clay-Webster struggles to render Union's appeal so powerful that there were no surpassing considerations.

Insisting that the Union legend would no longer disguise what Union had become—a curse to liberty—Calhoun offered his succinct summation: "So long as the Union, instead of being regarded as a protector, is regarded in the opposite character by not much less than a majority of the States, it will be vain to attempt to conciliate them by pronouncing eulogies on it." Observing that the cry of Union "comes commonly from those whom we cannot believe to be sincere," Calhoun announced that Washington's career indicated that he, too, would propose disunion in preference to submission beneath oppression. All of which allowed the South Carolinian to award a tyrannical North responsibility for preserving the Union.[35]

Laboring in the North to sacrifice Union before freedom was Calhoun's curious New England counterpart, Wendell Phillips, who had his own contrast to draw: "Put the Union into one scale and free speech into the other;" he suggested late in 1850, "it needs no ghost to tell which will kick the beam." The loss of freedom had wrought wonders in the past; now it again had to be rescued. According to Phillips, "It will be no matter of surprise if so great a work cost a Union or two; but what is that to us?" Like Calhoun, Phillips challenged the idolator: "See thou, creature of Union, knowing no 'higher law' than the parchment of 1789, to that!" [36] Or, as George William Curtis put it, "a political and commercial union" could indeed "be bought at too dear a price." It meant that "the Union had come to mean a league for the diffusion of slavery among men," [37] making slavery a loss for freedom more complex than simply involving humans in chattel status.

By the late 1850's, Calhoun's picture of the Union as a Hydra left several impressions. Jefferson Davis went home in 1859 to warn Mississippi that Republican success would at last pose the question: "Will you allow the constitutional Union to be changed into the despotism of a majority, will you become the subjects of a hostile Government, or will you outside of the Union, assert the equality, the liberty and sovereignty to which you were born?" Then Davis's conclusion: "let the Union be dissolved. . . . I love and venerate the union of these States—but I love liberty and Mississippi more." [38] Abraham Lincoln responded differently. Telling a New Hampshire audience that Southerners believed Union's destruction would be the North's deliberate choice, Lincoln observed: "This is cool. A highwayman holds a pistol to my ear, with 'stand and deliver, or I shall kill you, and then you will be a murderer.'" He added the analogy: "The threat of death to extort my money, and the threat of destruction to the

Union to extort my vote, can scarcely be distinguished in principle." [39] While Phillips would bid the highwayman depart to re-
pent alone the inevitable pangs of conscience, Lincoln wanted the
thief to surrender to principle. For Lincoln liberty and Union
were only salvageable together, while Phillips felt Union was so
badly tarnished as to mar the image of liberty whose reflection it
had to provide.

Confronted by this conflict between two concepts of Union, each
deeming the other a thinly-disguised menace to liberty, President
Buchanan's final message to Congress displayed the anguish of a
generation which hoped obedience to Union would resolve all
other matters. But now that generation's images of Union were
shouldered aside by long-avoided questions about sources and
purposes of power. In such a context Buchanan simply capit-
ulated by announcing, "The time has arrived so much dreaded
by the Father of his Country, when hostile geographical parties
have been formed," leaving the fount of national blessing, Union,
run dry. The President then reminded his auditors how society's
essence, the impulse for self-preservation, had once embellished
Union. But with Northerners bent upon molesting slavery, Union
no longer offered security. In such an event, Buchanan admitted,
the South, "after having first used all the peaceful and constitutional means to obtain redress, would be justified in revolutionary
resistance to the Government of the Union." [40]

When not everyone in the Democratic camp surrendered, the
party's ensuing distress showed the failure of Union's Absolute
guise. The latter, by sanctifying truce and skirting principle, glori-
fied the fact of Union. Yet when Stephen A. Douglas drew back
from the Dred Scott decison, it revealed how even he had to
mingle Union with certain considerations of the nineteenth century. Sympathetic acquaintances in Illinois could well warn Jefferson Davis in 1860 to "beware of such friends as Douglas who
cry out for union, when he sees the heel of the tyrant about to
be placed on your neck." [41]

Thus did Union bring disquietude, whether by exasperating
New England early in the story or by eroding Southern freedom
at the end. Logically, it occurred to some that disunion meant

advantage to all concerned. This is another relevant aspect of the Yoke concept. For Phillips and for Davis, both struck by this version, the sundering of Union held genuine advantages. But over this matter of disunion there was to be spectacular disagreement. The Yoke was not readily dislodged.

9: What of Disunion?

Union ideology responded in various ways to the idea of disunion. Some said that Union could be dismantled. Others saw dismemberment entailing dreadful consequences, either civil war or despotism. Another group insisted that any talk of dissolving Union was merely a contrived distraction. Beyond all of these, serving as a sort of epilogue to the drama of Union Absolute, was the belief of some that disunion was unthinkable, in fact, impossible.

I

Initially, when Union's paramount design was one of experiment, the possibility, if not the probability, of disunion was often discussed. For instance, Jefferson told President Washington, "the division of sentiment & interest happens unfortunately to be so geographical that no mortal can say that what is most wise & temperate would prevail against what is most easy and obvious." Of course the Secretary of State added: "I can scarcely contemplate a more incalculable evil than the breaking of the Union into two or more parts." But he had to admit the possibility and advantage of disunion, remembering that a great part of the South had opposed Union's creation.[1]

Before long, John Quincy Adams was having to deny that either Jefferson or Burr meant to dissolve Union; but he was also saying that "if they will break us up—in God's name, let the Union go. I love the Union as I love my wife. But if my wife should ask and insist upon a separation, she should have it, though it broke my heart." [2] Both Adams and Jefferson lived to see many extraordinary proposals for redesigning Union. While Adams's neighbors found the old family tie antiquated, preferring that Union's axis extend across the mountains, Southern willingness to see Union revised was appearing by 1820.

Speaking for a new generation of Virginians, Congressman William S. Archer explained what George Washington actually meant in recommending consolidation of the Union. "Not," he said, "assuredly consolidation *into unity*. Union did not imply unity. It implied exactly the reverse." Archer emphasized that "the unity of the States was their submergence," and then added a neat paradox: "Union, like other living things, had its condition of death, and this was unity." He advocated that the House abandon any voice in the Presidential choice, a surrender made for the "whole human race," since the "interests of freedom, in all countries and ages, are tied up, bound, and incorporated in our experiment." The latter would surely fail if the move toward consolidation were not halted. The Virginian saw disunion as better than consolidation, because, like a true son of Jefferson, he considered centralism intolerable.[3]

Archer had hardly finished speaking before the tariff controversy began, and many suggested the advantage of disunion. In 1827, Dr. Thomas Cooper announced that if the duties were raised, disunion was inevitable. South Carolina congressmen would be ordered home, and within the year the Palmetto State would become an independent nation. Gracious at this point, Cooper observed to Van Buren: "We shall separate in all amity; and assume conscientiously our share of the national debt; we have and shall have with you, no quarrel or dispute." Disunion was very simple, as Cooper told Van Buren, "we construe the terms of our present pact differently: We cannot exist under the construction you give it: we are compelled to separate." [4]

Three years later, the Charleston Fourth of July banquet found a similar deliberateness prevailing. The principal toast saluted

"The Union—the elements of its durability are to be found in its performing honestly, faithfully, and justly the beneficent purposes for which it was formed." After this, Colonel William Drayton warned the diners that disunion must be scrutinized closely, for it was "incalculably more to be deplored" than the tariff. He conceded, however, that "a crisis might arise, when the bonds of the Union ought to be broken. The right of the state to *secede* from the union, I, unqualifiedly, concede." Drayton simply continued the previous generation's pragmatic evaluation of Union. Granting that disunion would be "frought with more disastrous results" than participation, Drayton rested with the admonition: "We are bound by every social and moral duty to select the least of the evils presented to us." [5]

During the Jackson Adminstration, as Old Hickory's farewell address testifies, the nation took Drayton's judicious approach. Union's dismemberment for many was an alternative which, under conceivable circumstances, offered undoubted if not entirely un-mixed advantages. Visiting the United States in 1834, Michael Chevalier found the agony of issues like slavery expansion, tariff increases, and national banking such as to warrant saying, "The ear has become familiar with the ominous word *SEPARATION*. A habit has grown up of thinking, and even of declaring, whenever the interests of the North and South jar, that the cure-all will be a dissolution of the Union." [6]

However, as the Jackson-Webster appeals disclosed, the idea of a Union absolute and ordained was making its mark, and was leaving an ambivalence to characterize American thought for the next thirty years. On the one side there was devotion to a Union increasingly an end rather than a means; on the other dedication to ideals and securities not always discernible in Union itself. While Websterians sought a bridge by insisting nothing was possible beyond Union, such an Absolute caused much misgiving among many who agreed with Colonel Drayton.

An 1834 letter Whittier sent to the secretary of New England's anti-slavery society made this apparent. Writing just before the gag-rule controversy, Whittier told the society that, while Southerners must be treated as intelligent men, the prevailing ambiguity must cease. He pleaded, "for the love of peace and the harmony of the Union, let there be no more mining and countermining, no more blending of apology with denunciation, no more Janus-like systems of reform, with one face for the South and another for the North." Whittier's position, frankly stated, found principle the supreme determinant, to be maintained no matter what the cost; hence the poet's admonition: "although we may not be able to save our country from the awful judgement she is provoking, though the pillars of the Union fall and all the elements of her greatness perish, still let it be our part to rally around the standard of truth and justice." Conveniently, the defenders of righteousness could leave the Union's fate in God's hands.[7]

This outcome was delayed for nearly three more decades. Meantime, advocates of disunion's advantage continued to speak. A few instances may serve as reminders of those Southerners who, in swelling numbers, insisted that for their region separation was just and necessary. James H. Hammond told Calhoun in 1849 that dissolution was at hand. "I know that the value of the Union is now calculated hourly in every corner of the South," Hammond said, "for I rarely get into a coterie even in the streets of Augusta —a Yankee town you know—but it is discussed." Hammond saw endemic to the South the conviction "that the union has always been and will always be a disadvantage to us and that the sooner we can get rid of it the better." Noting that "I have thought this myself for twenty years," Hammond added, "but where I met one five years ago who agreed with me, I now meet fifty." Hammond's view employed the same authority Whittier recommended. He told Calhoun that circumstance "reveals the design of God to sever the Union—to rescue us from the licentious Sodom of Northern Mobocracy." Thus the accolade for disunion when Hammond proclaimed, "The fate of the Union is sealed. It is the order—the decree of Providence."[8]

More cautious, Calhoun said that dismemberment would have advantage for all concerned, since "the alienation between the two sections has . . . already gone too far to save the Union." Combining the concepts of spirit and immutableness, Calhoun asserted that, if the impending Nashville conclave did not impress the

North with the South's sense of Union, it would mean the end. Having made every effort to save the Union, "We would then stand justified before God and man to dissolve a partnership which had proved inconsistent with our safety, and, of course, destructive of the object which mainly induced us to enter into it." Just before he died, Calhoun said the concessions offered to the South by the Websterians meant "that the question may be adjusted, or patched up for the present, to break out again in a few years." This only strengthened his doubts about Union's attributes. "Indeed," said he, "it is difficult to see how two peoples so different and hostile can exist together in one common Union." [9]

Calhoun's view was unusual, coming from one who had grown up with Union. Most of his peers shared Clay and Webster's difficulty either in seeing the continent without Union or any genuine advantage in dismemberment. Calhoun's passage from one system of nationalism to another is well known, representing Southern Republicanism's move as its predominance over the Union faltered. But new men like Hammond and Rhett easily accepted the argument that dismemberment held advantage for all participants. One of them, South Carolina's Milledge L. Bonham, spoke in the vogue of the Experiment concept when he contended that the Constitution made it clear that Americans sought many goals other than Union. In asking, "is the Union the larger idea? Does that embrace all the rest?" Bonham challenged such apostles of Union Absolute as Clay and Lincoln.

For Bonham, as for many Southerners, America's statement of principle was the Constitution. Here were "objects . . . of greater importance than the preservation of the Union." Consequently, Union-worshippers must be suspect. Bonham himself was most shocked when men spoke of forcing the South back into the Union. The Union had life, he said, so long as it offered advantage and benefit. When force was mentioned, the Union had actually ceased.[10]

Bonham represented the renaissance of Union as a means, where it was easy to picture disunion as simple and advantageous for everyone. On the eve of his election, James Buchanan noted that many Southerners proclaimed that Frémont's victory would be a signal for dismemberment. Seeking the meaning of this staggering fact, the Democratic nominee reported to a friend: "One gentleman informs me that the men who were our contemporaries when the States lived in peace with each other ... have passed away." A generation come of age in the South, sensitive about slavery, "now deem that it would be for the mutual advantage of all parties to have a Southern Confederation in which they can live at peace." Buchanan could only remark on these insights: "I have received such communications with regret & astonishment." [11]

Regrettable, perhaps, but in view of Union's history as an idea Buchanan need hardly have been astonished. Where once Union had been a majestic harbor, now the South saw it as a place of peril. The success of the Bonham-Calhoun position is notorious. Less familiar is the idea that perhaps disunion was a prudent move. This view, so casual and calculating, was early espoused by Senator John Dix of New York. Conceding in 1847 that his state would have a profitable position should disunion come, Dix denied New York would ever appraise the Union's value. Union must never be pushed so far, however, as "to resist dismemberment by force—for disunion is better than intestine war." The latter, Dix argued, brought "pure unmixed demoralization," especially because "it renders selfishness more odious, by wedding it to hatred and cruelty." Thus his reiterated cry: "Less, far less than these, would be evils of disunion." [12]

Wendell Phillips and the Bonhams agreed, in spite of their distaste for each other, on the advantages of dismemberment. "A Union is made up of willing States," Phillips contended, "not of conquered provinces." He added a note reminiscent of John Quincy Adams's earlier despair: "There are some rights, quite perfect, yet wholly incapable of being enforced. A husband or wife who can only keep the other partner within the bond by locking the doors and standing armed before them, had better submit to peaceable separation."

Phillips wondered why American statesmen failed to recognize that homogeneous nations like France tended toward centralism,

whereas "confederacies like ours tend inevitably to dismemberment." Seemingly oblivious of the factors compelling Union which
Lincoln and others sensed, Phillips likened the nation to the Mississippi's mud, where "every flood shifts it from one side to the
other of the channel." Equally revealing was his comparison of
Union to a "herd of States" hunting together for food, making a
situation where one "must expect that any quarrel may lead to
disunion." Consequently, Phillips could only scoff as the idolators
of Union feared dismemberment, a process he felt only natural
and desirable.[13] What Phillips as well as many of his Southern
counterparts avoided was a misgiving which struck even the casual
Dix; might not Union's preservation exact the awful price of civil
war? Phillips's reluctance to include this possibility provides a
path into another uneasiness aroused by the Union.

II

Regardless of motive, many Americans considered the Union to
be the deity Phillips deplored. From such reverence, disunionism
provoked two significant responses, both recognizing the primacy
of Union Absolute. Of these, one was a conservative device, reminding the faithless that there was no alternative to Union but
civil war. It was often accompanied by allusions to a Gordian knot
which could be parted only by a crimsoned sword. This concept
opposed change in what was considered a given, immutable
system. Others, however, designated despotism as disunion's fearful result. Either prospect, civil war or despotism, would destroy
the great blessing that was Union.

This conservative appeal was so great that opposition to Union's
vital purposes was easily presented as support of anarchy, where
brother slew brother. Talk of doing away with Union provoked
predictions of civil war from the beginning. Thomas Jefferson's
uneasiness crept into a precaution sent to John Taylor during the
1798 crisis. The Vice President disliked thoughts of dismemberment. In a free society, he said, man's nature would make partisanship and discord inevitable. Because one faction commanded
the Union for a moment was no reason to contemplate disunion.

Jefferson then moved to a memorable question, one exposing the uneasiness over individualism which contributed to Union ideology. "If to rid ourselves of the present rule of Massachusetts and Connecticut, we break the Union," asked Jefferson, "will the evil stop there?" Were not Southerners also human? After disunion, even a fusion of Virginia and North Carolina could find enough cause for dispute to destroy their little union. These considerations brought the conclusion: "Seeing, therefore, that an association of men who will not quarrel with one another is a thing which never yet existed, from the greatest confederacy of nations down to a town meeting or a vestry; seeing that we must have somebody to quarrel with, I had rather keep our New England associates for that purpose, than to see our bickerings transferred to others." [14]

Not all of Jefferson's New England brethren were ignorant of this fact. A significant minority in both houses of the Massachusetts legislature protested the meeting planned for Hartford. The Senate cited the federal Constitution's objection to any state entering into compact with another without Congressional consent as showing how the Founders had "probably foreseen that disappointed and ambitious men, would attempt to form associations prejudicial to the general welfare and dangerous to the Union of the States." With Union seen as refuge against unprincipled individualism, the Massachusetts senators insisted that the Founding Fathers knew that such men "would excite local jealousies, and attempt geographical distinctions, and that despairing of governing the *whole,* they would attempt a severance that they might govern a part." Disunion would only play into the hands of the power-hungry demagogue, said these protesters: "In vain may we look for aid, except from the Union, energy and Heaven." [15]

Here, in the midst of disappointment with Union, was recognition that alternatives to Union could only prove worse. Such sentiment readily agreed that anarchy and intestine war would result from dismemberment. The urgency sounded by Jefferson and the Massachusetts lawgivers illustrates how Union, like the early medieval fortress, appeared the only succor for society.

Actually, Union and violence were set against each other as alternatives much earlier in contexts involving both the British empire and the colonists' union. The Declaration of Causes of 1775 to which John Dickinson contributed prayed for a renewal of the Union so that the Empire might be spared the calamities of civil war.[16]

Once separation had come, congressional delegates anticipated inter-state strife if the new nation lost its unity. In 1778, New Jersey's John Witherspoon told Congress of the "absolute necessity of union" to the "vigour and success" of their enterprise. While this was hardly news, Witherspoon was more original in wondering why some delegates insisted that any permanent Union was impossible or unlikely. Such admission could be disastrous to the country's morale, for, should it become generally known "that the delegates of the provinces consider a lasting union as impracticable, it will greatly derange the minds of the people, and weaken their hands in defence of their country." Witherspoon was horrified to think that, after blood had freed the states, there might come "a more lasting war, a more unnatural, more bloody, and much more hopeless war, among the colonies themselves." [17]

Early thoughts about Union's grim alternative were not limited to Congress. Connecticut's poet, Dr. Lemuel Hopkins, attacked dismemberment in lines appropriately called "The Anarchiad," written during Shays' Rebellion. The latter, for Hopkins, proved not only the need for unity as order's basis, but also the necessity of more effective union. In Hopkins' poem, discord calls from Hell to Shays, who represents not a regional so much as a social threat to the good society. The prospect of civil strife was not limited to inter-state war. Thus Hopkins' demand:

> Stand forth, ye traitors, at your country's bar,
> Inglorious authors of intestine war
>
> Ye sires of ruin, prime detested cause
> Of bankrupt faith, annihilated laws,
> Of selfish systems, jealous, local schemes,
> And union'd empire lost in empty dreams.

Hopkins saw only confirmation of Witherspoon's apprehension:

> Ye wanton states, by heaven's best blessings cursed,
> Long in the lap of fostering luxury nursed,
> What fickle frenzy raves, what visions strange,
> Inspire your bosoms with the lust of change?
> And frames the wish to fly from fancied ill,
> And yield your freedom to a monarch's will?

Having posed both fratricide and despotism as the alternatives, Dr. Hopkins took a more familiar form, depicting a split along regional lines:

> What madness prompts, or what ill-omen'd fates,
> Your realm to parcel into petty states?
> Shall lordly Hudson part contending powers?
> And broad Potomac lave two hostile shores?
> Must Allegany's sacred summits bear
> The impious bulwarks of perpetual war? [18]

It was often said in the 1786-7 crisis that either Union must be invigorated or civil war would ensue. Stephen Higginson warned Henry Knox that "the powers of the Union must be increased, and those of the States individually must be abridged; they cannot both be perfectly sovereign and independent at the same time." [19] Alexander Hamilton urged that Union be given an army strong enough to keep peace throughout the confederacy. If a state or states ever were allowed to challenge Union, the result would be dreadful. "When the sword is once drawn," he said, "the passions of men observe no bounds of moderation. The suggestions of wounded pride, the instigations of irritated resentment, would be apt to carry the States against which the arms of the Union were exerted, to any extremes necessary to avenge the affront or to avoid the disgrace of submission." Hamilton predicted, "the first war of this kind would probably terminate in a dissolution of the Union." [20]

Opinion ranged from Hamilton's extreme to quite the opposite, with the center remaining constant in its belief: preserve the Union to avert fratricidal war. An anonymous essayist, "Agrippa," attacked Hamilton's position by pleading, "Let us then be upon our guard, and do no more than the present confederation obliges. While we make that our beacon we are safe." And again, "Let us then cherish the old confederation like the apple of our eye ... that our union may outlast time itself. It is easier to prevent an evil than to cure it. We ought therefore to be cautious of innovations." To "Agrippa," the new system seemed a disguised wolf, for the new Union "must have an army to support it, and there can be no redress but by a civil war." [21]

Though the Union was strengthened, fears of violence lingered. With the first challenge in western Pennsylvania, the so-called Whiskey Rebellion of 1792, resolved inconclusively, misgivings veered from anticipations of "class" attack on Union toward the regional violence foreseen by Dr. Hopkins. When the Virginia and Kentucky resolutions reached the national community in 1799, young John Quincy Adams, far from home and hearing the news through Rufus King in London, felt civil war could be avoided if Union and public interest became so intimate that men "cannot tear one away without rending the other." Once this marriage was made, Adams could say that, "if after all we must come to disunion and civil war, the consciousness of pure unalloyed justice and right will be the bright ornament of our victory, or the most impregnable refuge of our defeat." The nuptials were troubled, and Adams was soon writing of how war with England would "be complicated with a civil war, and a desperate effort to break up the Union." [22]

Daniel Webster, then a youthful New Englander, saw "intestine feuds" likely, since Washington, "the great political cement," had just died. With only civil war able to destroy the Union, Webster considered the possibility real enough. "In my melancholy moments," he confessed to a friend, "I presage the most dire calamities. I already see in my imagination, the time when the banner of civil war shall be unfurled; when Discord's hydra form shall set up her hideous yell, and from her hundred mouths shall howl destruction through our empire; and when American blood shall be made to flow in rivers by American swords!" Allusions to blood and swords became common during the next sixty years, as did Webster's plea, "Heaven grant that the bonds of our federal union may be strengthened." [23] As Union's role of indispensability was stressed, so was the ghastly fate entailed by an unthinkable act, dismemberment. William Cocke, of Tennessee, typically equated peace with Union. But for the Union, "we should soon be plunged into all the horrors of civil war." Disunion, warned Cocke, meant "this country would be deluged with the blood of its inhabitants, and a brother's hand raised against the bosom of a brother." [24]

The association of fratricidal war with dismemberment persisted. During the Missouri debates, for instance, Senator Nathaniel Macon begged the elderly to recall the Revolution for some idea of civil war's evil. Pleading for Union, Macon insisted, "Nothing is to be got by American conquering American." [25] Not everyone agreed. John Quincy Adams now argued that such conflict would extirpate bondage from the continent, an end so glorious that, despite the vile means of disunion and civil bloodshed, Adams had to admit, "I dare not say that it is not to be desired." Curiously, this preoccupation with civil war offered few explanations why carnage must follow disunion. Adams himself suggested that if, "legislative acts of one or more states of this Union are passed, conflicting with acts of Congress, and commanding the resistance of their citizens against them," then what else "can be the result but war, civil war?" [26]

During the debate of Foot's Resolution, further attention was given to disunion's effect. Just before Edward Livingston became Secretary of State and shaped Jackson's proclamation on Nullification, he pleaded for a proper understanding of Union. Dismayed by the sentiments around him, Livingston deplored the "light manner" used to speak of dismemberment, "the greatest evil that can befall us." Wherever he turned, he found Union treated as "a knot of policy that might be unloosed familiar as a garter." Rather, Union was "a Gordian knot that can be severed only by the sword. The band cannot be unloosed until it is wet with the blood of brothers." Daniel Webster pushed on, calling Hayne's position "a dilemma, like that of another great general. He would have a knot before him which he could not untie. He must cut it with his sword. He must say to his followers, 'Defend your-selves with your bayonets,' and this is war—civil war." [27]

For some, the Livingston-Webster type of protest was too blunt. South Carolina was especially cautious. Fearing that the Found-ing Fathers' bequest might be lost, D. H. Huger said that a con-vention to consider Nullification was a serious move. It did not strengthen Union to threaten it. Whereupon Huger stressed the ambiguity which Union needed for endurance. A convention, he asserted, "must endanger this union, or wound the honor of my country." Thus, the terrible alternatives—if the Union backed away from the state, it was dishonored. If the state lost, it was disgraced. Even worse, if both held to their positions, the result would be civil war between "legatees of one political father, Washington the great." [28]

Others, like Pennsylvania's Senator George Dallas, chose to stress the opinion of later generations. He warned disunionists that they were surely deluded in feeling themselves defenders of human liberty. Instead, "If they recklessly involve the American people in the horrors, uncertainties, and fatal consequences of civil war . . . they must be content to receive, as a merited reward, an immortality of detestation." Posterity, Dallas said, would forget all the refined theories and virtuous passions in seeking, "amid the desolation of perpetual conflicts . . . to rebuild the edifice of our great, and glorious, and happy confederacy." He added that only the unscrupulous would use disunion. "Let no man, sir, seek elevation or renown, at the price of National Union." [29]

Jackson put it more simply in his Proclamation to South Carolina. Disunion and its tool, nullification, invited treason's grim punishment. Addressing the people of the state, and imply-ing that only misguided leaders could ignore Union's ultimate capacity, the President urged upon all the certainty "that com-pared to disunion all other evils are light, because that brings with it an accumulation of all." He warned of a primeval curse upon any man who shed a brother's blood in disrupting a Union which the Great Ruler of Nations "has chosen as the only means of attaining the high destinies to which we may reasonably aspire." [30]

Surrender to Union became the fashionable answer to these misgivings. John M. Clayton sent Henry Clay a note before Clay's 1833 effort to ease the tariff crisis, begging him to disclaim political advancement by describing his only desire as "the imperishable glory of preventing civil war." [31] Moved by the need for harmony, a Philadelphia journal acknowledged slavery a necessary evil. To tamper with it "would produce immediate dissolution of the Union," leaving the North with no influence on Southern institutions except to launch a civil war. This, the magazine asserted, was "a species of crusade not likely to be undertaken by all or any of the free states against their white brethren, in the cause of natural rights." [32]

Calhoun also contended that civil war might come if disunion were not permitted. In 1838 he described the issue of bondage as the only question "of sufficient magnitude and potency to divide this Union," and added that bloodshed was certain unless the South departed the Union. Angered by what he considered a gross unfairness, this apostle of True Union, Old Style, marveled at those who "saw no danger to the Union in the violation of all its fundamental principles," but who yet condemned others who disagreed as responsible for the consequences of that menace. When his daughter inquired about peacefully dissolving Union, Calhoun replied that such speculation misunderstood the act of dismemberment by underestimating the difficulty of making two people of a Union "which had been so long bound together by so many ties, political, social, and commercial." He reminded his daughter that this "is the most difficult process in the world." [33]

Another attitude was reflected in a plea made by Kenneth Rayner of North Carolinia: "We can never know the value of this Union until we have lost it." Yet what would the loss entail? Obviously, "fanaticism and the horrors of civil war ... when the brother's hand shall be reeking with the brother's blood, and the sun of freedom has gone down in blood." After this "then shall we only appreciate the value of this glorious Confederacy." [34]

Henry Clay often cited this dilemma, in spite of its pale, con-
jectural quality compared to Calhoun's cool calculations. A curious contrast existed between these two elder statesmen. Calhoun
had only unrealistic solutions for his candid appraisals, while
Clay's melodrama entailed shrewd tactics of evasion. In explaining his stand on bondage, Clay attacked the abolitionists who
dared "even to threaten our glorious Union with dissolution."
This "unhallowed object," if achieved, said Clay, would find the
perpetrators seeking "to light up a war between the dissevered
parts of the Union, and through blood, devastation, and con-
flagration, to march forward to emancipation." Dismissing "dia-
bolical means," Clay, the organicist, preached his beloved grad-
ualist approach and rejected extremism because it threatened
"the greatest of all possible calamities which could befall this
people, the dissolution of the union of these States." [35]

For advocates like Clay of a Union unimpeachable, the alternative of bloody strife had a nightmare's unreality, since the Absolute version was violated by positing any alternative. Neither
Clay nor Calhoun could accept Union and civil war as anything
but mutually exclusive, but where one anticipated the triumph of
Union's appeal, the other asserted that dismemberment alone
would prevent bloodshed. The Mexican War and David Wilmot's
proposal weakened both positions. Maryland's Reverdy Johnson
thought that choices now were either Union through civil war or
dismemberment. Even with fratricidal strife's "inconceivable
evils," Union's path seemed so directed: "The cement which keeps
us all together, in a Union which dispenses to all everything that
any contrivance of human society can dispense, is to be dissolved."

Reverdy Johnson, keeping to Clay's position, accepted disunion
in preference to a Union buttressed by civil war. Here was the
half-way house in Unionism's pilgrimage. Where once the alternative to Union was fratricide; as disunion became plausible,
civil war leaped to the side of Union's perpetuation. Few could
see the anachronism in this move of force to a concept of Union
which conveyed for many a mystical quality of omniscience and
omnipresence, an Absolute reposing on Spirit. Johnson had to
conclude, "This glorious and mighty republic, now the pride and

admiration of the world, will be broken into withered and scattered fragments; and all by suicidal hands." [36]

By 1850, the year of Clay and Calhoun's last great debate, technology had made civil war more plausible. Where Union's alternative once had been a series of Europe-like internal squabbles, involving small principalities, now Union itself seemed to mean that the majority would compel a segment of one-time companions to return to unity. But to a national mind steeped in the lore of Union as Spirit, both disunion and its new alternative, Union by force, seemed incredible. This brought Clay to try for clarification by using the Absolutist position. He contended no state had the right to secede, meaning that "war and the dissolution of the Union are identical and inseparable." Only violence would bring disunion, since consent to dismemberment could never be given. After describing the tragedy that dissolution, if successful, would bring, Clay said: "I am for staying within the Union, and fighting for my rights—if necessary, with the sword —within the bounds and under the safeguard of the Union." In contrast to John Quincy Adams's view in the age of experiment, Clay now called Union "a marriage that no human authority can dissolve or divorce the parties from."

Still, misgiving drove Clay, in concluding his great plea of February 6, 1850, to gaze horrified at a war-bound Union. Any struggle to contain Union, he warned, was hardly imaginable, since history gave no parallel. Yet the final result was certain, being "the extinction of this last and glorious light which is leading all mankind." Clay's Union Absolute depended upon the enlightened, free surrender of men and states. Enforcement by violence would strip Union of its divine purpose and its unique career. In such an event, Clay begged Heaven to allow that he would "not survive to behold the sad and heart-rending spectacle." [37] This confused quality of Union scarcely diminished; the prophets of war found advocates of peaceable parting undaunted. Both sides continued to seek a common concept of Union within the vast changes in the country brought about by passage of nearly a century's existence.

Some defenders of an Absolute version, though, found it difficult to reconcile Union's traditions with enforced perpetuation, and began calling insane those who argued for quiet dissolution. Two days after Clay's speech, the Senate eyed a petition for peaceful dismemberment. A glimpse of what ensued is revealing. Senator John Davis of Massachusetts advocated being discreet. The Senate was powerless to dissolve Union or to adopt measures for such a purpose; therefore it must ignore the petition. After calling the proposal offensive to the Senate, Jefferson Davis added, "If this Union is ever to be dissolved, it must be by the action of the States and the People." Ignoring momentarily the enormous implications of Davis's position, Senator Seward disavowed the petition, offering an optimistic word: "I have no fear of a dissolution of the Union. I believe that it was not made by madmen, nor can madmen destroy it; and I believe that none but madmen would petition for its dissolution." Seward advised never arguing with the insane. Thus, with reason on Union's side and madness astride dismemberment, there was little more said on the occasion.

Three days later, however, Lewis Cass resumed the subject, moved by what he considered the tendency to discuss disunion much "as we talk about dividing a township." Like his old foe, Clay, Cass proposed that there ought to be one unpronounceable word, "dissolution." The crisis arose because citizens did "not know how well we are off." As for advocates of bloodless disunion, Cass said they were "either already in an insane hospital or ought to be placed there." For him, a Union planted "in the heart's core of almost every American," could hardly be disturbed without the most violent wrench. Cass used a familiar allusion. "The Gordian knot that binds us together," he said, "will never be severed but by the sword. To talk then of a dissolution is to talk of war." With this admixture of hope and disbelief, Cass and his generation contemplated a collapse of the indispensable. What could be said, other than Cass's observation that the civil strife, certain to accompany dismemberment, would be the worst war man ever saw? [38]

The nation was equally perplexed. Philip Hone was incredulous, writing in his diary: "The South stands ready to retire from the Union, and bloody wars will be the fatal consequence. White men will cut each other's throats, and servile insurrections will render the fertile fields of the South a deserted monument of the madness of man." Yet in the North he also found those who would "listen to no terms of compromise. Equally regardless of the blessings of Union, they prefer to hold it of no value unless the power is conceded to them of restraining the extension of the great moral evil which overshadows the land." [39] Hone wrote before the most publicized event of 1850, Webster's speech of March 7, which actually brought little to clarify the problem of disunion and war but hoped, by its urgent tone, to drive most dissidents away from speculation.

Deploring any admission of dismemberment's possibility, Webster expressed "distress" and "anguish" at the mention of secession. He was especially pained because these references came from world-renowned patriots. Rejecting peaceful dismemberment, he said, "Sir, your eyes and mine are never destined to see that miracle." He attacked the idea in much the same way as some colleagues earlier had pronounced the notion insane. "The dismemberment of this vast country without convulsion," he marveled, "the breaking up of the fountains of the great deep without ruffling the surface! Who is so foolish, I beg everybody's pardon, as to expect to see any such thing?" But in this effort to prove peaceful disunion impossible, Webster did not join Clay in implying that disunion itself was impossible. He was content to encourage Union by stressing, "There can be no such thing as a peaceable secession. Peaceable secession is an utter impossibility." Disunion "must produce war, and such a war as I will not describe."

Webster preferred exploring the difficult dismemberment process with the calmness Calhoun had used a dozen years before. Under a voluntary separation, where would lines be drawn? Which states would secede? Who would still be an American? Where would the flag and the eagle soar? Then Webster abruptly seized Clay's favorite device, the linking of the present generation with the labor and love of the past and the future. Using the idea of timelessness to warn that ancestors and grandchildren alike would condemn the present age if it dishonored Union, Webster again dismissed talk of peaceable disunion. "I am sorry, sir, that it has ever been thought, talked of, or dreamed of, in the wildest flights of human imagination." Still evasive, Webster later told the New-York Historical Society that it would be better if America had no history, should it abandon such verities as Union, moral injunctions, eternal justice, and religious teachings: "Let the horrible narrative never be written." [40]

Many joined this determination to make wish father to fact, apparently hoping that disunion would go into hiding if sternly opposed. This response mostly ignored the complexity of Unionism and even the moral issues involved. Typical here was John A. McClernand's assertion that God's Union could never be dissolved peaceably. Every natural, civil, and historical factor pointed to civil war. The latter made McClearnand speak of rivers choked with blood as "the demon of disunion [would] flap his baleful wings and croak his discordant notes of fiendish joy over the ruins of this glorious Republic." Edward Everett compared contemplating disunion to peering into a volcano, the latter representing a vast, horrible, and unpredictable destruction. Everett also emphasized that dismemberment would cause "the sun of the republic [to] go down from the meridian and set in blood." [41]

Numerous Southerners now agreed. Stressing the states' importance and the Union's spiritual essence, they foresaw a bloody disruption, as in Judah P. Benjamin's 1856 statement that peaceful disunion was now impossible. Union's collapse would come when "brotherly feeling shall have been converted into deadly hate," and "dreadful will be the internecine war that must ensue." Benjamin's chief defense was the Spirit role, since wavering fellowship was more easily cited by Southern apologias than incautious mention of a divinely ordered Absolute. Said Benjamin: "Take away this league, convert it into a bond of distrust, of suspicion, or of hate, and the entire fabric which is held together by that cement will crumble to the earth, and rest scattered in dishonored fragments upon the ground." [42] It was much easier for the South to discover the transformation of brotherhood into enmity than to continue the more exasperating arguments over polity.

As the long-dreaded war drew near, misgivings over the alternative of violence began following a more consistent pattern. On the one hand were those joining Indiana's Congressman William H. English in depicting the coming horror. Emphasizing that "the American is essentially a restless, resentful, and belligerent race," English said, when "the dreadful event of collision" did occur, "it will be followed by a war as bloody and relentless as ever was recorded in the annals of time!" Others, like Seward, were more subtle, for they refused to believe what they saw. Disunion was incredible, said Seward, "for the Union is not more the body than liberty is the soul of the nation." The emotional shock was enormous, since "the American citizen has been accustomed to believe the Republic immortal. He shrinks from the sight of convulsions indicative of its sudden death." An even more eloquent summation of the misgiving over civil war came from an anonymous poem quoted during the crisis.

> Dissolve the Union! Be like France
> When 'Terror' reared her bloody lance,
> And man became destruction's child,
> And woman in her passions wild,
> Danced in the life-blood of her queen,
> Before the dreadful guillotine.
>
> Dissolve the Union! Roll away
> The spangled flag of glory's day;
> Blot out the history of the brave,
> And desecrate each patriot's grave,
> And then above the wreck of years
> Quaff an eternity of tears! [43]

The poem then went on through Union's ideology, incorporating man's transcendence of himself through obedience to Union; the anguish and tears as the only substitute for Union; the worthlessness of those who, in the face of the Founding Fathers, would ponder dismemberment; and finally, the bloody violation of nature itself, should Union be supplanted by strife.

With violence accepted as alternative to Union, its implication for American thought was clear. Once, dreading incessant war among fragmented, self-seeking states, Americans cultivated Union as a means of escaping this fate. When Union became a compelling fact, civil war was less the alternative to unity than the reply to disunion. It would be a war to restore and preserve what had been attacked by men bereft of sanity. Ironically, this meant that Union's career closed in 1861 as it had opened in 1776, on a tentative note. Despite the absolute character brought by time and technology, Union was still challenged. With its claim upon all Americans repudiated by some, Union's integrity had to be upheld in an ordeal by violence. The latter would release Unionism from the unease and doubt which had resorted to conservative versions. Yet, though there were battle appeals to God, the Founders, History, Nature and Mission, no one really replied to Seward's striking inquiry—what was the worth of a Union preserved by the sword?

In their misgiving, men like Seward glanced nervously at an alternative to Union which never equalled civil war's fascination for the public. This was despotism, ready to march into the nation from centuries of an alien past. Seward's alarm at a Union backed by force invited the nation to contemplate cohesion built upon the mailed fist and to wonder if a civil war would precipitate the tyranny a minority already claimed had mastered the character of Union. In the first federal Congress, Gouveneur Morris contended that without genuine Union Americans would "become the subjects of an usurping military despot." Morris made a moving cry: "What but the Union can save us from ruin?" Another generation replied through John Quincy Adams: "I speak in the sincerity and conviction of my soul in declaring that I look upon standing armies, intolerable taxes, forced levies, contributions, conscriptions, and requisitions, as the unavoidable and fatal chain of which disunion is but the first link." Joseph Story predicted invasion and the establishment of a monarchy should Union fall, and Mahlon Dickerson said that, if "the United States divided into parts by violence, these parts will not be free Republics, but will, of necessity, become military despotisms." [44]

Southern misgivings took readily to the idea, as when John C. Calhoun warned Duff Green that, unless national reform occurred, the nation faced either "the establishment of military despotism, or the disunion of these states. One or the other or both must follow without a great and timely change." [45] Fifteen years later, Calhoun recognized that disunion might not be accomplished by a single blow. He told the Senate, "The cords which bind these States together in one common Union are far too numerous and powerful for that." Then he added, as an apostle of Spirit might, "Disunion must be the work of time. It is only through a long process, and successively, that the cords can be snapped, until the whole fabric falls asunder." These cords, Calhoun said, "are not only many, but various in character. Some are spiritual, or ecclesiastical; some political; others social. Some appertain to the benefit conferred by the Union, and others to the feeling of duty and obligation." Within this system, dismemberment would proceed until "nothing will be left to hold the States together except force." Of such compulsion, Calhoun said, "But surely that can, with no propriety of language, be called a union." [46]

Another veteran of long years of service, Amos Kendall, said in 1856, that when disunion, the "grand explosion," came, the remnants would "dash against each other on a sea of anarchy, and finally sink and be lost beneath the calm of despotism." [47] Like Seward, Kendall found disunion's aftermath as frightful as the act of dismemberment. Most people, however, did not look beyond civil war. To talk of military or civil dictatorship, and especially of impending monarchy, seemed unreal after the age of Hamilton. By mid-century, faith in the success of Union allowed Americans to avoid inquiring how central authority would meet the issues of federalism. Men like Seward preferred to believe that the individual, sensing his responsibilities, would accept the need for Union. Since the failure of this individualism was unthinkable and the alternatives of civil war and despotism were even less comprehensible, Americans evaded the implications of reconciliation after violence.

III

The organic version also was used to answer disunion. Talk of
dismemberment was seen either as an effort to thwart the majority
or as a meaningless threat, a clever distraction. Disunion threats
were a method of slowing national expansion, and some supporters of this view even attributed disruption talk to some other
nation's effort to weaken America. Disunion appeared to be
merely a contrivance, a slightly absurd device which could hardly
hope to stay the ordained triumph of Union.

Those sharing this view accepted a dynamic and expanding
Union. Bravely they exuded confidence in Union's capacity. So
great was their reverence for the Absolute concept that talk of
dismemberment could be casually dismissed. This made loud
praise for Union and especially talk of its rescue seem in bad taste,
or perhaps even a sly tactic. The latter was scorned, since it implied dissident groups seeking to halt the majority's forward
motion.

Even as early as 1798, one observer felt there must be some
ulterior purpose in prayers that disunion might be averted followed by hossanahs for Union. *"Union.* This is a pleasing word,"
admitted Thomas Claiborne of Virginia to the House, but it
seemed that those who used it "wished rather to shake the Union
to its centre." Accusations of infidelity had to cease, he warned,
as he reminded Northerners that "No rebellious head had ever
been raised south of the Potomac." This point was frequently
repeated as regional strain persisted. New England had its turn
in objecting to the pious call for unity. Timothy Pickering complained that " 'Union' is the talisman of the dominant party;
and many Federalists, enchanted by the magic sound, are alarmed
at every appearance of opposition to the measures of the *faction,*
lest it should endanger the 'Union' " [48]

For many, disunion warnings seemed to stem from trifles. In
1820, for example, the proposal to publish journals of congress
under the Articles of Confederation was opposed by some representatives, who contended that sentiments uncovered might re-
open wounds dangerous to Union. These objections were an-

swered by the argument that Confederation leaders had possessed a national perspective. "Did they not look with a prophetic eye to the destiny of the nation?" asked George French Strother, who then added in disgust that it now seemed, whenever a new proposal was heard, immediately disunion was talked of. Yet this "is a spectre mere, which there is no danger of being converted into sober reality. Let the political gladiators use the prospect in their argumentation, the people are bound together by adamantine ties, not to be loosened by any one of the present day." [49]

In the Missouri debate, William Plumer spoke with similar confidence, noting how virtually everyone who favored the extension of slavery across the Mississippi predicted disunion if their course were threatened. Perhaps, Plumer observed, there would be more terror in these threats, except they had been repeated for years. He was certain that "if, unhappily, a dissolution of the Union should ever take place, it will not be for the sake of extending slavery." Plumer listened without belief to the warnings of dismemberment, "and therefore without dismay." The Union "is not easily destroyed; it is cemented by the mutual interests of all its members." Like his much-admired John Adams, Plumer waved disunion aside as small talk, since "the hearts of the people are knit together in the common bond of indissoluble Union." [50]

The House of Representatives seemed especially susceptible to frequent predictions or proposals of disunion. In 1826, the issue of amending the electoral college reappeared, immediately provoking talk of separation. Ichabod Bartlett of New Hampshire spurned this response: "In truth, all threats of dissolution of the Union, are too stale even to attract attention from any quarter; and, least of all, do they bring any alarm, when coming from a section whose salvation is the Union." Again, the public virtue was interposed against mere agitators. "The People have too much intelligence, and too much integrity, to enlist under the banner of rebellion, whatever may be the ostensible purpose." [51]

Congress continued to hear that both Northern and Southern members made disunion proposals a convenient departure for arguing about abolition. Typical of this increased disgust was Alexander Duncan's assertion, "I am induced to regard the whole question of abolition . . . as a miserable, contemptible hobby, too frequently introduced here for the purpose of making capital at home, by southern and northern gentlemen." And then: "Talk about dissolving the Union! Why, does any man suppose because a few individuals in this country cannot have their wishes gratified, that the Union is to be dissolved?" His reply was an echo of many previous assertions, "Sir, the Union does not stand on so slight a foundation. There is something more to keep together this Union, which as has been well remarked, was purchased by the blood of patriots. It has higher objects to hold it together." [52]

It was inevitable that those who loudly reproved talk of disunion should in turn be accused of seeking effect. In a revealing 1851 letter, John Greenleaf Whittier invited Charles Sumner to join with Bryant, Seward, Greeley, and others in an effort to rescue a distinguished national guest from the " 'Union savers.' " In the wake of Europe's 1848 uprisings Americans were welcoming the colorful Hungarian liberal, Louis Kossuth. What vexed Whittier was that Kossuth apparently had been persuaded to keep silent on such divisive issues as Negro bondage out of deference to the larger blessing, Union's perpetuation. Otherwise, said the poet, Kossuth would have condemned the institution which mocked American liberty: "Naturally he would deprecate a dissolution to this Union—but he ought to understand that it is not in the slightest jeopardy—that the solicitude of the 'Union savers' is all for political effect." [53]

Ben Wade became sarcastic over this trend: "We have had the Union saved five or six different times within my day, and it is the only thing I ever knew to suffer by salvation." Having amused his audience, the Ohioan continued: "The Union has a wonderful capacity for getting into trouble, and politicians have a wonderful knack of saving it." He added: "Let me say that the Union will not 'slide' half as quick as the politicians who are so patriotic in the efforts to save it. (Laughter.) It has more vitality than all the politicians who stick their right hand into the Treasury, at the same time they save the Union with the other." But despite the mirth provoked by Wade and the impatient complacency of Whittier, the sirens of Union generally succeeded, to the dismay of Georgia's Robert Toombs, who asked his fellow senators, "Is my State, a free State, to lie down and submit because political fossils raise the cry of the glorious Union? Too long already have we listened to this delusive song." [54]

In reviewing the history of disunionist threats for a Massachusetts audience, Charles Sumner said such maneuvers were merely distractions. Since there was sufficient sentiment in both sections for preserving the Union, let men keep to the fundamentals: those of freedom in the territories and the prostration of the slave oligarchy. Although concern over disunion talk cut several ways, the most apparent reply was Sumner's insistence that such alarms were an appeal *ad hominum,* using reverence for Union and distaste for the irreverent to overpower embarrassing questions.[55] Many agreed with Sumner that Union was strong enough to endure a national confrontation of any issue. The "Union savers" were thus accused of using love for unity to coerce a majority or a minority into accepting a condition which otherwise would be contested. The context mattered little; the implication was virtually the same. "Union savers" and cries of disunion alike were heaped together by those of dissimilar position, who nevertheless agreed that Union would survive and prosper the more because people were willing to speak out or act in its favor.

In 1814 Jared Ingersoll had admitted that "a dissolution of this Confederacy is a national misfortune, upon which I never think without great pain." The secret sin, however, was that of "deterring those States which hold a legitimate ascendancy ... from any measure whatever, by the threat of dismemberment as a consequence of it." Whenever this happened, said the Pennsylvanian, "the Union is virtually dissolved. The substance is gone, and nothing remains but the shadow." Unless the majority faced its duties, undaunted by paltry threats of dismemberment, then indeed would the Union be gone, "a cold and melancholy shade of authority, without warmth, without life—contemptible...." [56] As John Quincy Adams put it a few years later, "the Union is in the most imminent danger of dissolution from the old inherent vice ... anarchy in the members." He said, "one-third of the people is perverted, one-third slumbers, and the rest wring their hands with unavailing lamentations in the foresight of evil which they cannot avert." [57]

By 1860, Absolute Union was supported by charges that disunionism was merely a scheme to keep Union cowardly and passive. Now accusations of treason and warnings of violence could be brought against disunion advocates, where a few decades earlier such reprisals were rarely mentioned. In the youth of Clay and John Quincy Adams, an era of experimental Union, dismemberment talk produced regret and apprehension, but it was acceptable in polite society. For this older generation, the rising emphasis on the impossibility of separation was novel. At one time the physical challenge had been so staggering that many agreed when Fisher Ames said: "Our country is too big for Union, too sordid for patriotism, too democratic for liberty. What is to become of it, he who made it best knows." Although time stripped away the social conservatism, the misgiving persisted about Union's capacity to keep pace with physical growth. John Randolph might well wonder of Union: "Is it, like space, indefinite in its extent?" [58]

Even John Quincy Adams was impressed with this question. He filled his 1820 diary with concern over the Mississippi Valley's strain upon the Union. For the moment, he was joined by Henry Clay in dismissing a united future for America. Clay told Adams, then Secretary of State, that "it was a shocking thing to think of, but he had not a doubt that within five years from this time, the Union would be divided into three distinct confederacies." Soon, however, dreams of an American System allowed both men to reaffirm that only a difference of principle threatened Union. The physical challenge no longer seemed important. Said Adams: "There was no existing opposition of mere interest between any two parts of this country, which could possibly produce a dissolution of the Union." Here an important consideration within Unionism again emerged. Which face of Union's character ought men to find more appealing, a mutuality of interest or a mutuality of principle? [59]

For many, however, the alliance of Nature and the Machine justified such jubilation as that expressed by Ohio's Samuel F.

Vinton, when he saw the map disclosed "the wonderful network uniting the West with the North and the South." Said Vinton, "let any Northern or Southern man tell me where he would begin the work of its destruction." The Union's parts were so interdependent that dismemberment would bring ruin to the sundered segments. Actually, then, it was Union calling through an old version, in primitive setting with limited technology, which sounded in Lincoln's debate with Douglas at Galesburg. Although the Republican usually ignored this point, here he attacked Douglas's expansionism. Urging the nation to reflect before adding more territory, Lincoln warned such gain might "add to the one only danger that has ever threatened the perpetuity of the Union or our own liberties." [60]

The tentative character of Lincoln's statement mirrors the triumph of Nature and Destiny. By then, few persons anticipated dismemberment because of Union's diversity. The fear of disunion, which was abundant, stemmed not from uncertainty whether Union could in fact survive, but from the question as to how Union should survive. In asking this question Union's defenders ended its long travail, for when disunion was considered either impossible or incredible, the Absolute version became preeminent. Thereafter, those who dissented could not be reconciled, despite the nation's cultivation of both Spirit and Absolute roles in hope of retaining participation by the South. But when the latter departed unmoved, Unionism had no choice but to proceed as its Absolute self. The experiment could not fail, misgivings had not been confirmed. Rather, the heathen must be taught the sacred; the Union, calling upon Spirit, History, and Nature, had to demonstrate that it could not be disrupted. Yet Southerners stoutly defended their idea of Union, one which now had meaning mostly for them.

The Civil War revealed that Americans had never agreed upon a version of Union. Where circumstance had once tolerated diverse Union sentiment, it had been through cajolery and felt necessity. When fresh imperatives supplanted the old, they produced a new Union. The Civil War was, in a sense, an act of defiance, a repudiation of the past. Citizens of a new age were rejecting the paradise which Union once offered; namely, an assurance that scattered, self-sustaining communities would be free and secure. With economic complexity and social interdependence came the positive state, whose attributes bespoke activism, thus increasing the polity's importance for the individual. The triumph of this Union Absolute demanded the burial of misgivings lingering in Romantic memories of the eighteenth century.

Epilogue

The Union became so powerful a concept that Americans looked with horror on the violence, desolation, and darkness which dismemberment would bring. By embodying the agencies making for national awareness, Union appeared absolute. Union was a people's tradition, encompassing Security, Progress, Destiny, the Glorious Past, and a Divine or Natural Order. All this had grown from a frail experiment once invoked by a lonely America beset by geopolitical novelty and the absence of such familiar social instruments as monarchy, church, and feudal order.

Success for this experiment only increased the exertions of Union ideology. Fresh meanings had to be offered a community where socio-economic contrasts were increasing. Reliance upon consensus, spirit, supernaturalism, and nature could hardly disguise the impact of technology. The latter, by confirming the reality of Union, endorsed the belief that disunion was incredible. Cruel and bloody events after 1860 moved Union sentiment to a new dimension beyond the abstract realm so vital to the Jeffersonian age. When war compelled Union's acceptance as eternal and irrefrangible, a mystical ideology retreated. Traditional Unionism collapsed. Seward had dimly recognized this in his affirmation that a Union maintained by the sword was incomprehensible. While there had been some early feeling that disunion was inconceivable, the real significance of this view grew slowly.

Hope for a Union inviolable generally rested with John Adams's contention that the people would never tolerate anything else. There is no better glimpse of the vital role that Union acquired. American citizens sought a unity offering assurance and security. Serving as State, Ruler, and Church, Union allowed the uniqueness that history and physical fact taught was America's without requiring that Americans estrange themselves from the past, the divine, the natural, or the profitable. Consequently, at both the beginning and the end of Union's career in American thought, disunion could be dismissed, since "the prevailing sentiment of the people is in favor of their true interest, UNION." [1]

From everywhere resounded this reassurance: Union prevailed because the public embraced it as its own. It brought from an early poet the optimistic lines:

> Not diff'rent chimes, nor intervening seas
> Columbia's holy league shall break apart;
> Nor fraud, nor force, nor powers of earth, nor hell,
> Not Europe's potent arm nor brib'ry's magick spell.

And then, from another poet, a paraphrase of Washington's advice to the people:

> You should the infinite importance learn
> Of *Union* in a government like this
> To private, social, universal bliss.[2]

Put more prosaically by Nathaniel Macon, "It is our duty to take care of the nation, and not destroy it." Disunion was a horrid thought, he said, adding, "At the very idea I shudder" as should all men. After inquiring who would condone brother slaying brother, and pleading that, instead of "the arguments of bayonets," men should "rely on such as are drawn from truth and reason," Macon happily concluded that no leader could succeed in disunion, for "the people would laugh to scorn all those who wickedly make the attempt." [3]

During the War of 1812, staunch Hezekiah Niles expected every friend of Union would ignore "the raving paragraphs" which "occasionally appear" urging Union's weakening or dismemberment. Blaming these appeals upon Great Britain, Niles said of those who listened, "reason is lost upon them." Only a "dolt" would believe that a sizable segment of America desired disunion, for Niles insisted that the "people" would not be "disaffected to the Union." [4] Echoing Niles was John Forsyth of Georgia, who asserted contemptuously that the movement to disturb Union would fail because of "two powerful divinities—interest and fear." Said he, "The love of the Union is yet sufficiently strong, in defiance of artifice and falsehood," so that "the ruffian who dares to lift his sacrilegious hand" against Union would be destroyed.

By 1820, Edward Everett could write for a braver New England, as Union was buffeted by the Missouri storm. Everett believed disunion impossible, for it would have to "pierce through the great masses of the country, and set its individual atoms at war with each other." The sectional bitterness was no danger to the Union founded on the individual citizen.[5] James Madison put his agreement in a fable depicting the Union strengthened in spite of quarrels. The tale involved Jonathan and Mary Bull, North and South, fused in marriage. Mary developed a black-stained arm which offended Jonathan. The marriage grew stormy, and Jonathan thought of dissolving it. But Mary kept appealing to his reason and sense in defending their Union. Such family matters as managing estates like the Louisiana country or appointing the Head Steward influenced this domestic scene. Finally, Jonathan Bull responded, thus restoring this symbolical Union in even more affection and confidence.[6]

Such appeals to popular reason were prominent in the widening insistence that men would unfalteringly support Union. They invited the obverse contention that only madmen or vicious demagogues would think of dismemberment. From these assumptions came reassurance. Said George Holcombe: "Storms may assail, and the shadows of portending dissolution will assuredly encompass it," yet men could say of Union that "as long as virtue and intelligence continue to crowd its portals and officiate at its altars, the tempest will burst harmless around it." After the gloom of the moment had vanished, "the symbol of the Union will still be seen floating over it as resplendently as ever." [7] Young William H. Seward's Fourth of July oration at Auburn, New York, in 1825, was a more candid variation. He insisted that the people of the North and the South were too wise to surrender their Union. Any division would come between the authentic Union and the frontier. Faced by a young and powerful West, Seward felt "the North and South will soon forget all animosities." [8]

Agreeing that fear for Union was needless, another prominent New York citizen, James Fenimore Cooper, wrote in 1828: "My own opinion is, that the United States are now passing, or, in fact, have in a great measure passed, the ordeal of the durability of the Union." Citing the technological upheaval, Cooper emphasized that transportation now permitted Northern and Southern citizens to exchange ideas. No longer considered a threat to the states, Union now was seen as a "representation of the people in another form." [9] To assure this, President John Quincy Adams used memories of the Hartford Convention to call Union of "transcendent importance to every individual, to every family, to every community, throughout this nation." [10]

Adams's ally, Henry Clay, expressed this theme on a tour to the southwest. Speaking in 1830 at Natchez, Clay insisted that widespread fears of Union's dissolution were unfounded, arising from the people's commendable dread of such a calamity. Rumors of dismemberment circulating since 1787 stemmed from party passion, "rather than the reason of the people." Sweeping aside these tales, Clay acclaimed the public's wisdom: "I have seen nothing to give me any serious fears that such an evil would befall us." [11]

John C. Calhoun certainly utilized the people's Union to good advantage. Admitting that a state might conceivably abuse the power of interposition, Calhoun refused to take the possibility seriously. After all, he said, "the strongest feelings of our nature, and among them the love of national power and distinction, are on the side of Union." Beyond this, one could only ask "if those who voluntarily created the system cannot be trusted to preserve it, who can?" [12] On this score, at least, Madison agreed with Calhoun. Eying the tariff controversy, he considered it "painful" even to think that for such a cause, the "Union admitted to be the only guardian of the peace, liberty, and happiness of the people" should be broken up. Union being so crucial, Madison announced it was impossible that disunion "can ever be the deliberate act of the people," particularly if "the value of the Union be calculated by the consequences of disunion." [13]

Although the rumors Clay had mentioned persisted, the confidence in popular Union continued, especially in the insistence that internal anguish only heightened fondness for Union. During the conflict over slavery in the District of Columbia, Alfred Cuthbert, a Georgia Senator, lauded the people's patriotism. So extraordinary was this spirit that crisis actually contributed to Union's durability and strength: "As the lofty pine on the mountains becomes more firmly rooted as it is shaken by the tempest, so had the love for this Union taken deeper roots in our hearts." [14] Accepting such optimism, Francis Grund contended: "That the moral arguments in favour of the Union . . . and the dread of the calamities which would result from its dissolution, are daily more engrossing the public mind, is a fact beyond the possibility of doubt or controversy." Although conceding that dismemberment was talked about, especially in the North, Grund was supremely confident. "The union of America rests on a broader basis than mere individual speculation," he said; "it is founded on the material, moral, and political interests of the people." Furthermore, "the people understand these interests and are at liberty to follow their own judgement." [15]

More than one person supported this position when faced by the Haverhill citizens' petition for disunion. Representative Joseph R. Underwood, a Kentuckian, expected that the public in both North and South would be calm, since all men "were passionately fond of the Union; there were dear associations which made them love the Union . . . to the end of time." Disunion simply could not happen, since it would mean that the American people must "bring themselves to split from each other." Surely, said Underwood, "God never intended that this separation should take place." Therefore, "all the fury, madness, and . . . crime, in any portion of the Union, could not so far get the better of the good sense of this people as to allow this state of things to come to pass." [16]

A summary of this phase of Union appeal would be incomplete without at least one instance contributed by Daniel Webster, who often proclaimed that public sentiment made Union impregnable. Expressing pain that any state should even talk of taking "one stripe and one star and walk out of the Union with them," Webster anticipated what H. W. Bellows called "unexpected correctives," and predicted that somehow "patriotism and propriety" would return. "I cannot persuade myself," confessed the orator, "that honest and honorable men, ingenuous men, young men who wish to live for glory, and renown, and character, will ever leave that Union which their fathers established . . . when they come to sober moments of reflection." The same yearning influenced Webster's senatorial successor, Charles Sumner. Despite any momentary delusion, said Sumner, none of the Union could become separated permanently "from its well-compacted bulk." He added: "E Pluribus Unum is stamped upon the national coin, the national territory, and the national heart." [17]

Unwaveringly, this sentiment moved into the Union's deadliest hours, bolstering the Absolute idea and aiding Abraham Lincoln's demand for Union's perpetuation. With the South grumbling over Frémont's candidacy, one hopeful observer still referred to disunion sentiment as sheer demagoguery. "Why talk about an event which can never happen?" asked Samuel A. Purviance of Pennsylvania. "This Union is bound together by an indissoluble tie, which like the Gordian knot, cannot be unloosed; and to cut it would be treason." He suggested that only the "rankest, foulest treason" would seek Union's dismemberment; there was so much glory in Union that "the spirits of the gallant veterans of the Revolution would haunt the wretch" who envisioned its danger. Purviance preferred the positive approach: "No, sir, this Union cannot be dissolved. . . . It is the monument of that indomitable energy and enterprise for which our people are everywhere distinguished. In a word," he continued, "it is the monument of the greatest good and the greatest glory which could be conferred upon any nation." So powerful was Union's appeal to the people that Purviance insisted, "there is a talismanic influence and charm in the very name of Union." It would even "hush the demagogue to silence." [18]

On the eve of war, claims for Union's invulnerability rarely varied. "This Union was formed to be perpetual; and it will live through coming time." It was a Union, "hallowed by every feeling of national and individual pride and honor." In 1860, disunion fears were ascribed as a mere Democratic electioneering device, to which the typical reply was, "the Union of these States forms no debatable topic. . . . Its existence is a fixed fact, and lies down amid the foundations of our political superstructure, firmly and irrevocably, as lie the mountains which encompass about, the very impress of Divine beneficence and power." [19] In a final campaign plea, Seward drew upon Americans everywhere. Any person who believed "that this Union . . . can be dissolved, has no faith," he said, neither faith in Union nor faith in the people of that Union. Disunionists lacked confidence in the people's loyalty, which meant "no faith in reason, no faith in justice, no faith in truth, no faith in virtue." All of these Seward endorsed as basic to belief in the Union and the People.[20]

Grounded upon reason and instinct, this concept seemed to guarantee that Americans would recognize their unity. Nevertheless, preferring its own design for Union, the South rejected the creed espoused by Seward. Ensuing violence exposed the fragile quality of Union's theory. While a stern reply to disunion may have established Union in fact, it made revision in Union ideology mandatory. America was now one nation indivisible, but only through force. Thus, as a casualty of civil war, Union ideology became the first Jeffersonian aspiration victimized by the technological revolution. Americans supposedly designed to exist in unison had been unable to do so. A complicated system of values was thereby overturned. But few remembered Seward's misgivings about enforced Union.

Momentarily deluded by this ironical triumph, America sought new inspiration in economic individualism. But just as technological change had overwhelmed the Seward philosophy, it obviously would make atomized society an even greater disappointment. Far from ending America's insecurity, the Civil War merely presaged a more complex uneasiness. Confronted by machine-wrought human interdependence, American thought slowly returned to the question from which it had recoiled after Appomattox. Despite the sorrow and disillusion of a crimsoned Union's malediction upon brotherhood in reason and spirit, a new generation found more compelling need to confess society's claim upon the individual. The ideals once implicit in Seward's Union reappeared to challenge a modern America tortured by renewed doubt.

Notes

PREFACE

1. An exception is the published doctoral thesis by Dorothy Leeds Werner, *The Idea of Union in American Verse* (Phila., 1932), hereafter cited as Werner. This study is limited both in scope and interpretation. Helpful general studies are Merle Curti, *The Roots of American Loyalty* (N.Y., 1946), hereafter cited as Curti, *Roots;* Ralph H. Gabriel, *The Course of American Democratic Thought* (N.Y., 1956), hereafter cited as Gabriel; and Hans Kohn, *American Nationalism* (N.Y., 1957), hereafter cited as Kohn. Other work to which I am greatly indebted includes Henry Nash Smith, *Virgin Land, the American West as Symbol and Myth* (Cambridge, 1950), hereafter cited as Smith, *Virgin Land;* Max Lerner, "Constitution and Court as Symbols," *Yale Law Journal*, XLVI (1937), 1290-1319, hereafter cited as Lerner; Frank I. Schechter, "The Early History of the Tradition of the Constitution," *American Political Science Review*, IX (1915), 707-34, hereafter cited as Schechter; John William Ward, *Andrew Jackson, Symbol for an Age* (N.Y., 1955); Merrill D. Peterson, *The Jefferson Image in the American Mind* (N.Y., 1960), hereafter cited as Peterson. My guide has been Professor Louis Hartz's comment: "The task of the cultural analyst is not to discover simplicity or even to discover unity, for simplicity and unity do not exist, but to drive a wedge of rationality through the pathetic indecisions of social thought." Louis Hartz, *The Liberal Tradition in America* (N.Y., 1955), p. 63. Hereafter cited as Hartz.

2. Andrew C. McLaughlin, "Social Compact and Constitutional Construction," *American Historical Review*, V (April, 1900), 489. Hereafter cited as McLaughlin.

3. Professor Clinton Rossiter has said that "The American thinks highly of two essential conditions of the stable community: unity and loyalty,"

and he "has almost always put a higher call on *unum* than on *e pluribus.*" Clinton Rossiter, *Conservatism in America* (N.Y., 1955), p. 72. While Professor Kohn contends that American sentiment generally resisted the glorification of unity (Kohn, p. 128), I am convinced that the reverse is true.

PROLOGUE

1. *Writings and Speeches of Daniel Webster*, XIII (Boston, 1903), 432-3, 28 June 1851. Hereafter cited as *Webster*.
2. Howard Mumford Jones, *Ideas in America* (Cambridge, 1944), p. 30.
3. Hampton L. Carson, ed., *History of the Celebration of the Hundredth Anniversary of the Promulgation of the Constitution of the United States,* I (Phila., 1889), 439-67. Carson shows that early plans for union sought the well-being of both colonies and England. See also, Charles H. McIlwain, "The Historical Background of Federal Governments," in Roscoe Pound, *et al., Federalism as a Democratic Process* (New Brunswick, 1942), pp. 31-48, especially p. 47; Bernard Bailyn, "Political Experience and Enlightenment Ideas in Eighteenth-Century America, *American Historical Review,* LXVII (Jan. 1962), 351; Max Savelle, "Nationalism and Other Loyalties in the American Revolution," *American Historical Review,* LXVII (July 1962), 901-23.
4. *Niles' Weekly Register,* XII (7 June 1817), 228-30. Hereafter cited as *Niles'.* A search through the pages of the Charleston *Courier* for 1815 gives no clue to the orator's identity. The paper published notices of monthly meetings of the Literary and Philosophical Society of South Carolina, but offered no information as to participants in programs. The Society did advertise a special anniversary session for 10 May 1815, but posted no slate of speakers. Charleston *Courier,* 10 May 1815.
5. *Webster,* II, 80.
6. *Congressional Globe,* 36 Cong., 2 Sess., Appendix, 87. 23 Jan. 1861. Hereafter cited as *Globe.*

CHAPTER 1

1. Richard Frothingham, *The Rise of the Republic of the United States* (Boston, 1890), pp. 29-30. Hereafter cited as Frothingham.
2. William T. Hutchinson, "Unite to Divide: Divide to Unite: The Shaping of American Federalism," *Mississippi Valley Historical Review,* XLVI (June 1959), 5.
3. Jonathan Elliot, ed., *The Debates in the Several States On the Adoption of the Federal Constitution,* I (Phila., 1836), 69-70. Hereafter cited as Elliot.
4. John C. Fitzpatrick, ed., *The Writings of George Washington,* XXVI (Washington, 1931-44), 275. 31 March 1783. Hereafter cited as Washington.
5. Julien P. Boyd, ed., *The Papers of Thomas Jefferson,* VII (Princeton, 1950-), 356. To Madison, 1 July 1784. Hereafter cited as Boyd, *Jefferson.*

6. *Washington,* XXVIII, 328. To David Stuart, 30 Nov. 1785. Also, 336, 30 Nov. 1785.

7. Charles R. King, ed., *The Life and Correspondence of Rufus King,* I (N.Y., 1894-1900), 134-5. To Elbridge Gerry, 30 April 1786. Hereafter cited as *King.*

8. J. Franklin Jameson, ed., *Letters of Stephen Higginson* (Washington, 1897), p. 760. To Nathan Dane, 16 June 1787. Hereafter cited as *Higginson.*

9. Elliot, I, 487, 490. Governor Edmund Randolph to Speaker of Virginia House of Delegates, 10 Oct. 1787. See 482-91 for this curious letter.

10. Elliot, II, 527. 11 Dec. 1787.

11. Max Farrand, ed., *The Records of the Federal Convention,* III (New Haven, 1911-37), 146. 29 Nov. 1787. Hereafter cited as Farrand.

12. James C. Ballagh, ed., *The Letters of Richard Henry Lee,* II (N.Y., 1911-14), 463. To James Gordon, Jr., 26 Feb. 1788. Hereafter cited as *Lee.*

13. Farrand, I, 33, 38. Robert Yates's notes for 30 May 1787 and Madison's report.

14. Henry M. Johnston, ed., *The Correspondence and Public Papers of John Jay,* III (N.Y., 1890-93), 248-9. 4 July 1787. Hereafter cited as *Jay.*

15. *The Federalist* (Modern Library edition), pp. 46 and 86. Hereafter cited as *Federalist.* For interpretations of the Union seen as means, see Paul C. Nagel, "Democratic Thought and the Symbol of the Union: Early Phases," *Mississippi Quarterly,* XII (Spring 1959); and Gottfried Dietze, *The Federalist* (Baltimore, 1960), p. 35.

16. Elliot, III, 144; II, 124.

17. Henry Cabot Lodge, ed., *The Works of Alexander Hamilton,* II (N.Y., 1904), 28. 21 June 1788. Hereafter cited as *Hamilton.*

18. *Annals of the Congress of the United States,* 1 Cong., 1 Sess., (Washington, 1834), 774. 22 Aug. 1789. Hereafter cited as *Annals.*

19. Gaillard Hunt, ed., *The Writings of James Madison,* VI (N.Y., 1900), 104-105. From *The National Gazette,* 2 April 1792. Hereafter cited as *Madison.*

20. *Washington,* XXXV, 221-2.

21. George E. Baker, ed., *The Works of William H. Seward,* IV (N.Y., 1853-61), 274. Detroit speech of 2 Oct. 1856. Hereafter cited as *Seward.*

22. Edmund Quincy, *Life of Josiah Quincy* (Boston, 1869), p. 212. Speech delivered 14 Jan. 1811. Hereafter cited as Quincy, *Life.*

23. Henry Adams, *Documents Relating to New England Federalism* (Boston, 1877), 389. From a letter to Edward Pennington, 12 July 1812. Hereafter cited as Adams, *Documents.*

24. Quincy, *Life,* p. 349, Randolph to Quincy, 29 Jan. 1814; *Annals,* 18 Cong., 1 Sess., House, 2368. 15 April 1824.

25. *Webster,* XIV, 69. House speech on the Conscription Bill, 9 Dec. 1814.

26. *Annals,* 16 Cong., 1 Sess., Senate, 408.

27. *Niles'*, VI (9 Oct. 1814), 306. The writer was former N.Y. Congressman Gardiner.
28. Richard K. Crallé, ed., *The Works of John C. Calhoun*, VI (N.Y. 1853-55), 83. Hereafter cited as *Calhoun*.
29. *Webster*, VI, 74-5.
30. *Webster*, V, 258.
31. Joseph Story, *Commentaries on the Constitution of the United States*, I (Boston, 1833), 491, hereafter cited as Story, *Commentaries; Globe*, 31 Cong., 1 Sess., Appendix, House, 843, 5 June 1850.
32. *The New Englander*, VIII (May, 1850, New Haven), 293-4.
33. *Webster*, XII, 239. To G. W. Warren, chairman of the Bunker Hill Committee, 13 June 1850.
34. *North American Review*, LXXIII (Oct. 1851), 380, 385. The writer was Elizabeth Peabody.
35. Roy P. Basler, ed., *The Collected Works of Abraham Lincoln*, I (New Brunswick, 1953), 348. Hereafter cited as *Lincoln*.
36. Charles Eliot Norton, ed., *Orations and Addresses of George William Curtis*, I (N.Y., 1894), 73, 79, 90-91. An oration entitled "The Present Aspect of the Slavery Question," Oct. 1859. Hereafter cited as *Curtis*.
37. Three distinguished historians with varying points of departure have emphasized the ease and frequency with which Union's dissolution was once approached. Hermann von Holst, *The Constitutional and Political History of the United States*, I (Chicago, 1872-92), 77, hereafter cited as von Holst; Samuel Eliot Morison, *The Life and Letters of Harrison Gray Otis*, I (Boston, 1913), 267, f.n. 9, hereafter cited as *Otis;* Merrill Jensen, *The Articles of Confederation* (Madison, 1940), pp. 116-17, hereafter cited as Jensen.
38. Adams, *Documents*, p. 382. Hanson to Pickering, 17 Jan. 1810.
39. Charles Francis Adams, ed., *Memoirs of John Quincy Adams*, IV (Phila., 1874), 530-31, 24 Feb. 1820; V. 4, 12, 14, 3 and 5 March 1820. Hereafter cited as Adams, *Memoirs*.
40. *King*, VI, 342. Goldsborough to Rufus King, 30 May 1820.
41. *Niles'*, XXXIII (8 Sept. 1827), 32. Cooper's speech was delivered on 2 July 1827.
42. *Niles'*, XLIII (29 Sept. 1832), 97; Calvin Colton, ed., *The Private Correspondence of Henry Clay* (Cincinnati, 1856), p. 344, Southard to Clay, 1 Dec. 1832, hereafter cited as Clay, *Corr.*
43. *Webster*, VIII, 235. Second Sub-Treasury speech, 12 March 1838.
44. *Seward*, III, 18-20, 22. This oration, entitled, "The True Greatness of Our Country," was delivered at several places during 1844. It discloses Seward's continuing fear of an East-West split.
45. *King*, I, 158-60. Benjamin Lincoln to Rufus King, 11 Feb. 1786.
46. Paul L. Ford, ed., *Essays on the Constitution* (Brooklyn, 1892), p. 256. Clinton wrote as "Cato, III" in the New York *Journal*, 25 Oct. 1787;

   Hamilton, IX, 431, to Madison, 19 May 1788; see also 492, to Gouverneur Morris, 19 May 1788. Ford hereafter cited as *Essays*.

47. Elliot, II, 334-5, 27 June 1788; Henry Cabot Lodge, *Life and Letters of George Cabot* (Boston, 1877), p. 339, Pickering to Cabot, 29 Jan. 1799. Hereafter cited as *Cabot*.

48. *Niles'*, VII, 197.

49. Edward W. Emerson and Waldo E. Forbes, eds., *Journals of Ralph Waldo Emerson*, V (Boston, 1909-14), 328-9, entry for 15 Nov. 1839; VIII, 199. Hereafter cited as Emerson, *Journals*.

50. Edmund C. Burnett, *Letters of Members of the Continental Congress*, VII (Washington, 1921-36), 414-15. Osgood to John Adams, 14 Jan. 1784. Hereafter cited as Burnett.

51. Burnett, VIII, 305-06, Nathan Dane to Samuel Adams, 11 Feb. 1786; Lyman H. Butterfield, ed., *Letters of Benjamin Rush*, I (Princeton, 1951), 408, to Richard Price, 22 Oct. 1788. Hereafter cited as *Rush*.

52. *Washington*, XXVIII, 502, to John Jay, 1 Aug. 1786; XXIX, 152-3, to Henry Knox, 3 Feb. 1787.

53. *Washington*, XXIX, 176. To John Jay, 10 March 1787.

54. Charles Francis Adams, ed., *The Works of John Adams*, VIII (Boston, 1847-56), 439. To John Jay, 8 May 1787. Hereafter cited as *John Adams*.

55. Farrand, III, 302-03. Pierce Butler to Weldon Butler, 5 May 1788.

56. *Madison*, V, 373 f.n., 31 May 1789. The controversial issue of the Union's seat carried much concern for the Experiment. See *Annals*, 1 Cong., 1 Sess., House, 786ff.

57. George Gibbs, ed., *Memoirs of the Administrations of Washington and Adams Edited from the Papers of Oliver Wolcott*, I (N.Y., 1846), 28. Letter to his father, 2 Dec. 1789. Hereafter cited as *Wolcott*.

58. Timothy Dwight, *Travels in New England and New York*, IV (London, 1823), 513. Hereafter cited as Dwight.

59. *Wolcott*, I, 385. 3 Oct. 1796.

60. *Washington*, XXXV, 222-3. Washington here expressed an idea so popular later—that only the traitorous, the foolish, or the irreverent criticized Union.

61. *Annals*, 7 Cong., 1 Sess., House, 386. 5 Jan. 1802.

62. Paul Leicester Ford, ed., *The Works of Thomas Jefferson*, X (N.Y., 1904), 7. 29 Jan. 1804. Hereafter cited as Ford, *Jefferson*.

63. Seth Ames, ed., *Works of Fisher Ames*, II (Boston, 1854), 251. Hereafter cited as Ames. Certainly New England's uneasiness was an expression of experimentalist sentiment. The Salem *Gazette* put it clearly on 2 July 1812: "We suppose no person of observation had believed that the Union, in its present extent, would last for ages." Hervey Putnam Prentiss, *Timothy Pickering* (Essex Institute, 1933-4), p. 90.

64. *King*, VI, 287. From Richard Peters, a Pennsylvania jurist, 29 Feb. 1820.

65. Ford, *Jefferson*, XII, 159-60. To John Holmes, 22 April 1820. For a moving

appeal to reason, see *Register of Debates in Congress*, 20 Cong., 2 Sess., House, 247, 21 Jan. 1829. Hereafter cited as *Register*.

66. Clay, *Corr.*, pp. 347 and 383. Letters to Francis Brooke, 17 Jan. 1833 and 23 March 1834.

67. James Fenimore Cooper, *Notions of the Americans*, II (Phila., 1828), 153-4. Hereafter cited as Cooper.

68. *Democratic Review*, XXXVII (Jan. 1856), 1-2.

69. Charles Eliot Norton, ed., *Letters of James Russell Lowell*, I (N.Y., 1894), 307-08. To Charles Nordhoff, 31 Dec. 1860. Hereafter cited as *Lowell Letters*.

70. Wendell Phillips, *Speeches, Lectures, and Letters* (Boston, 1863), p. 351. Hereafter cited as Phillips.

CHAPTER 2

1. Useful insights into the political character of Union ideology are: McLaughlin, 467-90; Curti, *Roots*, passim; Gabriel; Lerner; Schechter; Charles M. Wiltse, "From Compact to National State in American Political Thought," *Essays in Political Theory Presented to George H. Sabine* (M. R. Konvitz and A. E. Murphy, eds., Ithaca, 1948); and Charles E. Merriam, *A History of American Political Theories* (N.Y., 1913), Chap. VII. The last is an excellent summation, although Merriam, like Curti, places the development of an organic concept rather too late. Another interesting effort is that of William W. Crosskey, *Politics and the Constitution in the History of the United States* (Chicago, 1953). See also Merle Curti, "Francis Lieber and Nationalism," *The Huntington Library Quarterly*, IV (April 1941), 290.

2. *Madison*, IX, 572, from essay, "sovereignty," 1835; IX, 573-607, in "Notes on Nullification."

3. *Annals*, 8 Cong., 1 Sess., House, 522-4. 8 Oct. 1803.

4. *Annals*, 13 Cong., 1 Sess., House, 333-41, especially 333 and 338, 15 Jan. 1813; *Annals*, 15 Cong., 1 Sess., House, 1091, 2 March 1818.

5. *Madison*, III, 210, from Journal for 19 June 1787; IX, 65, 29 June 1821; IX, 283, 13 March 1827.

6. *Madison*, IX, 347; 355-6 f.n. 15 Feb. 1830.

7. John Taylor, *An Inquiry Into the Principles and Policy of the Government of the United States* (Fredericksburg, 1814), p. 514. Hereafter cited as Taylor, *Inquiry*.

8. John Spencer Bassett, ed., *Correspondence of Andrew Jackson*, III (Washington, 1926-35), 187, 8 Feb. 1823, hereafter cited as *Jackson; Jackson*, IV, 504-05. 23 Dec. 1832.

9. *Register*, 19 Cong., 1 Sess., Senate, 426. 10 April 1826.

10. James D. Richardson, ed., *A Compilation of the Messages and Papers of the Presidents*, 1789-1907, IV (Washington, 1908), 336. Tyler's fourth message. Hereafter cited as Richardson.

11. *Seward*, II, 503, 509. 3 May and 8 June 1841.
12. *Webster*, VI, 57. Second speech on Foot's resolution. Webster had used these exchanges to attack the compact Union, esp. 77-80. An interesting essay in the *North American Review* of 1833 condemned Webster's concept of Union as emerging from fundamental law. The writer said that compact had to come before law, XXXVII, 215-45. Here compact and organic ideas converged early. It is a mistake, I think, to dismiss Webster as a legalist or contractualist, as does Curti in *Roots*, p. 175.
13. Randolph G. Adams, ed., *Selected Political Essays of James Wilson* (N.Y., 1930), p. 132. From Wilson's 1785 opinion, "Considerations on the Power to Incorporate the Bank of North America."
14. Farrand, II, 335.
15. *Hamilton*, II, 203, 209. Speech to N.Y. Legislature, 1787.
16. *North American Review*, XXI (July 1825), 128-38.
17. Alexis DeTocqueville, *Democracy in America*, I (N.Y., 1953, Phillips Bradley edition), 145-6. Hereafter cited as Tocqueville.
18. Clay, *Corr.*, pp. 311-13. 7 Sept. 1831. For interesting observations on the nature of a compact Union, see James Bayard, *A Brief Exposition of the Constitution of the United States* (Phila., 1834), pp. 41, 161. Hereafter cited as Bayard.
19. *Webster*, VI, 193, 211, 238. 16 Feb. 1833.
20. *Globe*, 28 Cong., 2 Sess., Appendix, House, 197. 25 Jan. 1845.
21. Richardson, V, 212-13. 5 Dec. 1853.
22. Edward D. Mansfield, *The Political Grammar of the United States* (Cincinnati, 1848), pp. 41-2, 203. Hereafter cited as Mansfield.
23. *Curtis*, I, 30, 33.
24. Dwight L. Dumond, ed., *Southern Editorials on Secession* (N.Y., 1931), the *Bee* of 15 Jan. and 22 Jan. 1861. Hereafter cited as Dumond.
25. *Globe*, 36 Cong., 2 Sess., 367, 369. 14 Jan. 1861.
26. Controversy over this matter continues. For one phase see *William and Mary Quarterly*, XIV and XV (1957-58), for an exchange between Max Saville and Irving Brant. In discussing work by Edmund Morgan, Saville insists that Morgan is wrong in believing that there was an early conscious sense of Union, of oneness among the new states. Defending Morgan, Brant asserts that for years he has noted the bountiful evidence suggesting the presence of Union throughout the Revolutionary period. See 609-18 and 137-9. I agree with Morgan and Brant that the evidence makes the Declaration of Independence a deliberate act of Union. See also Wesley Frank Craven, *The Legend of the Founding Fathers* (N.Y., 1956), pp. 59-63, for another concurring opinion. Professor Merrill Jensen also offers an interesting contribution by contending that Union was a means for colonial radicals who sought independence. Once independence was achieved, the conservative defenders of property became unionists as the means of achieving their end. Jensen, pp. 161-75.

27. Boyd, *Jefferson*, I, 269. To John Randolph, 29 Nov. 1775. A few sentences later, however, Jefferson comments: "There is not in the British empire a man who more cordially loves a Union with Gr. Britain than I do." Here appears the struggle between the union of the Atlantic community and the need for continental union. See also Jefferson's "Notes of Proceedings in the Continental Congress," I, 310.

28. Boyd, *Jefferson*, I, 326; Burnett, III, 114, Henry Laurens to Samuel Adams, 7 March 1778.

29. *Washington*, XXVI, 487-8. 8 June 1783. At one point Washington argued that only Union stood between the people and "a state of Nature." The latter for Washington was the certain road to tyranny. 489.

30. Burnett, VII, 224-5. Peters to Oliver Wolcott, 15 July 1783.

31. Farrand, III, 56off. See esp. 585.

32. Farrand, I, 129. 5 June 1787.

33. *Federalist* #2, pp. 9-10; see also 45, 303.

34. *Washington*, XXIX, 465; XXXII, 212; XXXV, 223-4.

35. Henry Wheaton, *Some Account of the Life, Writings, and Speeches of William Pinkney* (N.Y., 1826), pp. 550-51. Hereafter cited as *Pinkney*.

36. *Whig Review*, VI (Oct. 1847), 374-5.

37. *Pinkney*, p. 615.

38. William Rawle, *A View of the Constitution of the United States of America* (Phila., 1829, 2nd edition), p. 295. Hereafter cited as Rawle. Even so, Rawle remained at heart a states rights man, believing that should citizens of a state "determine to retire from the Union," federal intervention was unthinkable.

39. *Lincoln*, IV, 195-6. Bates House speech, 11 Feb. 1861. Lincoln's view was, of course, widely accepted in post-Civil war studies of Union's polity. Most notable here was von Holst, esp. I, 4ff. Frothingham says that the Declaration was Union's moment of birth as a concept, it was "a convenant of country in which the people recognized the providential development of Union. This Union had already been consecrated by precious blood and revered memories." The Declaration also "established Union as a fundamental law." In effect, "the transcendent fact of Union was now joined to the fact of a Republic. The Union was the country." See pp. 554ff.

40. Richardson, II, 643-4. 10 Dec. 1832. Jackson did not disguise his impatience with hair-splitting over Union's political guise, see esp. 648 and 650.

41. *Niles'*, XL (19 Jan. 1833), 351.

42. Everett wrote in the *North American Review*, XXXVI (Jan. 1833), 268-9; and in XXXIX (July 1834), 214-15.

43. *Webster*, XIII, 484. 23 Feb. 1852.

44. John Quincy Adams, *An Oration . . . On the Fourth of July 1831* (Boston, 1831), pp. 6, 17-18, 21-35 passim. Hereafter cited as Adams, *Oration*.

45. John Quincy Adams, *The Jubilee of the Constitution* (N.Y., 1839), pp. 10-17, 44ff. Hereafter cited as Adams, *Jubilee*.

46. *Calhoun*, VI, 106-08. Report of 1831.

47. *Calhoun*, VI, 116-17, 123, 136.

48. *Register*, 22 Cong., 1 Sess., House, 3349, 3353. 8 June 1832.

49. Rev. James Craik, *The Union National and State Sovereignty Alike Essential to American Liberty* (Louisville, 1860), pp. 34, 21. Hereafter cited as Craik.

50. *Lincoln*, IV, 265.

51. *Washington*, XXIX, 50. To Rev. William Gordon, 8 July 1783.

52. Elliot, I, 78. From Jefferson's notes, 1 Aug. 1777. Wilson admitted that laying aside state "individuality" for the citizen fraternity would potentially threaten the minority. But Wilson believed there was no earthly assembly where this danger could be prevented. Merrill Jensen records Wilson's early efforts to give heroic proportion to the idea of Union. Jensen, esp. p. 176. See also *Madison*, III, Journal, 221-2. King's speech was delivered on 19 June 1787.

53. *Madison*, V, 19, letter to Jefferson, 24 Oct. 1787; *Federalist* #39, pp. 245-7.

54. Elliot, II, 444, 425.

55. Emerson, *Journals*, VIII, 203. 1851 entry.

56. Griffith J. McRea, *Life and Correspondence of James Iredell*, II (N.Y., 1857), 484-5. 23 May 1796. Hereafter cited as *Iredell*.

57. Ames, I, 275. To John Ward Fenno, urging him to follow his father's editorial example, Feb. 1800.

58 *Annals*, 18 Cong., 1 Sess., House, 855. 22 Dec. 1823.

59. *Register,* 19 Cong., 1 Sess., House, 1375-6. 15 Feb. 1826.

60. *Annals*, 16 Cong., 2 Sess., Senate, 390. 15 Feb. 1820.

61. William W. Story, ed., *Life and Letters of Joseph Story*, II (Boston, 1851), 49-50. 13 Feb. 1831. Hereafter cited as Story, *Letters*.

62. Tocqueville, I, 158; J. P. Mayer, ed., Tocqueville, *Journey to America* (New Haven, 1960), pp. 246-7. Hereafter cited as Tocqueville, *Journey*.

63. *Niles'*, XLIII (19 Jan. 1833), 351.

64. *Webster*, XIV, 169, Senate speech, 26 Feb. 1833; II, 171, 12 Oct. 1835.

65. *American Quarterly Review*, XII (March 1833), 228-9.

66. *Whig Review*, X (Sept. 1849), 297-9. Author was H. W. Simms.

67. *Lincoln*, IV, 269, First Inaugural Address. See Harry V. Jaffa, *Crisis of the House Divided* (Garden City, 1959), p. 228, for useful comments on Lincoln's glimpse of a Union of people.

68. *Globe*, 36 Cong., 1 Sess., House, 174. 17 Dec. 1859, Congressman Larrabee.

69. George Ticknor Curtis, *History of the Origin, Formation, and Adoption of the Constitution of the United States*, II (N.Y., 1854), 123, hereafter cited as Curtis, *History;* Craik, p. 28.

70. *Globe,* 31 Cong., 1 Sess., Senate, 462. Helpful with the symbolical role of the Constitution are Edward Corwin, "Constitution as Instrument and Symbol," *The American Political Science Review,* XXX (1936), 1071-85; Carl Brent Swisher, *The Growth of Constitutional Power in the United States* (Chicago, 1946), esp. pp. 12-14; Lerner; and Schechter. None of these, however, finds it necessary to explore the Constitution's role in the Union's political version.

71. *Jay,* III, 315-16; *Madison,* V, 108, letter of 21 Feb. 1788. Patrick Henry was often described as leader of the disunion forces.

72. *Annals,* 1 Cong., 1 Sess., House, 514, 792-5.

73. *Annals,* 4 Cong., 2 Sess., Senate, 1581, special session, 4 March 1797.

74. *Madison,* VIII, 49, 4 March 1809. See also James Kirk Paulding, *Letters from the South,* I (N.Y., 1817), 212. Hereafter cited as Paulding.

75. *Annals,* 16 Cong., 1 Sess., House, 1008. 28 Jan. 1820.

76. *Niles',* XXIX (26 Nov. 1825), 207-08, Troup's message of 8 Nov. 1825; *Niles',* XXXIII (8 Dec. 1827), 232.

77. *Niles',* XXXVIII, 380 for reprint of Charleston *Mercury,* 5 July 1830; see also 392 and Calhoun's letter to Christopher Van Deventer in J. Franklin Jameson, ed., *Correspondence of John C. Calhoun* (Washington, 1900), 296-7, 5 Aug. 1831. Hereafter cited as *Calhoun Correspondence.*

78. Story, *Commentaries,* I, 2, 450.

79. *Webster,* XIII, 55, Concord, N.H. speech, October 1834; VIII, 237, second Sub-Treasury Speech, 12 March 1838; II, 265, 24 July 1838.

80. *Niles',* XLVIII (29 Aug. 1835), 455. Niles printed many descriptions of anti-abolitionist gatherings in the North, see passim.

81. *Globe,* 24 Cong., 1 Sess., Senate, 77. 7 Jan. 1836.

82. *Southern Quarterly Review,* VII (April 1845), 516; *Calhoun Correspondence,* 1139 and also 1157; *Democratic Review,* XXIII (Sept. 1848), 219.

83. *Globe,* 31 Cong., 1 Sess., Senate, 484; *Webster,* XII, 237-8.

84. *Webster,* XVIII, 424, 21 March 1851; XIII, 434, 437, 28 June 1851.

85. *Webster,* X, 394; XII, 260-61.

86. Rowland Dunbar, ed., *Jefferson Davis, Constitutionalist, His Letters, Papers and Speeches,* I (Jackson, 1923), 252, 579, 1 Jan. and 10 Nov. 1850; II, 237, July 1853; III, 327, 11 Oct, 1858. Hereafter cited as *Davis.*

87. *Whig Review,* XII (Dec. 1850), 556-60, "Plain Words for the North;" *Democratic Review,* XXXVII (June 1856), 435.

88. *Lincoln,* III, 103, 15 Sept. 1858. See also Jaffa, *Crisis,* for comments on Douglas's grasp of Union as polity, p. 330. Lincoln's views follow a curious development. Jaffa says that he denied that Union existed solely or mainly by virtue of the Constitution. But in his Galena speech of 23 July 1856, Lincoln pleaded that the Supreme Court be allowed to decide if slavery restriction was unconstitutional. If it so decided, it was certainly not legal. Meantime, said Lincoln, let both sides stop talking of disunion and await the Court's verdict. *Lincoln,* II, 355.

89. *Globe*, 34 Cong., 1 Sess., Appendix, House, 399, 9 April 1856; 36 Cong., 1 Sess., House, 45, 7 Dec. 1859.

90. Paul Leicester Ford, ed., *Pamphlets on the Constitution of the United States* (Brooklyn, 1888), p. 17. Gerry's "Observations on the new Constitution" by "A Columbian Patriot," Boston, 1788. Hereafter cited as Ford, *Pamphlets*.

91. *Annals,* 1 Cong., 2 Sess., House, 1325, 23 Feb. 1790; *John Adams,* IX, 573, to John Trumbull, 23 Jan. 1791.

92. Worthington C. Ford, ed., *Writings of John Quincy Adams,* IV (N.Y., 1913-7), 267, to John Adams, 31 Oct. 1811, hereafter cited as J. Q. Adams, *Writings;* Ames, p. 41, 23 Feb. 1809.

93. *Annals,* 10 Cong., 1 Sess., House, 892.

94. John Taylor, *Tyranny Unmasked* (Washington, 1822), p. 339, and also pp. 324-5. Hereafter cited as Taylor, *Tyranny.*

95. *Pinkney,* pp. 165-6; *Calhoun,* I, "Discourse," 239.

96. *Jackson,* III, 253, letter of 15 May 1824 to J. W. Lanier; Richardson, II, 488, 491, 27 May 1830.

97. Richardson, IV, 16.

98. *Webster,* III, 209, 223-4. 22 Dec. 1843.

99. Tocqueville, I, 59, 167-9.

100. *North American Review,* XXXVI (Jan., 1833), 230, 249. Alexander H. Everett.

101. *Whig Review,* X (July 1849), 47; and (Sept. 1849), 295.

102. Craik, pp. 16, 22-3.

103. Ford, *Jefferson,* VIII, 458ff.

104. Richardson, II, 148-50. 4 May 1822. Monroe's discourse was sent to Congress immediately following his veto of a bill for repairing and maintaining the Cumberland Road. Now Monroe moved closer to the view that Union was essentially a spirit.

105. *Calhoun,* VI, 98. Report prepared for the South Carolina Legislature's Committee on Federal Relations, Nov. 1831.

106. Herman V. Ames, *State Documents on Federal Relations* (Phila., 1900), p. 175, hereafter cited as Ames, *Documents; Calhoun Correspondence,* pp. 317-18.

107. *Democratic Review,* XIII (Nov. 1843), 546; XV (Sept. 1844), 320.

108. *Southern Quarterly Review,* VII (April 1845), 474.

109. Richardson, V, 249. Veto message of 3 May 1854.

110. *Globe,* 35 Cong., 1 Sess., Appendix, Senate, 167. During the Lecompton debates, 20 March 1858.

111. *Davis,* III, 276-8. Portland, Maine, 9 July 1858.

112. *Globe,* 36 Cong., 1 Sess., Senate, 917. 29 Feb. 1860.

113. Ames, *Documents,* p. 53. 11 Jan. 1811.

114. *Annals,* 18 Cong., 1 Sess., Senate, 201-02. 3 Feb. 1824.

115. *Register,* 19 Cong., 1 Sess., 1493, 1499, 2 March 1826; 1537, 1541, 6 March 1826.
116. George W. Pierson, *Tocqueville and Beaumont in America* (N.Y., 1938), p. 559. Hereafter cited as Pierson.
117. Reprinted by *Niles',* XL (26 March 1831), 69. Niles scoffed at this by pointing to the Preamble's reference to "We, the people" rather than we, the states.
118. Rawle, pp. 297, 302.

CHAPTER 3

1. Von Holst, I, 15-6, 25. For another glimpse of this complex guise, see Charles E. Merriam, *The Written Constitution and the Unwritten Attitude* (N.Y., 1931), p. 30.
2. *Washington,* XXVIII, 183-4, to George W. Fairfax, 30 June 1785; XXXIV, 60, f.n. 50.
3. Boyd, *Jefferson,* VI. 20 Feb. 1784.
4. *Washington,* XXIX, 465; XXXI, 28; XXXII, 133.
5. James DeWitt Andrews, ed., *The Works of James Wilson,* I (Chicago, 1896), 315-7. Hereafter cited as *Wilson.*
6. John Bassett Moore, ed., *The Works of James Buchanan,* VIII (Phila., 1909), 392. 19 Nov. 1850. Hereafter cited as *Buchanan.*
7. Werner, p. 13.
8. Elliot, I, 70-78 passim. As reported by Jefferson.
9. Elliot, III, 38. Pendleton's 5 June 1788 speech at the Virginia convention.
10. *Annals,* 1 Cong., 1 Sess., House, 107-09. 9 April 1789.
11. *Annals,* 1 Cong., 1 Sess., 225; *Madison,* VI, 68, "Consolidation" from *National Gazette,* 5 Dec. 1791.
12. *Annals,* 12 Cong., 1 Sess., House, 965-8. 25 June 1812.
13. Robert Y. Hayne, *An Oration . . . On . . . the 4th of July, 1814* (Charleston, 1814), p. 6.
14. Ford, *Jefferson,* XI, 461. To Lafayette, 14 Feb. 1815.
15. Henry Adams, ed., *The Writings of Albert Gallatin,* I (Phila., 1879), 700. To Matthew Lyon, 7 May 1816. Hereafter cited as *Gallatin.*
16. *Annals,* 15 Cong., 1 Sess., House, 1358-9, 13 March 1818; *Annals,* 15 Cong., 2 Sess., House, 1189-90; *Annals,* 16 Cong., 1 Sess., 1241.
17. *Niles',* XVI (3 April 1819), 106. Niles felt the widening veneration for Washington's memory augured well for a speedy triumph of the Spirit Union.
18. *American State Papers, Finance,* III, 579. Petition of Roanoke Agricultural Society, Mecklenburg County, Virginia.
19. *North American Review,* XXII (April 1826), 374, by Edward Everett; *American State Papers, Finance,* IV, 474, 30 Jan. 1824, an anti-tariff petition from the New York Chamber of Commerce.
20. *Annals,* 18 Cong., 1 Sess., House, 1387-8. 4-5 Feb. 1824.

21. *Webster*, I, 254. Bunker Hill Speech of 1825.

22. It was gratifying to have these conclusions confirmed by Professor Merrill Peterson. See Peterson, pp. 5-8.

23. Ford, *Jefferson*, XII, 350-1. 4 April 1824. See also *American Quarterly Review*, I (March-June 1827), 179. This Philadelphia journal began its career by calling for the Supreme Court to embody the Union spirit.

24. Reprinted in Charles M. Wiltse, *John C. Calhoun, Nullifier* (N.Y., 1949), p. 424, f.n. 45 to Chap. IV. Hammond's statement was printed in the first issue of *Southern Times*, 29 Jan. 1830.

25. *Register*, 21 Cong., 1 Sess., 90. Hayne's third speech, 27 Jan. 1830.

26. *Register*, 21 Cong., 1 Sess., Senate, 271. 15 March 1830.

27. Tocqueville, I, 166-7, 70; Pierson, p. 562.

28. William Ellery Channing, *The Works of William E. Channing, D.D.* (Boston, 1903), p. 805. Undated letter to Jonathan Phillips. Hereafter cited as Channing.

29. *Jackson*, V, 171-2, 208-09, Macon's letters dated 26 Aug. and 25 Sept. 1833; 177-8, 2 Sept. 1833.

30. John Greenleaf Whittier, "Justice and Expedience" (1833), as reprinted in Willard Thorpe, *et al.*, *American Issues*, I (N.Y., 1955), 460.

31. *North American Magazine*, IV (May 1834), 12. Published at Philadelphia.

32. *North American Review*, XLI (July 1835), 249-50.

33. *Webster*, VIII, 234-7. 12 March 1838.

34. Adams, *Jubilee*, pp. 69, 9.

35. Richardson, IV, 15.

36. *Globe*, 29 Cong., 2 Sess., 387-8, William F. Giles on 11 Feb. 1847; *Globe*, 30 Cong., 1 Sess., 66, 22 Dec. 1847.

37. Seward, III, 293, 26 Oct. 1848; IV, 123, 14 Sept. 1853.

38. Clay, *Corr.*, 593. To Leslie Combs, 22 Dec. 1849.

39. *Globe*, 30 Cong., 2 Sess., Appendix, House, 106-07, 10 Feb. 1849; *Globe*, 31 Cong., 1 Sess., 27-9.

40. George Bancroft, *Literary and Historical Miscellanies* (N.Y., 1857), p. 470. Hereafter cited as Bancroft, *Miscellanies*.

41. *Globe*, 31 Cong., 1 Sess., 203, 439. 22 Jan. and 28 Feb. 1850.

42. *Calhoun*, I, 395. From his "Discourse."

43. *Webster*, XIII, 389; XII, 242; X, 169; for an interesting endorsement, see Charles L. Woodbury, ed., *Writings of Levi Woodbury*, I (Boston, 1852), 592-3, hereafter cited as Woodbury.

44. Samuel Gilman Brown, ed., *The Works of Rufus Choate*, II (Boston, 1862), 313-5, 318, 326. 26 Nov. 1850. Hereafter cited as *Choate*.

45. *Globe*, 31 Cong., 1 Sess., House, 1702. 29 Aug. 1850.

46. Thomas Starr King, *Patriotism and Other Papers* (Boston, 1864), pp. 49-52. Hereafter cited as Thomas King.

47. *Davis*, II, 250. N.Y. speech, July 1853.

48. *Globe*, 33 Cong., 1 Sess., Appendix, House, 701. 9 May 1854. Cox was a Kentuckian. The Senate's Kansas-Nebraska debate displayed much less concern over its effect on the Spirit Union than did the House discussions. Perhaps this was because the Senate acted first, leaving the House confronted by rising public clamor.

49. *Lincoln*, II, 270-2, 276. 16 Oct. 1854.

50. John Greenleaf Whittier, *Works of John Greenleaf Whittier*, III (Boston, 1892), 202. Hereafter cited as Whittier.

51. *Choate*, II, 329-30. 31 Oct. 1855.

52. William Stickney, ed., *Autobiography of Amos Kendall* (Boston, 1872), p. 561. 7 Dec. 1856. Hereafter cited as *Kendall*.

53. *Lincoln*, III, 116 and 285.

54. *Globe*, 36 Cong., 1 Sess., House, 47-8. 7 Dec. 1859.

55. *Globe*, 36 Cong., 1 Sess., Appendix, Senate, 107-08; and House, 282. 31 Jan. 1860 and 2 May 1860.

56. Richardson, V, 636. Fourth annual message.

57. *Globe*, 36 Cong., 2 Sess., Senate, 29. 10 Dec. 1860.

58. *Lincoln*, IV, 271. See f.n. of 261-2 for Seward's suggestion that the inaugural message close with appeals to mystic chords and guardian angels.

59. *Seward*, I, 118. See also 89-91. Speeches of 11 March and 11 Sept. 1850.

60. Phillips, p. 316. "Lincoln's Election," 7 Nov. 1860.

61. Phillips, p. 317.

62. See Curti, *Roots*, for thoughts on the implication of commerce and industry for the evolving idea of Union. See esp. 111-7.

63. Boyd, *Jefferson*, I, 323-4, and passim; Burnett, III, 327.

64. Anon., *The Political Establishments of the United States of America* as reprinted in Crosskey, II, Appendix A, esp. 1186.

65. *Madison*, IV, "Journal," 264; Elliot, II, 142.

66. *Rush*, I, 473. To Elias Boudinot, 9 July 1788.

67. *Annals*, 11 Cong., 2 Sess., 1386-93. 8 Feb. 1810.

68. *Annals*, 12 Cong., 1 Sess., House, 950-52.

69. This memorial, 15 June 1813, was printed in *Annals*, 13 Cong., 1 Sess., 338-9.

70. *American State Papers, Finance*, III, 453, 10 Jan. 1820. See the fascinating anonymous pamphlet, *Plain Sense on National Industry* (N.Y., 1820), p. 42, for another expression.

71. N.Y. *Commercial Advertiser*, 11 Oct. 1823, as reprinted in *Niles'*, XXV (18 Oct. 1823), 103-110.

72. *Annals*, 17 Cong., 1 Sess., 1505, 1508. 9 April 1822.

73. *Register*, 19 Cong., 2 Sess., 947. 5 Feb. 1827.

74. Columbia *Telescope*, 2 July 1827, as reprinted in Dumas Malone, *Public Life of Thomas Cooper* (New Haven, 1926), p. 309. Hereafter cited as Malone, *Cooper*.

75. Robert J. Turnbull, *The Crisis* (Charleston, 1827), esp. pp. 9, 14, 148. Hereafter cited as Turnbull.

76. *Webster,* II, 46-7. Address of 10 March 1831.

77. Channing, p. 630.

78. Tocqueville, *Journey,* pp. 235-6. Entry dated 31 Jan. 1832.

79. Tocqueville, I, 164, 392, 406.

80. *American Quarterly Review,* XIX (March 1836), 164.

81. *Webster,* III, 206.

82. *Globe,* 28 Cong., 2 Sess., Appendix, House, 333. 11 Feb. 1845.

83. George Ticknor, *Life and Letters of George Ticknor,* II (Boston, 1876), 224. Hereafter cited as Ticknor.

84. Nahum Capen, *The Republic of the United States of America* (N.Y., 1848), pp. 19-20. Hereafter cited as Capen.

85. Joseph Bradley, *Progress—Its Grounds and Possibilities* (New Brunswick, 1849), pp. 14-15. Hereafter cited as Bradley.

86. *Globe,* 24 Cong., 1 Sess., Appendix, Senate, 226. 9 March 1836.

87. *Globe,* 31 Cong., 1 Sess., 29.

88. Richardson, V, 553-4. Buchanan's third message, 19 Dec. 1859.

89. *Globe,* 31 Cong., 1 Sess., Appendix, 1413. 22 July 1850.

90. Craven, *Legend,* p. 58.

91. Ames, I, 75-6, 80.

92. Richardson, I, 322-3.

93. Quincy, *Life,* p. 190. Letters from Desaussure, 21 Jan. 1809.

94. *Annals,* 12 Cong., 1 Sess., 1192. 9 March 1812.

95. *Otis,* II, 187-8. Lyman to John Treadwell, 14 Dec. 1814.

96. *Niles',* X (15 June 1816), 366. Message of 5 June 1816.

97. *Register,* 18 Cong., 2 Sess., House, 284-5, 17 Jan. 1825; *Annals,* 15 Cong., 2 Sess., House, 1225, 17 Feb. 1819.

98. Letter to U.S. *Telegraph,* 1 Nov. 1827, as reprinted in Malone, *Cooper,* p. 320.

99. Reprinted in *Niles',* XXXIV (5 July 1828), 300.

100. *Register,* 22 Cong., 1 Sess., 2177-81. 16 March 1832.

101. *Globe,* 23 Cong., 2 Sess., 140; *Webster,* XIII, 255; Richardson, IV, 376-7.

102. Richardson, IV, 376-7.

103. *Davis,* I, 378-9. 27 June 1850.

104. *Democratic Review,* XXVIII (Jan. 1851), 15-21.

105. *The New Englander,* XII (May 1854), 229.

106. *Globe,* 34 Cong., 3 Sess., Senate, 25. 4 Dec. 1856.

107. *Lincoln,* II, 461-2. This is the famous speech Lincoln made at the close of the Republican Convention at Springfield, 16 June 1858, after he had been nominated for the Senate. See Don E. Fehrenbacher, *Prelude to Greatness: Lincoln in the 1850's* (Stanford, 1962), passim, for splendid discussions of this and other episodes in Lincoln's early career.

CHAPTER 4

1. Von Holst, VII, 457-8.
2. Phillips, p. 64. 30 Jan. 1852.
3. *Seward*, III, 205, 4 July 1831 at Syracuse, N.Y.; II, 501, to J. M. Patton, Lt. Gov. of Virginia, 6 April 1841.
4. *Seward*, III, 78-9, 85, 87. Eulogy at Albany, 6 April 1848.
5. *Globe*, 31 Cong., 1 Sess., Appendix, Senate, 269. 11 March 1850.
6. *Seward*, III, 196. 4 July 1825.
7. *Seward*, III, 447. 5 April 1851.
8. *Seward*, III, 105ff. 30 June 1852.
9. *Globe*, 36 Cong., 2 Sess., 343, 12 Jan. 1861; *Seward*, I, 156, 27 Feb. 1851.
10. Curtis, *History*, I, 149-50.
11. *Washington*, XXVIII, 229.
12. Samuel Kettell, ed., *Specimens of American Poetry*, I (Boston, 1829), 281. Hereafter cited as Kettell. Excerpt is from Hopkins' "The Anarchiad."
13. *Madison*, III, 156-7, f.n., Carrington wrote on 13 June 1787.
14. Ford, *Pamphlets*, p. 269.
15. Elliot, II, 121. Mass. debates, 8 Jan. 1788.
16. Letter cited in Schechter, 717.
17. J. Q. Adams, *Writings*, II, 157. 3 April 1797.
18. Richardson, II, 10.
19. *John Adams*, X, 386. To Jefferson, 18 Dec. 1819.
20. Richardson, II, 86, 93. Second inaugural speech.
21. *Webster*, X, 90 n. Letter written from Boston, 14 May 1828, but Webster sent it to Gales and Seaton 15 Feb. 1851.
22. Channing, p. 739.
23. Rawles, pp. 306-07.
24. Richardson, II, esp. 500, 512-3, 515, 517, 6 Dec. 1830; *Jackson*, IV, 351, 18 Sept. 1831.
25. *Webster*, II, 44. 10 March 1831.
26. *Niles'*, XLI (22 Oct. 1831), 150. Dinner at Tuscaloosa, Alabama.
27. *Webster*, II, 81.
28. Tocqueville, I, 382.
29. *Kendall*, p. 429.
30. Ames, *State Documents*, pp. 184-5. Resolutions of Jan. 1833.
31. *Webster*, VI, 237.
32. Richardson, II, 631, message on S.C., 16 Jan. 1833; III, 293-4, Farewell Message, 4 March 1837.
33. Bayard, pp. 162, 164-5.
34. *Niles'*, XLVIII (29 Aug. 1835), 456.
35. *Globe*, 24 Cong., 1 Sess., Appendix, Senate, 139-40. 2 March 1836.
36. *Webster*, II, 162-3, 25 Aug. 1835; XIII, 82-3, June 1837.
37. Richardson, III, 296-7, 483; IV, 17.

38. Richardson, IV, 375-6.

39. Richardson, V, 201-03, 554. 19 Dec. 1859, third annual message.

40. *Webster*, IV, 99, 102, 26 May 1847; XIII, 494, 496, 13 Feb. 1852.

41. *Lincoln*, II, 341.

42. *Whig Review*, V (June 1847), 627.

43. *North American Review*, LXVII (Oct. 1848), 320-21.

44. *Whig Review*, XII (Aug. 1850), 174. For some of Everett's stirring observations in this connection, see Edward Everett, *Orations and Speeches*, IV (Boston, 1870), 247. Hereafter cited as Everett.

45. Mansfield, pp. 231-3; Capen, p. 24.

46. Howard C. Perkins, ed., *Northern Editorials on Secession*, II (N.Y., 1942), 571, from the *Daily Chicago Times*, 10 Dec. 1860. Hereafter cited as Perkins.

47. *Federalist* #3, p. 12; *Annals*, 12 Cong., 2 Sess., House, 812. 12 Jan. 1843.

48. Elliot, III, 25-6, 4 June 1788; and 85.

49. Ames, I, 65-6.

50. *Higginson*, p. 781. 7 April 1790.

51. *Iredell*, 387.

52. *Washington*, XXXV, 218-20, 58, 54.

53. *Annals*, 5 Cong., 2 Sess., House, 1142. 1 March 1798.

54. *Annals*, 12 Cong., 2 Sess., House, 764, 902.

55. *Annals*, 13 Cong., 3 Sess., House, 805-06. 9 Dec. 1814.

56. Richardson, III, 295.

57. *Madison*, IX, 610ff.

58. *Webster*, I, 271. 17 June 1843.

59. Richardson, IV, 639-42. Fourth annual message, 5 Dec. 1848.

60. *Globe*, 30 Cong., 1 Sess., House, 669. 25 April 1848.

61. *Lincoln*, II, 253, 270. 16 Oct. 1854.

62. Elias Peissner, *The American Question in its National Aspect* (N.Y., 1861), pp. 140-43. Hereafter cited as Peissner.

63. *Annals*, 10 Cong., 2 Sess., House, 1145-6. 20 Jan. 1809.

64. J. Q. Adams, *Writings*, III, 340-42. To William Plumer, 16 Aug. 1809.

65. *Niles'*, XVI (13 March 1819), 41-3; (3 April 1819), 104-05.

66. *Pinkney*, pp. 584-5, 588. Pinkney insisted that to limit Missouri was to make Union one between giants and dwarfs, thereby altering its nature. It was thus no longer "this Union."

67. *Register*, 19 Cong., 1 Sess., House, 1193. 29 March 1826.

68. Printed in *Niles'*, XXXIV (28 June 1828), 289. Adopted at Walterborough, 12 June 1828.

69. Turnbull, p. 147.

70. I have used *Niles'* account of the dinner, XXXVIII (24 April 1830), 153. The dinner took place on 13 April 1830, at Brown's Hotel.

71. *Niles'*, XXXIX (16 Oct. 1830), 129. Niles took the letter from the Columbia *Telescope*, letter dated 21 Sept. 1830.

72. *The Debates in the South Carolina Legislature in December, 1830 ...* (Columbia, 1831), p. 60. Hereafter cited as South Carolina Debates.
73. *Niles'*, XL (16 July 1831), 346.
74. *Calhoun*, VI, 61-5, 26 July 1831; 172, 178-9, 28 Aug. 1832.
75. *Globe*, 24 Cong., 1 Sess., Appendix, House, 287ff, esp. 291.
76. Richardson, III, 314-9. 4 March 1837.
77. *Globe*, 27 Cong., 2 Sess., House, 50. 22 Dec. 1841.
78. *Globe*, 28 Cong., 1 Sess., Appendix, House, 707. 21 May 1844.
79. *Globe*, 28 Cong., 2 Sess., Appendix, Senate, 329. 28 Feb. 1845.
80. *Whig Review*, I (March 1845), 278-9.
81. Richardson, IV, 607-10. 14 Aug. 1848.
82. *Globe*, 31 Cong., 1 Sess., Appendix, House, 949. 6 June 1850.
83. *Davis*, I, 596, 7 Nov. 1850; I, 599-600, 19 Nov. 1850.
84. Richardson, V, 92-3, 2 Dec. 1850; V, 79-80.
85. Richardson, V, 349-50. Pierce's third message, 31 Dec. 1855.
86. Emerson, *Journals*, VIII, 185-7. Entry for 12 Feb. 1851.
87. *Globe*, 33 Cong., 1 Sess., Appendix, House, 529. 6 April 1854.
88. *Lincoln*, III, 112-5. 15 Sept. 1858, Jonesboro debate.
89. *Lincoln*, III, 550. 27 Feb. 1860.
90. *Globe*, 36 Cong., 2 Sess., Senate, 75. 12 Dec. 1860.
91. Richardson, V, 655-9. Special message of 8 Jan. 1861.
92. *Globe*, 36 Cong., 2 Sess., House, 943. Daniel DeJarnette of Virginia on 15 Feb. 1861.
93. *Lincoln*, IV, 264-5. First Inaugural Address.
94. *Lincoln*, IV, 265.
95. Burnett, IV, 205. To Caesar Rodney, 10 May 1779.
96. *Washington*, XXVI, 265-6. To Arthur Lee, 29 March 1783.
97. Burnett, VII, 124. To Theophilus Parsons, Sr., 7 April 1783.
98. *Washington*, XXVIII, 228. To James McHenry, 22 Aug. 1785.
99. *Washington*, XXIX, 67, to Bushrod Washington, 15 Nov. 1786; 310-11, 10 Nov. 1787.
100. Ford, *Pamphlets*, p. 63.
101. *Gallatin*, I, 5-7. Sept. 1794.
102. Ames, *State Documents*, pp. 21-3. 9 Feb. and 5 March 1799.
103. J. Q. Adams, *Writings*, III, 193, 31 March 1808; 258-9, 5 Dec. 1808.
104. Ames, *State Documents*, pp. 158-9. 27 Jan. 1830.
105. Story, *Letters*, II, 123-4. To Rev. John Brazer, 4 Feb. 1833.
106. *Jackson*, V, 429. 13 Oct. 1836.
107. *Otis*, II, 272. 21 Aug. 1835.
108. Channing, p. 633. Essay on "Union," circa 1837. See pp. 633-41.
109. *Calhoun*, I, 311. From the "Discourse."
110. Richardson, IV, 563-4, 7 Dec. 1847; 660-63, Fourth Message.
111. Richardson, V, 6. 5 March 1849.
112. *Webster*, X, 97. 7 March 1850.

113. *North American Review,* LXXXIII (Oct. 1856), 534-5, by Edward Everett Hale.
114. Everett, III, 640-41, 645-6. 5 July 1848.
115. Quoted in Mary Scrugham, *The Peaceable Americans of 1860-61* (N.Y., 1921), p. 54. Hammond wrote to Simms, 10 July 1860.

CHAPTER 5

1. *Register,* 21 Cong., 1 Sess., 438. Emerson's observation about Union being part of American religion is from his *Journals,* VIII, 234.
2. *Niles',* XXIX (24 Sept. 1825), 17. 10 Sept. 1825.
3. Adams, *Jubilee,* p. 136.
4. *Democratic Review,* XXVIII (May 1851), 393.
5. Channing, p. 805 and p. 849.
6. Frank Moore, *Songs and Ballads of the American Revolution* (N.Y., 1855), p. 145. Hereafter cited as Moore, *Songs.*
7. *Washington,* XXX, 22. To Jonathan Trumbull, 20 July 1788.
8. *Federalist* #11, p. 69; #45, p. 298.
9. Ames, I, 237, 28 July 1798; *Annals,* 6 Cong., 2 Sess., 726.
10. *Register,* 19 Cong., 1 Sess., House, 1002. 17 Jan. 1826.
11. Turnbull, p. 15.
12. *Register,* 22 Cong., 1 Sess., 367. Tyler was then Senator from Virginia, 10 Feb. 1832.
13. Alexander H. Everett in *North American Review,* XXXVI (Jan. 1833), 270-73; and XXXVII (July 1833), 247.
14. Ames, *State Documents,* p. 181.
15. Harriet Martineau, *Society in America,* I (N.Y., 1837), 137, 143.
16. *Globe,* 28 Cong., 1 Sess., Appendix, 318. 23 Feb. 1844.
17. As quoted in Capen, pp. 24-5. Treasury Report, Dec. 1847.
18. Richardson, IV, 590. Message submitting peace treaty, 6 July 1848. For thoughtful insights, see Chapter III, "The Untransacted Destiny," in Smith, *Virgin Land.*
19. Henry W. Longfellow, *Complete Poetical Works* (Boston, 1893), p. 103. Hereafter cited as Longfellow.
20. *Whig Review,* V (1849), 235.
21. *Seward,* I, 58. Senate speech of 11 March 1850.
22. *Buchanan,* VIII, 290. Letter to a Philadelphia public meeting, 19 Nov. 1850.
23. Everett, III, 66; *Lincoln,* II, 126, 130; *Davis,* II, 252.
24. *Choate,* I, 555-6. 27 July 1853.
25. Richardson, V, 432. 4 March 1857.
26. *Globe,* 35 Cong., 1 Sess., House, 1339. 2 March 1858.
27. *Democratic Review,* XLII (July 1858), 56-7.
28. *Lincoln,* III, 68. Freeport, 27 Aug. 1858.
29. *Globe,* 36 Cong., 2 Sess., 344. 12 Jan. 1861.

30. Craik, pp. 5-7.
31. Henry Reed, *Two Lectures* ... (Phila., 1856), pp. 3-4, 68.
32. *Webster*, I, 265. Charlestown, Mass., 17 June 1843.
33. *Iredell*, II, 182. 17 Nov. 1787.
34. Elliot, IV, 233.
35. Ford, *Essays*, p. 47.
36. *Gallatin*, I, 1-2. 3 Sept. 1788.
37. *John Adams*, IX, 631. To Josiah Quincy, 9 Feb. 1811.
38. *Niles'*, XIII (7 Feb. 1818), 388. Address of 2 Dec. 1817.
39. *Register*, 20 Cong., 2 Sess., House, 290, 29 Jan. 1828; *Jackson*, III, 411-2.
40. *Jackson*, V, 15, 26-7. Jackson was sending encouragement to his agent in South Carolina, Joel Poinsett.
41. *Niles'*, XXXV (12 Dec. 1828), 263.
42. *Calhoun*, VI, 142-3.
43. *Madison*, IX, 353-7.
44. *Webster*, VI, 236-7 and II, 199. See also President Tyler's letter withdrawing from the 1844 contest in Lyon G. Tyler, *The Letters and Times of the Tylers*, II (Richmond, 1884-96), 349. Hereafter cited as Tyler.
45. Richardson, IV, 24.
46. *North American Review*, LXVII (Oct. 1848), 322; Francis J. Grund, *The Americans*, II (London, 1837), 243-4. Hereafter cited as Grund.
47. *Globe*, 30 Cong., 2 Sess., 319; 31 Cong., 1 Sess., 843.
48. Charles Sumner, *Charles Sumner, His Complete Works*, III (Boston, 1900), 163. Hereafter cited as Sumner.
49. *Webster*, IV, 287. 28 May 1851.
50. Curtis, *History*, I, xi; *Lincoln*, II, 383, 10 Dec. 1856.
51. Perkins, I, 112. Hartford *Evening Press*, 3 Dec. 1860.
52. Speech reprinted in *Democratic Review*, XXVIII (May 1851), 472, 475.
53. Elliot, IV, 330. Louis Hartz has perceptive comments on Pinckney, although he calls him a Virginian. Hartz, pp. 83-5.
54. Editorial in *National Gazette* (Philadelphia), 10 May 1792, as reprinted in Philip M. Marsh, ed., *The Prose of Philip Freneau* (New Brunswick, 1955), p. 276. Hereafter cited as Freneau.
55. *Annals*, 18 Cong., 1 Sess., House, 1262-3. 28 Jan. 1824. In this case the role of the Evil One was filled by an alien power—"'The Holy Alliance' would spread unassisted, their gloomy dominion over the universe," if Union was kept from fulfilling its purpose.
56. *Register*, 21 Cong., 1 Sess., 50-58 passim. 25 Jan. 1830.
57. *Register*, 22 Cong., 1 Sess., 3383, 8 June 1832; Ames, *State Documents*, p. 217, 16 Dec. 1835.
58. *Globe*, 29 Cong., 2 Sess., 388. 11 Feb. 1847.
59. *Buchanan*, VIII, 403 and 636.
60. *Globe*, 32 Cong., 1 Sess., Appendix, Senate, 176. 2 Feb. 1852.

61. *Globe,* 36 Cong., 1 Sess., Appendix, House, 175. Much of Lovejoy's comment was reported in incomplete sentences. 26 March 1860.
62. *Globe,* 36 Cong., 2 Sess., House, 629ff. Van Wyck of N.Y., 29 Jan. 1861.
63. *Globe,* 36 Cong., 2 Sess., Senate, 682. John C. Ten Eyck of N.J., 1 Feb. 1861.
64. *Annals,* 14 Cong., 1 Sess., House, 427. 2 Jan. 1816.
65. Tocqueville, I, 385.
66. *Hamilton,* I, 420-21, Sept. 1787; Washington, XXIX, 350-51, 1 Jan. 1788.
67. *Washington,* XXVII, 225, 235. See both the "Farewell Orders" of 2 Nov. 1783 and his address to Somerset County (N.J.) Militia.
68. As reprinted in Charles A. Beard, *The American Spirit* (N.Y., 1942), p. 150.
69. Richardson, III, 4-5. 4 March 1833.
70. Quoted in *North American Review,* LXXV (July 1852), 87.
71. Everett, I, 27, 33-4. 26 Aug. 1824.
72. *Washington,* XXVII, 12-3, 15 June 1783; Madison, VI, 115n, 21 June 1792.
73. *Iredell,* II, 495. Paterson to Iredell, 7 March 1797.
74. *Niles',* XVII (1 Jan. 1820), 290.
75. *American Quarterly Review,* XII (March 1833), 257, 259-60; Prescott wrote about Bancroft in *North American Review,* LII (Jan. 1841), 52, 81.
76. Woodbury, III, 191, 193. June 1845.
77. J. Q. Adams, *Writings,* I, 493-4. To Charles Adams, 9 June 1796.
78. J. Q. Adams, *Writings,* IV, 128. To Abigail Adams, 30 June 1811.
79. Richardson, II, 295-6. 4 March 1825.
80. Edward H. Tatum, Jr., ed., "Ten Unpublished Letters of John Quincy Adams, 1796-1837," *The Huntington Library Quarterly,* IV (April 1941), 382-3. To Charles W. Upham, 2 Feb. 1837.
81. *Federalist* #41, p. 263.
82. Ford, *Jefferson,* VIII, 286-7. 13 May 1797.
83. Abbott Lawrence, *Letters from the Hon. Abbott Lawrence to the Hon. William C. Rives of Virginia* (Boston, 1846), p. 23. 16 Jan. 1846. Hereafter cited as Lawrence.
84. *American Review,* I (Jan. 1845), 20.
85. Piessner, p. 134.
86. James Russell Lowell, *The Complete Writings of James Russell Lowell,* VI (Boston, 1904), 61-80. Hereafter cited as Lowell, *Writings.*
87. *Globe,* 36 Cong., 2 Sess., House, 1069. 20 Feb. 1861.

CHAPTER 6

1. Pamphlet reprinted in *Whig Review,* XII (Dec. 1850), 602. "Union or Disunion" by "A Southron."
2. *Rush,* II, 966. To John Adams, 13 June 1808. Many provocative ideas are in a paper read by Professor Keith Berwick at the 1962 meeting of the Mississippi Valley Historical Association (Milwaukee, 26-9 April),

"A Preface to Nationality, the Mythic Imagination in American History." According to Berwick, while America failed in its search for a single mythic figure, an American demigod which might encompass the needed national ethos, still the pursuit of such a symbol revealed America's recognition that powerful leadership was not incompatible with American democracy.

3. *Federalist* #2, p. 9.
4. *Federalist* #7, p. 231.
5. *Washington*, XXIX, 409-10, 7 Feb. 1788; XXX, 10, 28 June 1788.
6. *Annals*, 18 Cong., 1 Sess., House, 138, 4-5 Feb. 1824; 15 Cong., 1 Sess., House, 1128, 1168, 6-7 March 1818.
7. *Whig Review*, V (March 1847), 234-5.
8. *Democratic Review*, XXI (Sept. 1847), 103.
9. Everett, III, 30, 17 June 1850; George Bancroft, *History of the United States*, I (Boston, 1837), 4.
10. Craik, pp. 17-21.
11. Reed, pp. 17-67 passim. For a good, brief treatment of this German appeal, see Harvey Wish, *The American Historian* (N.Y., 1960), pp. 73ff.
12. Moore, *Songs*, p. 194.
13. Elliot, II, 419-20. Penn. debate, 26 Nov. 1787.
14. Ford, *Essays*, p. 47. "Cassius" in *Massachusetts Gazette*, 25 Dec. 1787.
15. *Jay*, III, 296-7. Address to the people of N.Y., 1788.
16. *Annals*, 1 Cong., 1 Sess., 102. 8 April 1789.
17. *Annals*, 10 Cong., 2 Sess., 1324-5. 2 Feb. 1809.
18. *Niles'*, II, 307-08. Orator was William H. Winder who was substituting for William Pinkney.
19. Everett, I, 37, 39. Harvard, 1824. For glimpses of how the simultaneous deaths in 1826 of Jefferson and Adams strengthened the Founders' legend, see *A Selection of Eulogies ... Of ... John Adams and Thomas Jefferson* (Hartford, 1826), esp. p. 128. Hereafter cited as *Eulogies*.
20. Richardson, II, 590, 10 July 1832; *Globe*, 27 Cong., 1 Sess., Appendix, House, 48, Reyner of N.C. speaking on 15 June 1840.
21. *Niles'*, LXIV (1 July 1843), 282. 17 June 1843.
22. *Globe*, 28 Cong., 1 Sess., Appendix, 408. Pennsylvania's Brodhead on 27 April 1844.
23. *Globe*, 28 Cong., 2 Sess., Appendix, Senate, 154. 3 Feb. 1845.
24. *Globe*, 29 Cong., 1 Sess., Appendix, House, 217. 6 Feb. 1846.
25. *Globe*, 31 Cong., 1 Sess., Appendix, Senate, 98-9. 8 Feb. 1850.
26. *Globe*, 31 Cong., 1 Sess., Senate, 332. 11 Feb. 1850.
27. *Davis*, I, 580. 10 Nov. 1850.
28. *Webster*, XII, 257-60. Letter of 27 Jan. 1851 to citizens of Westchester, N.Y.
29. *Seward*, IV, 171. 26 July 1854.
30. *Globe*, 36 Cong., 1 Sess., 1042-3. 7 March 1860.

31. Perkins, I, 38. Cincinnati *Daily Times*, 22 Sept. 1860.
32. Peissner, pp. 61, 131.
33. *Globe*, 36 Cong., 2 Sess., 269. 7 Jan. 1861.
34. Story, *Commentaries*, III, 759.
35. Grund, II, 364.
36. *Globe*, 27 Cong., 2 Sess., House, 175ff. Wise's speech was on 26 Jan. 1842. Adams continued his attack on the Gag Rule (21st Rule) with a delicious sense of the ironical.
37. *Calhoun Correspondence*, p. 625. 14 Oct. 1844.
38. *Globe*, 30 Cong., 1 Sess., Appendix, House, 955-6. Congressman Wallace on 26 July 1848.
39. Ames, *State Documents*, p. 256. Adopted 6 March 1850.
40. Everett, III, 29. 17 June 1850.
41. *Globe*, 33 Cong., 1 Sess., Appendix, House, 583-4. 9 May 1854.
42. *Lincoln*, II, 251-2. Peoria, 16 Oct. 1854.
43. From "Stanzas" by William Ross Wallace, in *Democratic Review*, XL (Oct. 1857), 353.
44. *Globe*, 35 Cong., 2 Sess., 353-5.
45. Ernst Cassirer, *The Philosophy of Symbolic Forms*, II (New Haven, 1955), 235.
46. Malone, *Cooper*, p. 389. To J. H. Hammond, 2 March 1836.
47. *Globe*, 26 Cong., 1 Sess., Appendix, 849-55. 20 Jan. 1840.
48. *Globe*, 31 Cong., 2 Sess., Appendix, House, 256. 9 Dec. 1850.
49. Sumner, III, 164. 14 May 1851.
50. Phillips, 85ff., 1852; and 375-6, 1861.
51. Dumond, p. 140. *Enquirer* of 10 July 1860.
52. Ralph L. Rusk, ed., *The Letters of Ralph Waldo Emerson*, V (N.Y., 1939), 18. March 1856.
53. Curti, *Roots*, pp. 43ff; Smith, *Virgin Land*, pp. 43, 138-9, 186-9. Smith has an excellent discussion of William Gilpin.
54. William Gilpin, *The Central Gold Region* ... (Phila., 1860), pp. 18-22, 71, 110, 119. Hereafter cited as Gilpin.
55. Gilpin, pp. 119, 113, 194. 15 Nov. 1858.
56. Boyd, *Jefferson*, IX, 218. 25 Jan. 1786.
57. Boyd, *Jefferson*, VIII, 442. 25 Aug. 1785.
58. Richardson, II, 6.
59. Richardson, II, 46-7.
60. Richardson, II, 74-5. Fourth annual message.
61. Richardson, II, 248. 7 Dec. 1824.
62. Richardson, II, 177-8.
63. *Calhoun Correspondence*, pp. 266-7.
64. *Annals*, 1 Cong., 1 Sess., House, 253-4. 5 May 1789.
65. *Niles'*, XVIII (11 March 1820), 26; King, VI, 79, to Rufus King, 24 July 1817.

66. *Annals*, 17 Cong., 2 Sess., House, 416-7, 681-3, 688. 18 Dec. 1822 and 24 Jan. 1823.
67. *Annals*, 17 Cong., 2 Sess., 693. 25 Jan. 1823. Breckinridge argued that there was a population shortage in the Union, so why drain the precious supply even lower? 695.
68. Cooper, II, 153.
69. Richardson, II, 545, 6 Dec. 1831; Clay, *Corr.*, p. 358. Lawrence's letter dated 26 March 1833.
70. Channing, pp. 891, 893; also 805-07.
71. Smith, *Virgin Land*, pp. 174-5, cites Walker's *Letter of Mr. Walker of Mississippi, Relative to the Annexation of Texas* (Wash., 1844), p. 5.
72. Richardson, IV, 380.
73. *Calhoun*, I, 314. "Discourse."
74. *Globe*, 30 Cong., 1 Sess., Senate, 157. 12 Jan. 1848.
75. *Webster*, IV, 224; XII, 241, 17 June 1850; XII, 274, 6 Oct. 1851.
76. *Webster*, X, 94-5.
77. *Lincoln*, III, 12-8. Ottawa debate, 21 Aug. 1858.
78. *Davis*, IV, 63. 6 July 1859.
79. Thomas King, pp. 39-43. 2 June 1851.
80. From a letter to the Boston *Palladium*, 14 Feb. 1814, reprinted in *Niles'*, VI (5 March 1814), 9-10.
81. *Niles'*, VI (21 May 1814), 191; XI (25 Jan. 1817), 357. Claiborne's address of 20 Nov. 1816.
82. S. Putnam Waldo, *The Tour of James Monroe* (Hartford, 1818), pp. 270-72.
83. *The Western Citizen* (Paris, Ky.), 15 Nov. 1823. The *Citizen* relied upon the *Kentucky Reporter.*
84. Francis Lieber, *Manual of Political Ethics*, II (Boston, 1839), 533, hereafter cited as Lieber; Tocqueville, I, 394-6.
85. Lawrence, pp. 34-5. 23 Feb. 1846.
86. *Seward*, IV, 99, 134. St. Paul speech, 18 Sept. 1860 and St. Joseph speech, 22 Sept. 1860.

CHAPTER 7

1. *Globe*, 36 Cong., 2 Sess., Appendix, House, 87. 23 Jan. 1861.
2. Herbert Read, *Icon and Idea* (Cambridge, 1955), pp. 111, 140. See also Erwin Panofsky, *Studies in Iconology* (N.Y., 1939), pp. 3-16 passim, and Alfred North Whitehead, *Symbolism, Its Meaning and Effect* (N.Y., 1927), pp. 75-7. Hereafter cited as Whitehead.
3. All students of American thought are much indebted to the provocative work of Merle Curti, Henry Nash Smith, R. W. B. Lewis, John William Ward, Merrill Peterson, and Leo Marx. Their efforts, while supported by others, come immediately to mind in this field.
4. Peterson, pp. 69-70.

5. *Annals,* 1 Cong., 2 Sess., House, 1380. 1 March 1790.

6. *Annals,* 9 Cong., 1 Sess., House, 694. 10 May 1806.

7. *Madison,* IX, 356-7. To Nicholas Trist, 15 Feb. 1830.

8. *Webster,* XIII, 42. 17 Dec. 1832.

9. Adams, *Jubilee,* p. 123. This poem was never placed in any collection of Bryant's writings. Nevertheless, the lines were frequently repeated, although not always with due credit to the poet. See, for example, *Globe,* 28 Cong., 1 Sess., Appendix, 543; 29 Cong., 1 Sess., 187; 34 Cong., 1 Sess., 1093. In the last instance, Hannibal Hamlin did preface his use by observing "in the inimitable language of our own distinguished poet."

10. Whittier, VIII, 298-9.

11. *Choate,* I, 125, address at Salem, Mass., 17 Oct. 1848; *Webster,* XVIII, 361, 28 March 1850.

12. Whittier, III, 163-5.

13. *Webster,* IV, 289. 28 May 1851, at Albany.

14. Quoted in William Alfred Bryan, *George Washington in American Literature* (N.Y., 1952), p. 162.

15. *Globe,* 34 Cong., 1 Sess., Appendix, House, 1033. 2 Aug. 1856.

16. *Globe,* 36 Cong., 2 Sess., Appendix, House, 52. 16 Jan. 1861. Isaac N. Morris of Illinois.

17. Ford, *Jefferson,* IX, 201. 6 March 1801.

18. *Pinkney,* p. 189. The report in the *Annals* has Pinkney call Union a "sacred bark." 16 Cong., 1 Sess., Senate, 390. 15 Feb. 1820.

19. Mary Lee Mann, ed., *A Yankee Jeffersonian* (Cambridge, 1958), p. 238. To Susan Lee, 12 Jan. 1834.

20. *North American Review,* LIV (Jan. 1842), 212-3.

21. Longfellow, p. 103.

22. *Globe,* 31 Cong., 1 Sess., House, 444-8. 4 March 1850.

23. Tyler, II, 489. Public letter to Senator H. S. Foote, 21 May 1850.

24. Thomas Foster, ed., *Eulogies...On...Calhoun* [and] *Webster* (Washington, 1853), Part II, p. 21. Hereafter cited as Foster.

25. Foster, Part II, p. 24.

26. *North American Review,* LXXIII (Oct. 1856), 380.

27. *Lincoln,* IV, 215-6, 15 Feb. 1861; 233, 20 Feb. 1861.

28. *North American Review,* XCII (April 1861), 492-4. I have been unable to discover the author of this essay.

29. Ford, *Jefferson,* VIII, 377. To Peregrine Fitzhugh, 23 Feb. 1798.

30. *Annals,* 9 Cong., 1 Sess., House, 146-7. 11 Dec. 1806.

31. *Register,* 21 Cong., 1 Sess., Senate, 145, 8 Feb. 1830; *Webster,* V, 259.

32. *Webster,* XIII, 500. 24 Feb. 1852.

33. From J. Q. Adams's "Appeal," printed in Adams, *Documents,* p. 329.

34. Matthew Carey, *The Olive Branch* (Phila., 1817, 8th edition), p. 21, hereafter cited as Carey; John Bigelow, ed., *The Works of Benjamin Franklin,* X (N.Y., 1904), 199, to David Hartley, 22 Oct. 1783.

35. This appeared in the *Pennsylvania Packet*, 29 Dec. 1787 and is reprinted in George E. Hastings, *The Life and Works of Francis Hopkinson* (Chicago, 1926), pp. 397-8. Hereafter cited as *Hopkinson*.

36. Published in the *American Museum*, July 1788, and reprinted in *Hopkinson*, pp. 410-11.

37. For a typical instance of the Temple image, see Augusta (Ga.) *Courier*, 3 July 1828, as reprinted in *Niles'*, XXXIV (26 July 1828), 355-6. Described in *Niles'*, XXXVI (14 March 1829), 40, the dinner was in Washington, 7 March 1829.

38. *Madison*, IX, 541. To Edward Coles, 29 Aug. 1834.

39. *Globe*, 30 Cong., 1 Sess., Appendix, House, 668. 20 June 1848.

40. Quincy, *Life*, p. 497. Letter to Delaware's ex-Senator, James M. Broome, 27 March 1848.

41. *Choate*, II, 330.

42. *Globe*, 36 Cong., 1 Sess., Senate, 914, 29 Feb. 1860; 36 Cong., 2 Sess., Senate, 341, 12 Jan. 1861.

43. *John Adams*, IX, 538-9. 10 Sept. 1785.

44. Mason L. Weems, *The Life of Washington* (Cambridge, 1962), p. 122.

45. Robert Treat Paine, "Eulogy on Washington at . . . Newburyport, January 2, 1800," as used by Schechter, 727.

46. *Annals*, 7 Cong., 2 Sess., Senate, 169. 24 Feb. 1803.

47. *Niles'*, II (1 Aug. 1812), esp. 364 and passim; VI (5 March 1814), 1.

48. *Annals*, 18 Cong., 1 Sess., House, 1458. 9 Feb. 1824.

49. *Register*, 22 Cong., 1 Sess., House, 1785. 13 Feb. 1830.

50. *Register*, 22 Cong., 1 Sess., House, 1788-97. 13 Feb. 1830.

51. *Webster*, II, 79-80. 22 Feb. 1832.

52. Adams, *Memoirs*, VIII, 479. 22 Feb. 1832.

53. *North American Review*, XLVII (Oct. 1838), 323.

54. *Woodbury*, I, 534. 15 Nov. 1850.

55. Sumner, V, 95. 19 Feb. 1856.

56. *Globe*, 36 Cong., 1 Sess., Senate, 104, 12 Dec. 1859; *Lincoln*, III, 550, 27 Feb. 1860.

57. *Globe*, 36 Cong., 2 Sess., 342-3. 12 Jan. 1861.

58. Whitehead, *Symbolism*, p. 88.

CHAPTER 8

1. Phillips, pp. 360-61, "Disunion." 20 Jan. 1861.

2. Burnett, VII, 602-03.

3. *Cabot*, p. 445. Pickering wrote to his kinsman, Theodore Lyman, 11 Feb. 1804.

4. *Cabot*, pp. 453-4. Letter of 17 March 1804.

5. For an interesting discussion, see *Cabot*, pp. 440, 479-80.

6. Ames, II, 350.

7. Quincy, *Life*, p. 206. House speech of 14 Jan. 1811.

8. *Otis*, II, 179. Charles W. Hare to Otis, 15 Oct. 1814.
9. *Otis*, II, 227. To William Sullivan, 13 Feb. 1820.
10. King, VI, 274. Tudor wrote on 12 Feb. 1820.
11. *Annals*, 16 Cong., 1 Sess., 1436-9.
12. *Annals*, 16 Cong., 1 Sess., 1485-6; *Columbian Centinel*, 24 Nov. 1819, 1 Dec. 1819, 25 Dec. 1819, as well as 8 and 11 Dec. 1819.
13. *Columbian Centinel*, 8, 11, 25 March 1820.
14. Quincy, *Life*, p. 388.
15. Claude H. Van Tyne, ed., *Letters of Daniel Webster* (N.Y., 1902), pp. 83-4, Webster's italics. Hereafter cited as Van Tyne.
16. Adams, *Memoirs*, V, 4, 15.
17. C. J. Clark, ed., *Memoir, Autobiography, and Correspondence of Jeremiah Mason* (Kansas City, 1917), 246-7, 240-41, hereafter cited as *Mason;* Van Tyne, pp. 84-5.
18. Everett S. Brown, ed., *The Missouri Compromise and Presidential Politics, 1820-1825* (St. Louis, 1926), pp. 18-21, 23-4, 32-3, 36-7.
19. *Annals*, 14 Cong., 1 Sess., 962.
20. As cited in Joseph Dorfman, *Economic Mind in American Civilization*, I (N.Y., 1946), 384; see esp. *Columbian Centinel*, 1 Jan. 1820, and the Boston *Intelligencer and Evening Gazette*, 29 Jan. 1820; *Webster*, XIII, 6-8. Nevertheless, Webster blamed an ill-informed public pressure for causing many of his colleagues to swerve in their stands. He insisted that two-thirds of the House would oppose protection "if it were not for instruction and other nonsense." XVII, 348-9.
21. Boston *Patriot*, 23 Oct. 1824, also 23 Aug. 1823; Boston *American Statesman and Evening Advertiser* as cited in the Lexington *Kentucky Reporter*, 27 Jan. 1823. The sectional animosities were intense in a campaign usually considered a contest in personalities. For a brief analysis of the implications of this campaign for Unionist ideology, see Paul C. Nagel, "The Election of 1824: A Reconsideration Based on Newspaper Opinion," *Journal of Southern History*, XXVI (Aug. 1960), 315-29.
22. *Register*, 21 Cong., 1 Sess., Senate, 147. 9 Feb. 1830.
23. *Webster*, VI, 48, 60-61.
24. For this extraordinary exchange between Adams and his fellow New Englanders, see Adams, *Documents*. Adams began his assault in the *National Intelligencer*, 21 Oct. 1828.
25. Allan Nevins, ed., *The Diary of Philip Hone* (N.Y., 1936), p. 581, entry for 25 June 1841. Hereafter cited as *Hone*.
26. Petition printed in Whittier, VIII, 179-80. See *Globe*, 27 Cong., 2 Sess., passim, for the spectacular effect of this phase of New England agitation.
27. S. G. Goodrich, *Recollections of a Lifetime*, I (N.Y., 1856), 512-4. Hereafter cited as Goodrich.
28. Goodrich, II, 11ff., esp. 48, 60-61.
29. Elliot, III, 57; II, 405; Ford, *Jefferson*, VIII, 470, 10 Nov. 1798.

30. Ford, *Jefferson*, XII, 425-6. To William B. Giles, 26 Dec. 1825.
31. *Register*, 19 Cong., 1 Sess., Senate, 596. 20 April 1826.
32. Malone, *Cooper*, reprints this letter on p. 330. 24 March 1829.
33. *Niles'*, XL (29 Sept. 1832), 77; *Globe*, 27 Cong., 2 Sess., House, 182 *et seq.*, for a debate which stressed that civil war was inevitably the companion of disunion.
34. *Calhoun*, I, 390-91.
35. *Globe*, 31 Cong., 1 Sess., 453-5. 4 March 1850.
36. Phillips, p. 36. 15 Nov. 1850.
37. *Curtis*, I, 29.
38. *Davis*, IV, 86-7. Speech at Jackson, Miss., 6 July 1859.
39. *Lincoln*, III, 553. Dover, N.H., 2 March 1860.
40. Richardson, V, 626-30. 3 Dec. 1860.
41. *Davis*, IV, 554. Letter of 12 Dec. 1860.

CHAPTER 9

1. Ford, *Jefferson*, VI, 492. 23 May 1792.
2. J. Q. Adams, *Writings*, II, 525-6. 7 April 1801.
3. *Register*, 19 Cong., 1 Sess., House, 1457-8, 1461. 23 Feb. 1826.
4. Letter reprinted in Malone, *Cooper*, p. 319. 31 July 1827.
5. For an account of this celebration, see *Niles'*, XXXVIII (17 July 1830), 375-6.
6. Michael Chevalier, *Society, Manners, and Politics in the United States* (Boston, 1839), p. 96.
7. Whittier, VII, 92. To Samual E. Sewall, 10 Jan. 1834.
8. *Calhoun Correspondence*, pp. 1193-4. Hammond wrote on 19 Feb. 1849.
9. *Calhoun Correspondence*, p. 765, 13 April 1849, and p. 784, 10 March 1850.
10. *Globe*, 36 Cong., 1 Sess., House, 167. 16 Dec. 1859.
11. *Buchanan*, X, 92-3. 14 Sept. 1856.
12. *Globe*, 29 Cong., 2 Sess., Senate, 543. 1 March 1847. Dix could seem calm for he was certain at this point that civil war would never come.
13. Phillips, pp. 350ff. 20 Jan. 1861.
14. Ford, *Jefferson*, VIII, 430-33. 1 June 1798.
15. Resolutions of 15 Oct. 1814, printed in *Niles'*, VII (12 Nov. 1814), 153-4.
16. Boyd, *Jefferson*, I, 197, 206, 211, 217.
17. Burnett, III, 508-09. 25 Nov. 1778.
18. Kettell, I, 278-81.
19. *Higginson*, pp. 745-6.
20. *Federalist* #16, pp. 96-7.
21. Ford, *Essays*, pp. 102-03. 18 Jan. 1788.
22. J. Q. Adams, *Writings*, II, 495-6, 27 Jan. 1801; III, 248-51, 17 Nov. 1808.
23. *Webster*, XVII, 78-9. 5 Feb. 1800.

24. *Annals,* 7 Cong., 1 Sess., 77, 14 Jan. 1802. See passim for similar comments aroused by the attempt to repeal the Adams administration's judiciary act. See also S. C. Carpenter, *Select American Speeches,* II (Phila., 1815), 65, 87-8 for Gouverneur Morris's speech in which he too warned that without Union civil war would surely come, when "a brother's hand be raised against a brother." Hereafter cited as Carpenter. Timothy Dwight also asserted that disunion would lead to war among regional units. Dwight, IV, 512-13.
25. *Annals,* 16 Cong., 1 Sess., Senate, 219. 20 Jan. 1820.
26. Adams, *Memoirs,* V, 210, 29 Nov. 1820; Adams, *Documents,* p. 53.
27. *Register,* 21 Cong., 1 Sess., Senate, 270, 15 March 1830; *Webster,* VI, 71-2.
28. South Carolina Debates, p. 47.
29. *Register,* 22 Cong., 1 Sess., Senate, 486. 27 Feb. 1832.
30. Richardson, II, 654-6. 10 Dec. 1832.
31. Clay, *Corr.,* p. 350. 20 Feb. 1833.
32. *American Quarterly Review,* XII (June 1833), 446.
33. *Globe,* 25 Cong., 2 Sess., Appendix, Senate, 29, 5 Jan. 1838; *Calhoun Correspondence,* 291, 25 Jan. 1838.
34. *Globe,* 27 Cong., 2 Sess., Appendix, House, 50. 15 June 1841. Again, the issue was abolitionist petitions.
35. Clay, *Corr.,* pp. 463-6, esp. 465-6. 25 July 1842.
36. *Globe,* 29 Cong., 2 Sess., 338, 6 Feb. 1847. For an interesting variation, see Isaac Strohm, ed., *Speeches of Thomas Corwin* (Dayton, 1859), pp. 387-8, 11 Feb. 1847.
37. *Globe,* 31 Cong., 1 Sess., Appendix, 127. 6 Feb. 1850.
38. *Globe,* 31 Cong., 1 Sess., Senate, 321-3, 331. 8 and 11 Feb. 1850.
39. *Hone,* p. 801. Entry for 18 Feb. 1850.
40. *Webster,* X, 93-4; XIII, 492-3. 7 March 1850 and 13 Feb. 1852.
41. *Globe,* 31 Cong., 1 Sess., Appendix, House, 701, McClearnand was from Illinois; Everett, III, 65, 22 Feb. 1851.
42. *Globe,* 34 Cong., 1 Sess., Senate, 1093-5. 2 May 1856.
43. *Globe,* 36 Cong., 1 Sess., Appendix, House, 282, 2 May 1860; 36 Cong., 2 Sess., 341, and Appendix, House, 52.
44. Carpenter, pp. 87-8; J. Q. Adams, *Writings,* II, 501-02; Story, *Letters,* I, 182; *Annals,* 15 Cong., 1 Sess., Senate, 179.
45. *Calhoun Correspondence,* p. 344. 30 Aug. 1835.
46. *Globe,* 31 Cong., 1 Sess., Senate, 453. 4 March 1850.
47. *Kendall,* p. 560. 19 Aug. 1856.
48. *Annals,* 5 Cong., 2 Sess., House, 1117-8, 1 March 1798; *Cabot,* p. 535, Pickering to Gouverneur Morris, 29 Oct. 1814.
49. *Annals,* 16 Cong., 1 Sess., House, 1060-61, 3 Feb. 1820. Strother was a Virginian.
50. *Annals,* 16 Cong., 1 Sess., House, 1435-6. 21 Feb. 1820.

51. *Register,* 19 Cong., 1 Sess., House, 1927. 31 March 1826.
52. *Globe,* 28 Cong., 1 Sess., House, 112. Alexander Duncan of Ohio on 6 Jan. 1844.
53. Whittier, VIII, 363-4. To Charles Sumner, Dec. 1851.
54. *Globe,* 34 Cong., 1 Sess., House, 220, 11 Jan. 1856; 36 Cong., 2 Sess., 271.
55. Sumner, VII, 25ff. 39-40. 11 Oct. 1860 speech at Framingham, Mass.
56. *Annals,* 13 Cong., 3 Sess., House, 209-10. 9 Dec. 1814.
57. Adams, *Memoirs,* VIII, 229, 1 June 1830; 262-3, 4 June 1831.
58. Ames, I, 328, 26 Oct. 1803; *Annals,* 12 Cong., 1 Sess., 712, 9 Jan. 1812.
59. Adams, *Memoirs,* IV, 517, 526; V, 68; VII, 63. 4 and 13 Feb., 13 April 1820, 26 Nov. 1825.
60. *Globe,* 28 Cong., 2 Sess., 333; *Lincoln,* III, 236-7, 7 Oct. 1858.

EPILOGUE

1. *Hamilton,* II, 465. To Washington, 18 Aug. 1792.
2. As quoted in Warner, p. 25. George Richards, 1793, and Jonathan Sewall, 1801.
3. *Annals,* 7 Cong., 1 Sess., House, 716-18.
4. *Niles',* IV (8 May 1813), 166; V (4 Sept. 1813), 3.
5. *North American Review,* X (July 1820), 75.
6. *Madison,* IX, 77-85. Written in 1821.
7. *Annals,* 18 Cong., 1 Sess., House, 1016. Holcombe was from N.J., 13 Feb. 1824.
8. *Seward,* III, 194-5. "The Union," 4 July 1825.
9. Cooper, II, 341-2.
10. Adams, *Documents,* p. 289.
11. *Niles',* XXXVIII (17 April 1830), 143-4.
12. *Calhoun,* VI, 68. From the Address of 1831.
13. *Madison,* IX, 480. To Nicholas Trist, May 1832.
14. *Globe,* 24 Cong., 1 Sess., Appendix, Senate, 143. Cuthbert of Georgia on 7 March 1836.
15. Grund, II, 368-9.
16. *Globe,* 27 Cong., 2 Sess., House, 181. 27 Jan. 1841.
17. *Webster,* X, 398-9, speech at Annapolis, 1851; Sumner, III, 163, to Mass. Legislature, 14 May 1851.
18. *Globe,* 34 Cong., 1 Sess., Appendix, House, 1211-2. 4 Aug. 1856.
19. *Globe,* 36 Cong., 1 Sess., House, 1167, Killinger of Pennsylvania, 14 March 1860; 35 Cong., 1 Sess., Appendix, House, 260.
20. *Seward,* IV, 420-21. 2 Nov. 1860.

Index